D0068924

Creating a New Racial Order

Creating a New Racial Order

HOW IMMIGRATION, MULTIRACIALISM, GENOMICS,
AND THE YOUNG CAN REMAKE RACE IN AMERICA

Jennifer Hochschild
Vesla Weaver
Traci Burch

PRINCETON UNIVERSITY PRESS   PRINCETON AND OXFORD

Copyright © 2012 by Princeton University Press

Published by Princeton University Press, 41 William Street, Princeton, New Jersey 08540
In the United Kingdom: Princeton University Press, 6 Oxford Street, Woodstock,
Oxfordshire OX20 1TW
press.princeton.edu

Library of Congress Cataloging-in-Publication Data

Hochschild, Jennifer L., 1950
    Creating a new racial order : how immigration, multiracialism, genomics, and the
young can remake race in America / Jennifer Hochschild, Vesla Weaver, Traci Burch.
        p. cm.
    Includes bibliographical references and index.
    ISBN 978-0-691-15299-8 (alk. paper)
    1. United States—Population—History—21st century.   2. United States—Race
relations—History—21st century.   I. Weaver, Vesla M., 1979–   II. Burch, Traci R.,
1979–   III. Title.
    HB3505.H635 2012

    305.800973—dc23

British Library Cataloging-in-Publication Data is available

This book has been composed in Sabon

Printed on acid-free paper. ∞

Printed in the United States of America

10 9 8 7 6 5 4 3 2 1

TO THE NEXT GENERATION,

WHOM WE ARE COUNTING ON TO WORK

FOR A BETTER RACIAL FUTURE

Old deeds for old people, and new deeds for new.

—Henry David Thoreau

Contents

List of Figures and Tables _____

Figures

Tables

Introduction _____

A RACIAL ORDER—the set of beliefs, assumptions, rules, and practices that shape the way in which groups in a given society are connected with one another—may seem fixed. Racial orders do change, however. The change may be gradual, as when America evolved over two centuries from being a society with slaves to a slave society, or cataclysmic as when slavery or serfdom is abolished or apartheid instituted. A racial order can change for some groups but not others; the Immigration Act of 1924 denied all Asians and most Europeans and Africans, but not Latin Americans, the right of entry to the United States. Change in a racial order is most visible when it results from severe struggle, but it may also occur unintentionally through thousands of cumulative small acts and thoughts. And a racial order can change in some but not all dimensions; American Indians gained U.S. citizenship in 1924 but few have reacquired the land lost through centuries of conquest and appropriation.[1]

Variation in pace, direction, activity, and object makes it difficult to see major change while it is occurring. Nevertheless, we argue that the racial order of the late twentieth century that emerged from the 1960's civil rights movement, opening of immigration, and Great Society is undergoing a cumulative, wide-ranging, partly unintentional and partly deliberate transformation. The transformation is occurring in locations and laws, beliefs and practices. Its starting point was the abolition of institutional supports and public commitments of the pre-1960s racial order, such as intermarriage bans, legally mandated segregation, unembarrassed racism, and racial or ethnic discrimination. Once those props were removed, the changes broadly signaled by "the 1960s" could develop over the next forty years. They included a rise in immigration, Blacks' assertion of pride and dignity, Whites' rejection of racial supremacy (at least in public), a slow opening of schools, jobs, and suburbs to people previously excluded, and a shift in government policy from promoting segregation and hierarchy and restricting interracial unions to promoting (at least officially) integration and equality and allowing interracial unions.

As a consequence, in the first decade of the twenty-first century, new institutions and practices have been moving into place: official records permit people to identify with more than one race, anti-discrimination policies are well established in schools and workplaces, and some non-Whites hold influential political positions. At the same time, the late twentieth century's understanding of the very meaning of race—a few exhaustive and mutually exclusive groups—is becoming less and less tenable as a consequence of new multiracial identities, immigrants' rejection of conventional American categories, and genomic science. Social relations, particularly among young Americans, are less driven by stereotypes, more fluid and fragmented, and more susceptible to creation rather than acquiescence. Even deeply seated hierarchies of income, educational attainment and achievement, prestige, and political power are easing for some groups and in some dimensions of life. Race or ethnicity, though still important, is less likely to predict a young person's life chances than at any previous point in American history; today's young adults will move through adulthood with the knowledge that one need not be White in order to become the most powerful person in the world.

These and other changes are best organized and understood through analysis of four powerful transformative forces. Immigration, as it has done throughout American history, is changing the raw materials of the racial order as well as the mixture and positioning of those materials. Multiracialism is changing our almost century-long convictions that a person belongs to one and only one race and that one's race is fixed at birth and remains static. Genomic science is reopening the old question of whether race has a biological component at the same time that it offers the possibility of dissolving race into individual profiles and transforming the criminal justice system. For young adults, marches, riots, and grape boycotts are what they study in history books; their collective memories include the New Orleans' Superdome in 2005, the immigrant rights march in 2006, and Barack Obama's Grant Park speech in 2008. Because, we predict, the cohort of young adults will retain this new set of views and perspectives, young adults are the preeminent transformative force. They disproportionately comprise and engage with immigrants, they are most likely to identify as multiracial, they will be most affected by genomic innovations, and they have the broadest set of life chances. They may create a new American racial order.

Thus the late twentieth-century racial order captures less and less of the way in which race and ethnicity are practiced in the United States today and may be practiced in the foreseeable future. If transformative forces persist and prevail, the United States can finally move toward becoming the society that James Madison envisioned in *Federalist* #10, one in which no majority faction, not even native-born European Americans, dominates the political, economic, or social arena.

The Madisonian vision must not blind us to two concerns. If it persists, creation of a new racial order will not have only beneficial results. Some Americans are likely to be harmed by these changes and will thereby suffer relative or even absolute losses. Continuing the venerable American pattern, they will be disproportionately African American or Native American, supplemented by undocumented immigrants. All Americans are likely to lose some of the joys and advantages of a strong sense of group identity and rootedness. The greater concern, however, is that the newly created racial order will not persist and prevail. Black poverty and alienation may be too deep; White supremacy may be too tenacious; institutional change may be too shallow; undocumented immigrants may not attain a path to belonging; genomic research may usher in a new era of eugenic discrimination. In short, Americans may in the end lack the political will to finish what demographic change, scientific research, young adults' worldviews, and the momentum of the past decade have started.

Promoting the gains and reducing the costs of a transformed racial order are the driving motivations behind this book. We aim to contribute to understanding and explaining creative forces, provide warnings against their harms as well as extol their virtues, and generally help strengthen the political will to attain Madison's vision of a country of majority-less factions.

Our exploration of transformative forces and their blockages is spread over three parts and seven chapters. Part 1, "The Argument," has one chapter. Chapter 1 explicates the five components of a societal racial order and suggests what is at stake in the ongoing reinvention of the American racial order. Examples show how immigration, multiracialism, genomics, and cohort change are transforming each component of the late twentieth-century racial order. Chapter 1 also points to elements of American society that could distort or block transformation of the racial order. Perhaps most important, it provides analytic justification for our expectation that creative forces will outweigh blockages, so long as Americans take steps to incorporate those now in danger of exclusion and to improve the life chances of those at the bottom.

Part 2, "Creating a New Order," consists of five chapters. Chapters 2 through 5 respectively analyze immigration, multiracialism, genomics, and cohort change, in each case using the five components of a racial order to organize the discussion. Despite variation in the content and process of change, a consistent pattern emerges: each transformative force independently (and all of them interactively) is changing how Americans understand what a race is, how individuals are classified, how groups are relatively positioned, how state actions affect people's freedom of choice, and how people relate to one another in the society. Chapter 6 looks at the opposite side of the creative dynamic—that is, features of the American racial order that reinforce the late twentieth-century order of clear racial and ethnic boundaries, relatively fixed group positions, intermittently prohibitive state actions, and hostile social relations. Chapter 6 focuses on four issues that directly challenge the transformative forces—the costs of a loss in group identity, wealth disparities, unprecedented levels of Black and Latino incarceration, and the possibility that illegal immigrants or Muslims might become the new pariah group. It warns that effective creation of a new racial order can itself deepen the disadvantage of the worst off even while moving toward a more racially inclusive polity.

Finally, part 3, "Possibilities," consists of one chapter. Chapter 7 concludes by considering the likelihood that the current American racial order will look very different by the time our children reach old age. It also sketches some political and policy directions necessary to promote transformation, expand its benefits, and reduce the proportion of Americans who are left out or harmed.

The issues of this book are personally as well as professionally important to the authors; we live them as well as study them every day. We have family members who identify with a different race or ethnicity from our own; two of us are second-generation immigrants; we vary in phenotype and complexity of racial identity; two of us are children of intergroup marriages. Our DNA ancestry tests reveal these varied backgrounds. Although Hochschild had taken a test several years ago that showed Native American and East Asian ancestry, to her and her parents' surprise, the recent test reported 100 percent European heritage. It is presumably the more accurate and a good early warning signal about not taking these results too seriously. Weaver has 82 percent European ancestry (a little higher than she had anticipated but not a lot), 16 percent African, and 2 percent Asian background; like most other Americans of comparable background, she identifies as Black and multiracial but seldom as White despite how people sometimes see her. Burch has 85 percent African, 12 percent European, and 3 percent Asian ancestry. Her reaction: "Both the test and my own research happen to draw the same conclusion that I am mostly Black, so no surprises there."

Parts of this book have been published elsewhere, generally in quite different form. We provide references to our own articles or chapters where an argument rests on a fuller analysis and richer evidence already in print. Much of chapter 3 was published in "'There's No One as Irish as Barack O'Bama': The Policy and Politics of American Multiracialism," *Perspectives on Politics* 8 (3) (September 2010): 737–59, © 2010 by the American Political Science Association. Some of chapter 5 was published as "Destabilizing the American Racial Order" in *Daedalus* 140 (2) (spring 2011): 151–65, © 2011 by the American Academy of Arts and Sciences. We thank the publishers of both pieces for allowing us to use the material from these articles here.

We could not have finished this book—or perhaps even begun it— without the extraordinary help of family, friends, colleagues, and students. Over the course of too many years and too many drafts, the following people read and commented on sections, gave us suggestions after hearing a talk, or provided us with crucial evidence: C. Anthony Broh, Kimberly DaCosta, Suzann Evinger, Reynolds Farley, Richard Ford, Michael Fortner, Jacob Hacker, Ian Haney López, David Hollinger, Jeffrey Isaac, Anthony King, Philip Klinkner, Robert Lieberman, Arthur Lupia, Keith Maddox, Melissa Nobles, Matthew Platt, Kenneth Prewitt, Lydia Saad, James Sidanius, John Tryneski, Katherine Wallman, Stephen Wasby, and Kim Williams. In addition, Adam Hochschild and William Julius Wilson gave us wisdom, enthusiasm, and backbone-stiffening advice when we were in need of all three. We are grateful for and honored by the friendship and colleagueship of all of these people and tried to take full advantage of their terrifically useful comments.

We presented various versions and stages of the argument at City University London, Harvard University (several departments), the University of California at Berkeley, at Los Angeles, at San Diego, and at Irvine, the University of Manchester, the Miller Center of Public Affairs at the University of Virginia, the Russell Sage Foundation, Oberlin College, and at Brown, Columbia, Duke, Emory, Princeton, Stanford, and Yale universities. Participants in these seminars made observations and asked questions that pushed us to develop claims more clearly and fully, or occasionally to abandon them altogether, as did auditors and discussants at a string of annual conventions of the American Political Science Association and Midwest Political Science Association. To all of these helpful colleagues, we are grateful.

A long list of undergraduate and graduate student research assistants contributed invaluably to the book's eventual appearance. We would be embarrassed by the length of this list if it did not indicate the quality and commitment of students at Harvard University, Northwestern University, and the University of Virginia. These students include: Andrew Benitez, Claire Burks, Sara Burwell, Richard Coffin, Tiffany Jones, Miriam Kirubel, Daniel Koh, Jay Lundy, Maavi Norman, Sally Nuamah, Natalie Padilla, Alan Potter, Brenna Powell, Meg Rithmire, Joshua Robison, Emily Sydnor, and Sarah Talkovsky.

Institutional support was also essential to our efforts. We offer deep thanks to the Radcliffe Institute for Advanced Study, the Andrew W. Mellon Foundation, the Center for American Political Studies at Harvard University, the John Simon Guggenheim Memorial Foundation, the John W. Kluge Center at the Library of Congress, the American Bar Foundation, and the Miller Center of Public Affairs at the University of Virginia.

Princeton University Press has done its usual superb job in shaping and producing this book. Editor Chuck Myers has shown faith in it over the many years since we started, on what was then a book about the same general topic with almost entirely different content. He is helpful, wise, patient, expert—just what anxious authors need. Princeton University Press's staff, especially Nathan Carr, Julia Livingston and Jennifer Backer, enhanced the Press's enviable reputation for excellent production values. Anonymous reviewers for Princeton and another terrific university press supported us with their enthusiasm and prodded us with their questions and criticisms.

In addition to the many people who helped improve this book, we each want to thank individuals who enhance our lives. Vesla Weaver is grateful to Chris Lebron for his unmatched intellectual support, including countless conversations and epiphanies related to this project. She thanks her parents, Britt Vesla Weaver and Gary Weaver for supporting her through many years of school and for braving an interracial marriage when it was not yet mainstream. She thanks Kristin and Tyler Cole for their pride in her work on "disenfranchised Negroes." She's utterly grateful for Delancia Weaver, who saw a very different time and persevered so the rest of us could have it easier.

Traci Burch is grateful to Alfred and Freddie Burch for their love and encouragement and to Marquis Parker for his patience and understanding. She would also like to thank her family and friends, particularly Jean Hodge, Susie Hodge, Ophelia Burch, Andrea Lewis, Russell Ellis, Garani Nadaraja, Ana Aparicio, Nitasha Sharma, Todd Coleman, Melanie Penny, Francesca Soria Guerrero, and Lauren Roberts, for their support.

Jennifer Hochschild offers love and admiration to her parents, Barbara and George Hochschild, who in their tenth decades of life have better memories, more wisdom, and deeper humanity than anyone she knows. She thanks Tony Broh for everything they have shared together for many years of marriage. She writes in loving memory of Judy Gruber, and of Olive and Paul Colburn.

The authors jointly dedicate *Creating a New Racial Order* to the next generation, whom we are counting on to work for a better future. We mean that generally, invoking all of the Americans and would-be Americans who are young enough to fix the problems that we older Americans have made or not yet fixed. We also mean it more concretely, invoking our students who challenge us when we fall down and make it worthwhile to come to work each day. And we mean it very specifically, invoking Vesla's relatives, Chloe Britt and Blakely Tyler, Vesla's son, Lennox Grey Lebron-Weaver, and Jennifer's children, Eleanor and Raphael Broh. They are the light of our lives.

PART I

THE ARGUMENT

1

Destabilizing the American Racial Order

There are many . . . variables that are *not* matters of degree. And it is these variables that define what it means to be black in America. . . . Police do not stop whites for "driving while black," but police do stop blacks, particularly wealthy blacks, for this offense. . . . Thus, it would be wiser to regard "driving while black" and being black not as two variables but, instead, as part of the same condition. It is this second type of variable that forces one to conclude that by definition blacks and whites do not occupy the same social space.
    —Samuel Lucas

Does race exist? Of course it does. We see it every day. Guy steals a purse, the cop asks, What did he look like? You say, He was a six-foot-tall black guy, or a five-and-a-half-foot-tall Asian man, or a white guy with long red hair. . . . We hold these vague blueprints of race in our heads because, as primates, one of the great tools of consciousness we possess is the ability to observe patterns in nature. It's no surprise that we'd train this talent on ourselves.
    —Jack Hitt

It is possible that, by 2050, today's racial and ethnic categories will no longer be in use.
    —*Migration News*, 2004

MANY AMERICANS, LIKE the first two people quoted above, believe that we must recognize, and should perhaps celebrate, clear differences among racial and ethnic groups in the United States. Even if race is "merely" a social construct with no biological basis, it has a huge impact on the quality and trajectory of individual lives and on American society and politics more generally. Whether group boundaries are intended to include or exclude, everyone apparently knows where to draw the lines and what the lines imply.

But group boundaries that seem fixed, even self-evident, at a given moment are surprisingly unstable across a period of years. A Harvard anthropologist's 1939 textbook titled *The Races of Europe* showed eighteen races spread across the continent. In an elaborately overlapping swarm of lines and hashmarks, Carleton Coon showed how the "Partially Mongoloid," "Lappish," "Brünn strain, Tronder etc., unreduced, only partly brachycephalized," "Pleistocene Mediterranean Survivor," "Neo-Danubian," Nordic, and (separately) Noric, and a dozen other groups were distributed among those whom we now designate as "White."[1]

This is not how we now view Europe, nor was this image itself stable. As Jack Hitt points out, "the number of races has expanded and contracted wildly" over the past few hundred years, "growing as high as Ernst Haeckel's thirty-four different races in 1879 or Paul Topinard's nineteen in 1885 or Stanley Garn's nine in 1971." One hundred and thirty years earlier, Charles Darwin had made the same point in some exasperation:

> Man has been studied more carefully than any other organic being, and yet there is the greatest possible diversity amongst capable judges whether he should be classed as a single species or race, or as two (Virey), as three (Jacquinot), as four (Kant), five (Blumenbach), six (Buffon), seven (Hunter), eight (Agassiz), eleven (Pickering), fifteen (Bory St. Vincent), sixteen (Desmoulins), twenty-two (Morton), sixty (Crawfurd), or as sixty-three, according to Burke.[2]

And the number and nature of what we call races may again change, as the third epigraph reminds us.

What constitutes a race or ethnic group has been no more stable over time than how many there are. People in the nineteenth century spoke of the race of Yankees, the "criminal race," or the "race of Ushers" (in Edgar Allen Poe's famous ghost story). The concept of ethnicity emerged early in the twentieth century, but in 1936 the chair of Yale University's board of admissions rejected an increase in the freshman class on the grounds that Yale might admit "too large a proportion of candidates who are undesirable either racially or scholastically." He was referring in the first instance to Jews.[3] One author of this book is the child of what was once an interracial marriage—between an immigrant German Jew and a New England Congregationalist descended from the Puritans.

Nor is the concept of race or ethnicity coherent even at one moment in time. One of us used to teach undergraduates that Asians were a single race with many ethnicities and that Latinos were a single ethnicity with many races—but scholars now dispute whether race is best understood as distinct from ethnicity (as that lesson implies), a subset of it, or a synonym. Consider the U.S. census, typically thought of (if at all) as the epitome of neutral bureaucratically inflected science. Figure 1.1 shows the two key questions on the 2010 census.

The first question implicitly asks about ethnicity—but only for Hispanics and, curiously, Spaniards. Swedes, Koreans, Arabs, or Nigerians, never mind the Portuguese or Brazilians, have no official ethnicity. The second question first defines race as a color—"White" or "Black." But there is no Brown, Yellow, or Red; instead the answer category shifts to race as a tribe—but only for Native Americans. Race then appears as a nationality—but only for nations that are, roughly speaking, in South or Pacific-rim Asia. Finally, the question gives up, allowing the respondent to de-

→ **NOTE: Please answer BOTH Question 8 about Hispanic origin and Question 9 about race. For this census, Hispanic origins are not races.**

8. Is Person 1 of Hispanic, Latino, or Spanish origin?

☐ **No,** not of Hispanic, Latino, or Spanish origin

☐ Yes, Mexican, Mexican Am., Chicano

☐ Yes, Puerto Rican

☐ Yes, Cuban

☐ Yes, another Hispanic, Latino, or Spanish origin — *Print origin, for example, Argentinean, Colombian, Dominican, Nicaraguan, Salvadoran, Spaniard, and so on.* ⟋

[   ]

9. What is Person 1's race? *Mark* ☒ *one or more boxes.*

☐ White

☐ Black, African Am., or Negro

☐ American Indian or Alaska Native — *Print name of enrolled or principal tribe.* ⟋

[   ]

☐ Asian Indian	☐ Japanese	☐ Native Hawaiian
☐ Chinese	☐ Korean	☐ Guamanian or Chamorro
☐ Filipino	☐ Vietnamese	☐ Samoan
☐ Other Asian — *Print race, for example, Hmong, Laotian, Thai, Pakistani, Cambodian, and so on.* ⟋		☐ Other Pacific Islander — *Print race, for example, Fijian, Tongan, and so on.* ⟋

[   ]

☐ Some other race — *Print race.* ⟋

[   ]

Figure 1.1. Ethnic and racial categories on the 2010 census.

clare "Some other race," defined only by the person filling out the form. And since a respondent may now "mark one or more boxes" (as well as choosing a Latino ethnicity), one's official race can be a combination of color, nationality, tribe, and "some other" thing. There are, in fact, 63 possible racial combinations and 126 possible combinations including ethnicity. Through all of this, the word "race" appears seven times on the document. As one highly knowledgeable statistician puts it (though not for attribution), "race on the census is a rat's nest."

Incoherence in census categories simply reflects the realities of American racial and ethnic politics. In fact, given the opportunity people define themselves in even more ways.[4] Asked on a 2007 survey to indicate their "ancestry, nationality, ethnic origin, or tribal affiliation," about 40,000 American citizen students at several dozen selective colleges and universities provided over 3,200 responses. Many chose what we think of as conventional categories: African American, English, European American, Chicano, Chinese, and so on. But others hinted at ways in which group boundaries get blurred—"gay Jewish Cuban American," "adopted Chinese into an Indonesia and Filipino Family," "Mixed between American slave descendants and native Liberians, Liberian," or "usually Black, sometimes biracial."

The American racial order is unsettled substantively as well as conceptually. It used to be easy to identify groups' relative positions. On a vertical dimension of more to less, Whites held the overwhelming share of desirable resources and statuses and Blacks were at the bottom of most distributions (although other groups were occasionally worse off). On a horizontal dimension of insiders to outsiders, Whites and possibly Blacks held the status of quintessential insiders, while Asian Americans seemed to be perpetual foreigners and Latinos were admitted to the United States only temporarily or instrumentally.[5] (Native Americans were so much insiders that they had to be pushed out to make room for the new insiders.)

Those relative positions persist, but new patterns and trajectories are beginning to bend the rule to the point where it may become overwhelmed by the exceptions. Asian Americans still lack positions at the center of the political or economic mainstream, but—with crucial exceptions—most nationalities have on average more education and higher incomes than do White Americans. A man plausibly understood to be either multiracial, Black, or a second-generation immigrant defeated an array of White candidates for the American presidency. "A Mexican middle class is thriving in Southern California and . . . this population defied the range of predicted outcomes for the children of Mexican immigrants." Young Asian Americans marry Whites at very high rates. African Americans remain the most residentially segregated of all conventionally defined groups, but in 2010 one newspaper headline read, "Black Segregation in US Drops to Lowest in Century." According to the 2010 census, "for the first time, a majority of all racial/ethnic groups in large metro areas live in the suburbs."[6] If it continues, this sort of structural change could generate a society in which group identification predicts less and less about status or life chances.

Social relations among and within groups are also being transformed. Almost all Americans claim to be willing to vote for a Black, Hispanic, or woman presidential candidate, though they remain skeptical of Mormons, atheists, and Muslims. Two-thirds of teens in California have dated someone of another race or ethnicity and almost all would consider marrying someone of another group. Of the 3.7 million people newly registered to vote in California from 1990 to 2010, only 400,000 were non-Hispanic Whites. The Minnesota State Colleges and Universities system publishes a recruitment brochure in nine languages. Gallup Poll's "life evaluation index" found not only that young adults and the affluent became more optimistic from 2008 to 2009, and again by 2010, than did older or poorer respondents, but also that in all three years Blacks and Asians showed more optimism than did Whites, Hispanics, or "Others."[7] Genomic science is both demonstrating that human beings share almost all of their genetic inheritance and enabling research on the tiny fraction of genetic difference in search of group-specific diseases or aptitudes.

Not all recent changes in the racial order indicate progress toward a more fair society; some undermine it. Young, poor Black men are much more likely to be stopped by police, arrested, convicted, and imprisoned than under legal segregation or in the post–civil rights decades. Even government agencies charge that a federal program deputizing local police officers to enforce immigration law, while perfectly legal, facilitates discrimination against dark-skinned or "foreign-looking" Americans. New Yorkers carry signs at protests against a Muslim community center and mosque with the slogan, "Everything I need to know about Islam I learned on 9/11." Protestors at Tea Party rallies carry other signs depicting Barack Obama as a monkey or announcing that "The zoo has an African lion and the White House has a lyin' African." As William Faulkner, and later Thomas Sugrue, put it, the United States' racist past is "not even past."[8]

Making Sense of Change

These facts and trends give the sense that something is afoot. Many scholars, politicians, journalists, and commentators seek to characterize the growing sense of racial and ethnic change in American society. Depictions range from claims that the United States is now a post-racial society,[9] in which group-based identification no longer shapes life chances and racial identity should be abandoned, to claims that the United States is developing a more subtle and therefore even more pernicious regime of racism than existed through the twentieth century. In this book, we aim to make sense of this debate, harnessing theory and evidence to show what is changing, what is not, and how Americans might create a new order that retains the best features of their racial and ethnic history while jettisoning the worst.

Our core argument is that Americans are creating a new racial order as a consequence of increasing heterogeneity in the constituent racial and ethnic groups of the United States. When groups' salient features remain fairly homogenous, or when heterogeneity within groups is not salient, a given racial order is more likely to remain stable. However, increasing and increasingly important differences within groups, and the entrance of new groups, can over time put pressure on existing understandings of which groups exist, who fits into them, how they relate to one another, and how their members are characterized. Increasing and salient differences within groups and the entrance of new groups can also generate changes in voters' willingness to elect people from another race or ethnicity, investors' or clients' willingness to put economic control in the hands of people from another group, people's willingness to live and work near members of other groups, and other changes in access to power, resources, and status.

During the late twentieth century, racial or ethnic groups remained largely homogenous in their level of economic well-being, amount of political power, and presentation to outsiders. They also remained fairly separated from one another in neighborhoods, schools or universities, social interactions, and jobs. That relative stasis enabled the racial order that developed after the upheavals of the 1960s to remain quite stable. But the turn of the twenty-first century witnessed four new drivers of rising heterogeneity: high levels of immigration, public recognition of multiracialism, the growth of genomic science, and the emergence of a distinctive cohort of young adults with new memories, new attitudes, and new behaviors. Through these four forces, American racial and ethnic groups are becoming more internally differentiated by class, ideology, political attitudes, ancestry, perceptions of discrimination, nationality, social connections, political and economic power, levels of optimism or cynicism, and even genes. They are also becoming more linked to other groups in personal interactions, schooling and jobs, residence, culture and attitudes, and organizations. As a result, the race or ethnicity with which a person identifies or is identified is becoming less and less predictive of his or her views, behaviors, and, eventually, life chances.

Increasing heterogeneity will lead to long-term and lasting transformation of the American racial order only if societal structures and conditions change to promote the new understandings and practices rather than reinforce old ones. Thus we examine laws, governmental policies and practices, and actions of important institutions for evidence of behavior that does or does not reinforce other sorts of transformation. We find that, despite many policies and practices that accord with the existing racial order and inhibit change, other powerful forces encourage instability and heterogeneity. Innovations in policy are enabling a new fluidity in the meaning and practice of race; institutional actors from employers to politicians to real estate agents are acting in ways that lower segregative barriers; immigration laws and local institutions sometimes permit newcomers to join and thereby transform the American racial order; and findings in genomic science are creating new structures and practices for mediating among race, medicine, law, and self-definition. Demographic shifts do not themselves create social or political transformation, but in conjunction with changes in attitudes, behaviors, laws, and policies, demography is a powerful force for change. How much structural change is actually occurring and whether it is cumulating— along with demographic, attitudinal, and resource change—into a coherent and intelligible transformation of the American racial order is the subject of the next five chapters. Whether the creation of a new racial order is fully desirable and whether it is on a firm path to completion is the subject of the final chapter.

The American Racial Order

Our analysis of the forces leading to the new heterogeneity is organized through the concept of the American racial order. As we use the term, a society's racial order is the widely understood and accepted system of beliefs, laws, and practices that organize relationships among groups defined as races or ethnicities. We derive this basic concept and its more specific components from research by Brenna Powell. She argues that boundary rigidity and status distance between groups structure any society's racial or ethnic stratification system and determine the opportunities for coordinated action within it.[10] From that starting point and her further development of it, we identify five components of any racial order: an authoritative typology of the society's racial categories, classification of individuals within those categories, relative positions of the racial and ethnic groups, permissions or prohibitions created and controlled by the state, and social relations within and among groups.

We can illustrate how this conception of a racial order helps make sense of stasis and change by briefly characterizing the two most recent racial orders in the United States. Many historians have written about race in the twentieth century, so here we need only specify their outlines. The earlier of the two most recent racial orders occurred roughly from the 1910s through the mid-1960s, and the second ran from the mid-1960s through the end of the twentieth century. During both periods, most Americans agreed that there were four races—Caucasian, African, Asian (often termed Mongoloid), and American Indian.[11] Regardless of any mixture in his or her ancestry, each person had only one race, fixed at birth. During the first period, most politically relevant Americans—that is, Whites—agreed that Whites not only were but should be the quintessential insiders and at the top of all status hierarchies; other groups were either lower in status and resources, outside the American mainstream, or both. The federal government and many states reinforced that group positioning by prohibiting actions such as interracial marriage, Asian immigration and citizenship, and non-Anglo voting. Government-mandated segregation was pervasive.[12] Social relations across groups might be polite but were usually distant and frequently hostile if not violent. Whites were seldom challenged and almost never with impunity.

By the end of the 1960s, through the combination of Supreme Court decisions, the civil rights movement, the 1965 Hart-Celler amendments to the Immigration and Nationality Act, and the Great Society, significant elements of the Jim Crow racial order had been destroyed. The most important change was the abolition of federal and state prohibitions against intermarriage, physical intermingling, employment in certain positions, voting, and Asian immigration and citizenship. As a consequence of these structural and social changes, a new racial order emerged over the rest of the twentieth century. There were still only four races, and people were still born into and remained within only one. But relative group positions began to shift somewhat, as poverty levels declined, Blacks were able to develop and maintain a small middle class, and most Asians attained more education and income. Social relations sometimes became more friendly, at least within organizations and political entities. Despite the western hemispheric quotas in the 1965 immigration act, ever larger numbers of Hispanics entered the United States; as the demography of the country changed, so did—slowly—the political incentives of elected officials and political parties. Despite these developments, however, groups continued to appear to outsiders to be largely homogenous.

This is a relatively consensual historical summary. Our contention, which will not be consensual, is that the United States is undergoing yet another transformation of its racial order through increasing heterogeneity and interaction, underlain by demographic and legal changes. Over the next four chapters, we lay out the evidence for this argument, which includes the following:

- changing definitions of race and ethnicity, so that the meaning of or elements encompassed by the term "race" are unclear and people differ on the number of or boundaries around races;

- changing classification of individuals, so that racial identity might be fluid or idiosyncratic, self-definition might differ from others' definition, or classification may cross conventional racial boundaries;
- shifting relative positions within and among groups, so that one's capacity to accurately predict people's life chances by knowing their race or ethnicity remains but is weaker now than ever before in American history;
- strong sanctions against the twentieth century's sweeping group-based prohibitions and permissions, combined with the emergence of implicit or explicit new rules for new, smaller groups; and
- changes in social relations among individuals and groups so that stereotypes, daily encounters, political coalitions, and social norms are less predictable and more interactive than they have heretofore been.

Thus sentiments within an individual, connections between persons, interactions across groups, and social, economic, and political structures are all changing. The pace of change is uneven, it is moving in several directions, and it is not the same for all groups or all components of the racial order. On balance, the new heterogeneity is most visible and potent at the level of conceptual changes involved in defining races and classifying individuals, and fairly visible in changing social relations. Change is slowest to arrive in relative group positions, though even here some evidence suggests growing momentum.

How would we know that these forces are together creating a new racial order in the United States? Signals would include a larger share of people marrying across group lines and/or identifying as multiracial, abandonment of the racial classification system shown in figure 1.1 in official (and unofficial) documents, more non-White elected and appointed officials with genuine and widely dispersed political power, decreasing group-based disparities in educational attainment and achievement, persistence of non-White families in the middle class over generations, laws and policies that incorporate immigrants into the mainstream society and polity, use of genomic science to make medical diagnoses and prescribe treatments without using crude racial classifications but taking into account variations associated with ancestral inheritance, and use of genomic science to offset racial biases in the criminal justice system. A new racial order would be most clearly manifested if we saw young adults understanding and practicing race in ways that grow out of their collective memories of the 2000s rather than remaining imprinted on memories of the 1960s.

In the most hopeful case, a new American racial order would include less separation in schools and neighborhoods, a decline in the deep poverty and isolation of the worst-off decile or quintile of non-Whites, a decrease in group-based disparities in involvement with the criminal justice system, and an end to the persistent, petty, demoralizing acts of discrimi-

nation or racism that dog the lives of so many non-Whites. In the least
hopeful case, the new order would substitute Muslims and illegal immigrants for Blacks at the bottom of status hierarchies and as outsiders to
the American mainstream. It would also include the loss of racial solidarity with the consequent abandonment of poor, poorly educated, unemployed Blacks in devastated inner-city neighborhoods.

Although all usages of the term are related, prior study of racial orders
differs from ours in important ways. Rather than focusing on a single
dominant order with some deviations and holdovers as we do, Desmond
King and Rogers Smith envision simultaneous rival racial orders, manifested in competing institutions and ideologies. They describe "meaningful development" as a period when the prevailing order's relatively more
inegalitarian racial goals, rules, roles, and boundaries are substantially
revised, usually in response to a more egalitarian and successful opposition. They point, for example, to the moment when most White suprema-
cists felt compelled to abandon slavery, or when racial egalitarians began
to insist on equal voting rights, not just on civil rights. Claire Kim defines
a racial order in terms of two orthogonal dimensions of insider to outsider and high to low status. We find that framework compelling and will
use it over the next few chapters. To George Fredrickson, a racial order
connotes longer and deeper stasis than we see, since his time frame is
centuries rather than decades. He defines it as "a permanent group hierarchy that is believed to reflect the laws of nature or the decrees of God."
Michael Omi and Howard Winant, in contrast to Fredrickson, emphasize
the fragility and rapid change of any given racial order; in their eyes,
"race is an unstable and 'decentered' complex of social meanings constantly being transformed by political struggle. . . . We define racial formation as the sociohistorical process by which racial categories are created, inhabited, transformed, and destroyed." Unlike us, they see two
successive racial orders in the late twentieth century—the almost revolutionary 1960s, followed by the neoconservative 1980s—and they are especially attuned to not only the "disruption" but also the "restoration" of
a given order. In their view the racial state is an "unstable equilibrium" in
which progress and retrenchment are constantly battling.[13] There is, of
course, no correct definition; what matters is how the analyst uses the
concept, and our use has been sharpened by considering it in relation to
these others.

Other scholars who have influenced our thinking focus less on what a
racial order is and more on the institutions and practices that characterize a given period. As in our formulation, changes in key structures, attitudes, and practices signal a move away from stasis. The crucial institution might be racial segregation, the condition of unskilled surplus labor,
or the prevalence of anti-miscegenation statutes. It might be the growth

disproportionate share of Black men's genomic samples. Law en-
~nt officers use biobanks to identify people whose DNA matches
~nd at a crime site, and they are beginning to use biobanks to iden-
tial matches, who may be family members of the person whose
~as found at the crime site. Whether this use of biobanks turns out
~t another form of racially biased surveillance and control, not just
~icted felons but also of their relatives, or whether biobanks will
~ore objective and less biased evidence than eyewitness reports or
investigations remains to be seen. Either way, genomics will be
implicated in the development of state permissive or prohibitive
~ that affect different groups differently.

~ng adult Americans' choices will do a great deal to determine
~ relative positions over the next few decades. Overall, they are
~ing more egalitarian. For example, in 1976 young White adults
~ore likely to claim that Blacks had too much influence in "Ameri-
~e and politics" than to claim that they had too little influence. By
~even after the election of Barack Obama to the presidency, young
~adults were four times more likely to say that Blacks have too
~fluence than to say that they have too much. Older Whites moved
~same direction over the period but to a much smaller degree. To-
~oung adults will also change social relations among groups in the
~on of more heterogeneity and more interaction of all types. In
~for example, less than a quarter of young adults "completely dis-
~l" that they "don't have much in common with people of other
~; that figure rose to 57 percent by 2009. In California, two-fifths
~ino and African American teens and young adults, and over half of
~s and Anglos, report that most of their friends are of a different
~r ethnicity.[15]

~these vignettes show, immigration, multiracialism, genomics, and
~t change each independently is putting pressure on one or more
~onents of the current American racial order. Immigration brings
~people into the mix; multiracialism makes definitions of race and
~ties much more fluid; genomics may change the relationship be-
~ race and law enforcement; cohort change enables the Obama or
~generation to view the world differently from the civil rights or
~anomics generations. Even more important, however, immigration,
~racialism, genomics, and cohort change interact such that change
~e force reinforces and helps cause change in others. They may even
~ply one another's effects, combining to increase each other's mo-
~um. High levels of immigration by young adults from many coun-
~make intergroup marriage more likely and increase the proportion
~oung adults who practice race differently from twentieth-century
~ricans. When individual genomic profiles become widely available,

of a stable middle-class community or the attainment of political or social power in a local community.[14] All of these foci matter, and across the
next few chapters we attend to most, if not all, of them.

Transformative Forces

Our central focus, however, is the four transformative forces: the entry of
large numbers and new kinds of immigrants into American society, the
rise of multiracialism understood as a political movement and public
identity, the growing impact of genomic science on American medicine,
law, and society, and the way in which the current cohort of young adults
is reconfiguring Americans' collective racial memory and racial interactions. These are the subjects, respectively, of chapters 2 through 5; here
we provide snapshots of the kinds of change that these forces are producing in the components of the racial order.

Whether one understands race and ethnicity to be distinct or synonymous concepts, the presence of an increasing number of immigrants to
the United States complicates the definition and categorization of races.
Figure 1.2 shows two very different efforts from the early 2000s to accommodate this new heterogeneity. The University of California at Berkeley aims at precision in its job applications through detail, while Pennsylvania State University aims at precision through minimalism. Both mix
race and ethnicity on a single list; Berkeley adds the complications of
ancestry while Penn State hints that its main interest lies in legal statuses
with budgetary implications. (Neither, however, permits the complexity
of choosing more than one category.) Berkeley acknowledges both biological and cultural components of race; Penn State is silent on the cul-
ture/biology dimension.

Like immigration, multiracialism blurs conventional racial classifications, with potentially important implications for public policy and for
our understanding of relative group positions. Consider American Indians. The 1980 census asked, "Is this person XX?" (with a long list of
races and nationalities). It also asked if the person is of "Spanish/His-
panic origin or descent" and "What is this person's ancestry?" Given the
extent of interracial mixture among Native Americans, this combination
of questions yielded widely varying counts, shown in table 1.1.

Which of these five rows contains the "real" American Indians? The
question is unanswerable because any answer is arbitrary. And yet one's
choice has important policy implications. The number of people recognized as Indian affects federal policy toward tribal governance, while the
reported socioeconomic status of those recognized as Indians affects
levels and amounts of federal support. However, people in row 3 had
an average of 10.7 years of education and average earnings in 1979 of

University of California, Berkeley
Race/ethnicity *Please choose one category. If more than one choose the one with which you most closely identify.*

☐ **White, not of Hispanic origin:** *persons having origins in any of the original peoples of Europe, North Africa, or the Middle East*

☐ **African American, not of Hispanic origin:** *persons having origin in any of the Black racial groups of Africa*

☐ **American Indian or Alaskan native:** *persons having origins in any of the original American Indian peoples of North America, including Eskimos and Aleuts, or who maintain cultural identification through tribal affiliation or community recognition*

☐ Unknown

Hispanic (including Black individuals whose origins are Hispanic)

☐ **Mexican / Mexican American / Chicano:** *persons of Mexican culture or origin, regardless of race*

☐ **Latin-American / Latino:** *persons of Latin American (e.g., Central American South American, Cuban, Puerto Rican) culture or origin, regardless of race*

☐ **Other Spanish / Spanish American:** *persons of Spanish culture or origin, not included in any of the Hispanic categories listed above*

Asian or Pacific Islander

☐ **Chinese / Chinese American:** *persons having origins in any of the original people of China*

☐ **Japanese / Japanese American:** *persons having origins in any of the original people of Japan*

☐ **Filipino / Pilipino:** *persons having origins in any of the original people of the Philippine islands*

☐ **Pakistan / East Indian:** *persons having origins in any of the original people of the Indian subcontinent (India and Pakistan)*

☐ **Other Asian:** *persons having origins in any of the original people of the Far East (including Korea), Southeast Asia, or Pacific islands (including Samoa), not included in any of the Asian categories listed above.*

Figure 1.2a. What is a race?

The Pennsylvania State Universit
Affirmative Action Data Card

PLEASE CHECK THE APPLICABLE CATEGOR
(Group definitions can be found on the back of this

☐ American Indian or Alaska Native   ☐ Asi

☐ Black (non-Hispanic)   ☐ Hisp

☐ White (non-Hispanic)

☐ Disabled   ☐ Disa

☐ United States Citizen or Permanent Resident

Figure 1.2b. What is a race?

$8,307, whereas people in row 4 enjoyed 12
$10,680 in 1979 earnings. Which set of figures
federal support? How people are racially class
yond personal identity or social identification.

Genomic science is becoming deeply involve
system in ways that could reinforce or could I
disparities in imprisonment. By now, every stat
ment collect DNA samples from people convic
them in biobanks that can be linked across si
Given conviction rates over the past few years,

Table 1.1
Variations in American Indian Identity, 1980.

Response category

1. Persons reporting American Indian race
2. Persons reporting American Indian ancestry, possib among other ancestries
3. Persons reporting American Indian race and Americ Indian ancestry only
4. Persons reporting American Indian race and non-Inc ancestry or ancestries
5. Persons reporting non-American Indian race and Inc ancestry, possibly among other ancestries

Source: Snipp 1986.

---

clude
forcem
that fc
tify pa
DNA
to be
of cor
offer
police
deepl
polici
You
grou₁
becor
were
can l
2008
Whit
little
in th
day's
direc
1987
agre
races
of L
Asia
race
A
coho
com
new
iden
twe
9/1
Rea
mu
in c
mu
me
trie
of
An

this new knowledge will influence young adults' self-definitions, understanding of race, engagement with the criminal justice system, and medical treatment. As the twenty-first century's young adults mature into political and social power at the same time that demography and science are being transformed, the magnitude and pace of racial change may increase at ever faster rates. They may, in short, create a new racial order.

Blockages to Transformation

This image of a snowball gaining girth and speed as it tumbles down a hill does not, however, complete our argument. The racial terrain has roadblocks and boulders that can block, deflect, or even explode the rolling snowball. That is, some features of the current American racial order have remained stable, and some may even be solidifying. Homogeneity is not yielding fully to heterogeneity, and on some dimensions it may not be yielding at all.

We distinguish among three kinds of blockage. The first is particular events that show continuing injustice against or harm to particular groups. Private individuals may be responsible—but so may government officials, as the killing of Amadou Diallo by New York City police and the pink underwear of Sheriff Joseph Arpaio's inmates (discussed below) make all too clear. A second kind of blockage is laws and policies that disproportionately harm one group. Examples include laws permitting police to check the immigration status of people arrested for disturbing the peace, racial profiling on highways or in airports, and forensic biobanks that inadvertently target African American families of people convicted of a felony.

Events and laws can be frightening and destructive, but they can also be fought and sometimes overcome through judicial action or further legislation. A third kind of blockage is deeper, less visible, and less available for political contestation. Structural impediments to transformation of the American racial order include huge and persistent wealth disparities among groups, the legal purgatory of unauthorized immigrants, the effects of very high levels of incarceration concentrated in a few non-White communities, and the risk of creating a new pariah group of Muslims in America.[16] Racially inflected persistent poverty and isolation among people with no "hooks" into mainstream society is another structural impediment to creation of a new order. Whether these blockages are powerful enough to halt or distort transformation of the American racial order is the subject of chapter 6; the answer to that question depends on political and policy choices that we outline in chapter 7.

A final flaw of the transformative model has a different flavor. Transformation may in fact succeed, but its very success will engender harms as well as gains. For example, as racial boundaries blur and as state-sponsored prohibitions become more focused or subtle, advocacy groups and others with strong group identities could deplore the decline in race-based solidarity. They may mourn the anticipated loss of connection with a rich and deep heritage, or they may believe that only a unified group can challenge persistent disadvantage and bias. They might be right if, as they fear, racial inequality persists along with the positive aspects of a newly created order.

Indeed, transformation of the American racial order will probably increase class disparities within each racial and ethnic group even as it lessens disparities across groups. In the new American racial order, the better-off majority of each group will enjoy more freedom to define oneself, more geographic and economic mobility, a broader array of friends and colleagues, greater political influence, while the life chances of the worst-off minority of each group are diminished, relatively if not absolutely. The solution to this problem, as to the various forms of blockage, will be yet more transformation that moves in the direction of more overall equality, not just more equality across groups—but no one should imagine that we envision a society with no losers. We only anticipate that the proportion of Americans with genuine freedom of choice will expand considerably and that the United States will move closer to Madison's vision of no dominant faction. That seems to us a worthy, even if partial, goal.

PART II

CREATING A NEW ORDER

2

Immigration

Blacks are the central metaphor for otherness and oppression in the United States. . . . [But] we're in the United States and [from our perspective] blacks are Americans. They're Anglos. . . . They're Anglos of a different color, but they're Anglos.
  —Jorgé Klor de Alva

Being a Latina immigrant can be difficult—especially these days, when immigration is such a controversial issue. There are some people who treat me poorly once they hear my accent; they are angry at Hispanics, thinking we have taken away their job opportunities. But they are the exception, and overall I love being an American. I love the fast pace of this culture, the ability to do a million things at once, and most of all, the sense that there are infinite possibilities out there—all you have to do is grab hold of the one you want.
  —A student

When do I just get to be American? Why do I always have to carry the burden of my ancestors' origins when I have nothing to do with them?
  —A student

IMMIGRATION IS DESTABILIZING and changing all five components of the American racial order—Americans' understanding of what a race is, their system for classifying individuals, the relative position of groups, official or quasi-official permissions and prohibitions, and social interactions among groups. It is making each racial or ethnic group more heterogeneous as well as adding new ones to the mix. Elites' political action more or less accidentally opened the doors to massive immigration; individuals' decisions to start a fresh life in a new country turned the anticipated trickle into a rush. What the political implications will be remains unclear. The United States may practice an updated version of the last century's assimilation of immigrants into the extant order. But the evidence suggests that the powerful demographic changes resulting from immigration, especially in conjunction with multiracialism and cohort change, are more likely to usher in a new racial order.

The Growth of Immigration

The 1965 Immigration Act and Its Successors

No one, at least on the public record, intended or expected the 1965 Immigration and Nationality Act to transform the American racial order.[1]

President Lyndon Johnson was clear on that point: "This is not a revolutionary bill. It will not reshape the structure of our daily lives or add importantly to our wealth and power." A chief sponsor of the bill, Representative Emanuel Celler (D-NY), was equally explicit: "the bill would not let in great numbers of immigrants from anywhere at all. . . . [T]here will be some shift of immigration to countries other than the ones in Northern Europe which are now favored . . . but quota immigrants will have to compete and to qualify to get in, and quota immigration will not be predominantly from Asia and Africa." Secretary of Labor W. Willard Wirtz testified that the new act would bring in only 24,000 new workers a year and perhaps 100,000 nonworking family members; in a workforce of up to 86 million by 1970, this change "would have no appreciable impact." (The new attorney general, Nicholas Katzenbach, made the same observation.)

Debates over a proposed new western hemispheric quota were more intense than discussion of the loophole of family reunification. Senator Jacob Javits (R-NY) described it as "most unwise and improvident in terms of United States' relations with Latin America"; President Johnson shared that concern. But labor unions feared job competition from Latin American immigrants and the American Legion, the American Coalitions of Patriotic Societies, and other groups feared too many immigrants from a disfavored race, ethnicity, or nationality. Quota proponents won, especially since legislators expected an annual quota of 120,000 to slightly decrease western hemispheric immigration compared with the recent past. As the authoritative *Congressional Quarterly* article put it, the law "closed off the possibility of a very substantial increase in future immigration from the one area on which there previously had been no numerical restrictions. In this sense, [it] . . . could be described as a bill which . . . foreclosed any long-term upward trend in the number of immigrants."

Nor did the American public expect or want substantial new immigration. National surveys in 1964–65 asked twenty-five questions on the subject, with clear results. On three of three questions, respondents overwhelmingly rejected increased levels of immigration—and if there were to be immigrants, vanishingly small percentages wanted more Asians or Latin Americans. But the issue hardly registered among Americans. Before passage of the new law, only 10 percent "felt bad because of U.S. strictness in limiting immigration"; a majority admitted to knowing nothing about immigration policy; only a third knew that the law had passed; and barely any found the law "important . . . personally" or deemed it one of President Johnson's major accomplishments. Had citizens and politicians been told that the 1965 immigration law would have as much influence on the American racial order as civil rights laws or Great Society legislation, they would have been dumbfounded.[2]

The bill's opponents made better predictions. Representative Joe Skubitz (R-KS) warned that it would raise unemployment and "place . . . increased demands upon education, housing, health facilities, and transportation." Senator Sam Ervin (D-NC) feared that it would be "just one little hole in the dike for unrestricted immigration." (However, he predicted only 66,000 new job seekers a year.) The president of the Republican Committee of One Hundred cautioned that the new law would "enormously increase the number of immigrants permitted to enter the United States annually for permanent residence."

Antagonists were also more accurate in predicting the law's effects on the U.S. racial order. The president of the Daughters of the American Revolution argued that "abandonment of the national origins system would drastically alter the source of our immigration," while the president of the Republican Committee of One Hundred asked if we are "willing . . . to permit the American population makeup to be based rather on the makeup of foreign lands whose native can get in line fastest, in the greatest number, under a first-come first-served scheme of entry."

The final bill passed with a lopsided vote of 320–69 in the House and a voice vote in the Senate. President Johnson signed it, despite his opposition to western hemispheric quotas.

Subsequent immigration laws have been no more effective in controlling the flow of immigrants to the United States than was the 1965 law; some did not even try to do so. Sweeping immigration controls in 1986 were intended to curb illegal immigration at the border. The law imposed fines and even jail terms on U.S. employers for knowingly hiring unauthorized foreign workers. It also created a mechanism for giving amnesty to illegal immigrants who had lived in the United States for four or more years and expanded the guest worker program for up to 350,000 farm workers. Whatever its (mixed) intentions, subsequent years saw more, rather than less, legal as well as unauthorized immigration. The 1990 immigration reform permitted legal immigration to climb from 500,000 to 675,000 people per year; both legal and illegal immigration subsequently rose even higher. A 1996 law again sought to control illegal immigration through pressure on employers, strengthened rules for deportation of undocumented criminals, and limits on appeals. It restricted not only illegal but also legal immigrants' access to social welfare benefits. It, too, made no noticeable dent in the trend lines, which continued to rise.

Demographic Change

Proponents of all of these laws were presumably neither foolish nor deceptive, and the legislative process was apparently neither corrupt nor misguided. Experts and lawmakers were acting on the best information

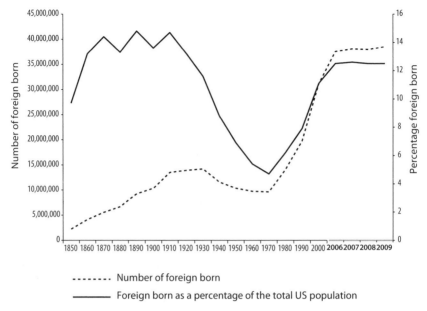

Figure 2.1. Foreign-born people in the United States: number and share of the population, 1850–2009.
Source: Migration Policy Institute, MPI Data Hub.

available. But overwhelming the laws was the fact that immigration around the world began to increase in the mid-1960s and accelerated over the next few decades. The number of migrants rose from about 75 million in 1960 to about 214 million in 2010—from 2.5 percent to over 3 percent of the world's population. The United States absorbed the largest number of immigrants by an order of magnitude.[3] Almost two million people attained legal permanent residence in the United States in 1991, and over a million did so annually in six of the eight years between 2000 and 2008.[4] Unauthorized immigration adds hundreds of thousands more people annually; we address it separately below and in chapter 6.

Figure 2.1 shows the scale of demographic change through legal immigration to the United States since the mid-1800s (using the earliest data available). As the figure shows, immigrants have swelled the American population in recent decades. After a decline resulting from the stringent 1924 law, by 2008 the proportion of legal permanent residents was approaching 1910's high point of almost 15 percent.

Any country's racial order would be challenged by the arrival of such a large number of newcomers. It will be even more destabilized if immigrants and their children are perceived to be of a different race or ethnicity than the native-born population. That was the case a century ago, and

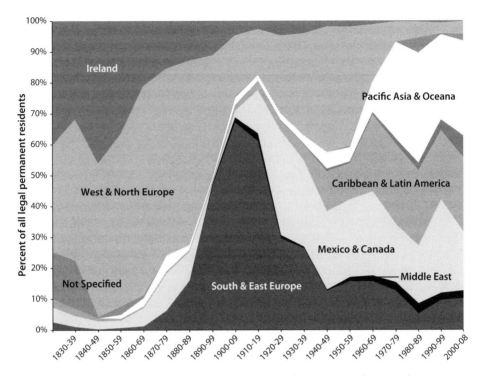

Figure 2.2. Persons obtaining legal permanent resident status in the United States: regions of the world, 1820–2008.
Source: Authors' analysis of Department of Homeland Security, *Yearbook of Immigration Statistics; 2008*, table 2.

it is the case now. Figure 2.2 shows the regions of origin for people obtaining legal permanent resident status to the United States since 1820. It does not include undocumented immigrants; if they were included, the proportion of migrants from Mexico especially would be almost twice as large for the past two decades. Nevertheless, it shows the dramatic changes in newcomers' origins over time.

Figure 2.2 depicts the demographic consequences of both policy choices and individual migrants' choices. The 1882 Chinese Exclusion Act had an impact that was not reversed until the 1970s; eastern and southern Europeans have never regained the position they held before the 1924 immigration act. Not only did the 1965 immigration law unintentionally allow a drastic rise in immigration overall (see figure 2.1), but it also unintentionally permitted immigration from countries that now seem as foreign as Slovakia or southern Italy used to seem. Most important, as figure 2.2 illustrates, the 1965 law and its successors are making race and ethnicity in the United States more heterogeneous and dynamic in various ways:

- "Four out of 10 children and young adults are minorities, compared with three out of 10 baby boomers and only two out of 10 seniors. New-immigrant minorities . . . are both younger and more likely to have children than the native white population."
- Non-Hispanic Whites below age six will be in the minority by 2021. Eighteen- to twenty-nine-year-old non-Hispanic Whites will be in the minority by 2028. Hispanics will then comprise over a quarter of young adults and Blacks 13 percent. But non-Hispanic Whites over age sixty-five will remain about 60 percent of their age cohort through 2050.
- In 2007, 7.7 percent of marriages were across group lines—twice as many as in 1990. Almost half of those marriages involved a Hispanic. Looked at from the other direction, about one-third of marriages involving either Hispanics or Asians were outside their respective group. (The African American rate of interracial marriage is lower but also double what it was in 1990.)
- "Immigration accounted for three-quarters of population growth during the decade [after 2000]. Census Bureau data found 13.1 million new immigrants (legal and illegal) who arrived in the last 10 years; there were also about 8.2 million births to immigrant women during the decade." Assuming continuation of current laws, new immigrants will account for about half of the U.S. population growth by 2050, and their U.S.-born children will account for another third.
- "Immigrants are everywhere." Since 1990, the population of foreign-born has more than doubled outside the original six magnet states, and by 2005, the population of more than fifteen states was at least one-tenth foreign-born. "Population growth in the largest twenty-five cities has been disproportionately driven by foreign-born residents in recent years."
- During the 2000s, "the number of non-Hispanic whites fell in 46 states and 86 of the 100 largest metropolitan areas. In 10 states, white children are now a minority among their peers, including six that tipped between 2000 and 2010. Others will follow soon."[5]

Despite the fact that "immigrants are everywhere," demographic changes resulting from immigration vary dramatically by state and region as well as by age. The number of (predominantly White) baby boomers rose during the past decade in all Mountain and western states except for California. These are precisely the states, especially Nevada, Arizona, and New Mexico, in which the proportion of children who are White is relatively low. Some states have much higher intermarriage rates than do others—Hawaii, New Mexico, and other Mountain states are on one end of the spectrum and Mississippi, Vermont, and Maine are on the other end.[6] Thus group-based politics in southwestern states will occur in a context of older Whites, intermarried adults, and minority children, while group-based politics in New England will occur in a context of White predominance. These regional differences will complicate the politics of immigrant incorporation at both state and national levels.

Unauthorized Immigration

Unauthorized entries complicate contemporary immigration politics in a way that even the 1924 and 1965 contenders did not have to deal with. The United States had almost twelve million undocumented migrants in 2008—just under a third of the foreign-born residents. Net annual increases averaged up to 500,000 from the mid-1990s to 2008, although almost 800,000 undocumented immigrants arrive in the United States each year (the difference is due to death, return migration, or attainment of legal status). From 1998 through 2004, more unauthorized than legal immigrants entered the country. After the economy failed and unemployment rose in 2008, the number of unauthorized residents declined slightly to 10 or 11 million in 2010.[7]

Like legal immigrants, the unauthorized come disproportionately from a few countries or regions. As of 2008, roughly seven of the twelve million were from Mexico; put another way, almost three-fifths of Mexican immigrants to the United States are unauthorized.[8] The next largest groups of unauthorized immigrants, about 2.6 million, are from various countries in Latin America and the Caribbean; the home countries of the rest are scattered around the world.

Immigrants' Impact on the American Racial Order

Oscar Handlin famously wrote in 1951, "once I thought to write a history of the immigrants in America. Then I discovered that the immigrants *were* American history." The Cato Institute responded in 1995, "they still are."[9] That exchange is not quite right; it leaves out American Indians, Mexicans who inadvertently joined the United States when their homelands were acquired, and enslaved Africans or contract labor Chinese who were not immigrants as that term is commonly used. Nevertheless, it captures the essential truth that most Americans are migrants, in one way or another, or descendants of newcomers. That fact is globally unusual, and the current surge of newcomers is transforming the distinctive American racial order that had been created by earlier surges of newcomers and their offspring. In different ways and to different degrees, all five components of the racial order are affected.

What Is a Race?

Awkward locutions provide an initial signal of the shifting definitions of what counts as a race in the United States: non-Asian minority, non-Hispanic White, Pacific-rim Asian, NHOPI, AIAN, A.O.I.C,[10] mixed-race Black children.[11] More generally, the rapid increase in new Americans from all over the world makes a mockery of any attempt at precise and consistent definition. In the mid-1990s, the Office of Management and the Budget (OMB) conducted a "comprehensive review" of then current definitions of race and ethnicity, in response to "increasing criticism" of the fact that they "do not reflect the increasing diversity of our Nation's population that has resulted primarily from growth in immigration." The agency described its new categories as "a social-political construct designed for collecting data on the race and ethnicity of broad population groups in this country, and [they] are not anthropologically or scientifically based." An influential National Academy of Sciences' report spelled out the implications: "perhaps the largest degree of consensus at the workshop was that any revision in the standard will itself need to be able to adapt to change."[12] Nevertheless, "using appropriate scientific methodologies, including the social sciences," the OMB prescribed definitional boundaries around these social-political constructs.

The logic of these boundaries is hard to discern. Congress has mandated two categories in the census, neither at the core of the traditional American racial order: Hispanic and "some other race."[13] Beyond them, the report specifies seventeen groups in the new category of "Native Hawaiian or Other Pacific Islander." Some are geographic—Solomon Islander, Tarawa Islander—and some tribal or ethnic—Fijian, Kosraean, Tongan—although the census form itself instructs users to "print race." The redefined Asian category identifies ten countries, six of which are given check boxes on the 2010 census form; people from elsewhere are asked to check "other Asian" and "print race." Even the redefined category of "American Indian or Alaska Native" shows the influence of immigration in its modification "to include the original peoples from Central and South America" along with North Americans.[14] "White," which applies to roughly two-thirds of the American population, all of whom are immigrants or descendants of immigrants, is the only category on the census form with no synonyms or specifications.

Controversy attended the OMB's racial classification; as the *Revisions to the Standards* tactfully puts it, "the OMB decisions benefited greatly from the participation of the public that served as a constant reminder that there are real people represented by the data on race and ethnicity and that this is for many a deeply personal issue." For example, "several comments from the American Indian community opposed" including Central and South American Indians in the category of American Indian—but thousands of Native Hawaiians, the Hawaiian congressional delegation, and the Hawaiian state legislature objected to their exclusion from this group. Despite pressure, the OMB declined to add an ethnic category for "Arab or Middle Eastern" on the grounds that "there was no agreement on a definition for this category"; the same decision rule obtained for Cape Verdean. Hispanics remain the only official ethnicity in the United States.

Parsing the criteria for federal data collection on racial and ethnic groups is not an arid word game; the official rules and the counts they generate are used by activists, litigators, politicians, school systems, survey researchers, scholars, advertisers, store buyers, manufacturers, and myriad others to whom racial classification in the U.S. racial order matters. Volumes many times longer than the *Revisions to the Standards*, such as the Department of Education's 2008 *Managing an Identity Crisis: Forum Guide to Implementing New Federal Race and Ethnicity Categories*, are published in order to show users just how to implement the rules. Most important for our purposes, the OMB's 1997 update documents official recognition that what were understood to be homogeneous and fixed racial groups through most of the twentieth century were becoming heterogeneous, fragmented, augmented, and otherwise problematic for that understanding. And despite years of expert struggle for coherence, the result was, inevitably, a hodgepodge. There are simply too many Americans associated with too many different countries and ancestries—and too many political choices and contradictory demands about classification—to fix the definition of a race systematically.

How to classify Hispanics is an especially vexed question. Mexicans have been variously identified as mulatto, a distinct race, White,[15] and a legislatively sanctioned ethnicity. Once it was mandated to enumerate Hispanics in 1970, the census bureau struggled with the complexities of defining race and ethnicity. Figure 2.3 shows its first effort.

Enumeration rules have been streamlined since the 1970's flowchart, but the debate over whether and how to distinguish race from ethnicity has intensified as the number of immigrants to the United States has grown. Some would abjure any separate designation of newcomers; as Orlando Patterson put it, "the census . . . is up to its age-old mischief of making and unmaking racial groups. As it makes a new social category out of the sociologically meaningless collection of peoples from Latin America and Spain, it is quietly abetting the process of demoting and removing white Hispanics from the 'true' white race—native-born non-Hispanic whites."[16] In contrast, the census bureau's Hispanic Advisory

**Detailed Tabulation Plan According to the Spanish Heritage Definition,
1970 Census of Population and Housing**

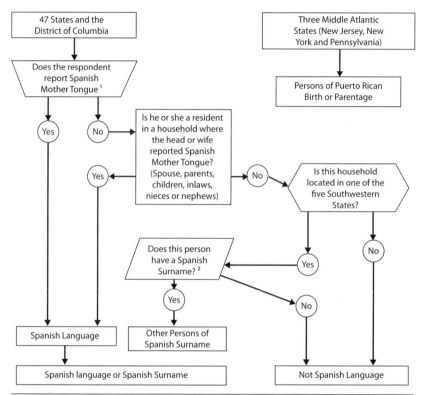

[1] Spanish Mother Tongue: all persons who reported that Spanish was spoken in the home
when they were a child.

[2] Spanish Surname: coded only for Arizona, California, Colorado, New Mexico and Texas by
matching surnames recorded in the questionnaire with those included in a list of over 8,000
Spanish surnames.

Figure 2.3. Procedural flow chart for enumerating people of Spanish heritage,
1970 census.
Source: Hernandez et al. 1973, 675

Committee promotes the official distinction between Hispanic ethnicity
and race on the grounds that many immigrants and their descendants do
not think of themselves in American racial categories.

A third position calls for identifying Hispanics as a race rather than an
ethnicity: "conceptualizing Latinos/as in racial terms is warranted. . . .
[A]bandonment of racial language and its replacement with substitute
vocabularies, in particular that of ethnicity, will obfuscate key aspects of

Latino/a lives." Still others fear rather than urge the view that Latinos are a race: Congressman Thomas Tancredo (R-CO) observed in 2006 that "a lot of people come here . . . not with a desire to disconnect . . . from a previous culture, linguistically, familially, culturally, or even politically. This is a problem. . . . A lot of people [are] coming and saying, 'I don't want to be part of it [American society] anyway.' This is a dangerous thing."[17]

So all plausible views about how to understand Latino immigrants in relationship to race and ethnicity are alive and well in American elite political discourse. The views of ordinary citizens are probably no more settled. Just over half of the respondents to the 2006 Latino National Survey (LNS) agreed that Latinos or Hispanics "make up a distinctive racial group in America"—but they were not offered alternative framings so it is hard to know what to make of this agreement. Just under half of people who identified as Latino or Hispanic on the 2000 census also chose White in the race question; only a few percent identified as Black and the rest called themselves Hispanic or a nationality in the Some Other Race write-in line. In 2010, more identified as White (53 percent), about the same proportion as Black, and fewer as Some Other Race (37 percent). Observers described that change, variously, as "assimilation," "learning," "allowing more to identify as white without feeling that they are . . . in denial about their Hispanicity," being "confused," and irrelevant to their real identity.[18]

Since immigrants come from a wide array of countries, Hispanics are not the only subjects of definitional disputes and intragroup disagreement. At a meeting with Representative Barney Frank (D-MA) in preparation for the 2000 census, "a Vietnam War veteran, Mr. DePina, asked how 'Vietnamese' was listed as a category, yet Cape Verdeans must write in their answer. 'To me, it's a kick in the teeth to Cape Verdean Vietnam vets,' he said." Another Cape Verdean contrasts violence among "*our* people" with that of "other races such as whites, blacks, and Hispanics." Haitians in southern Florida have sought federal recognition as a group distinct from African Americans in order to carve out a space between "firmly entrenched" Black and Cuban American voting blocs.[19]

In our view, there is no correct or most desirable definition of a race; what matters for our purposes is that immigration is making Americans more heterogeneous in ways that challenge the settled understandings of the meaning of race that prevailed for most of the twentieth century. How much one believes that destabilizing conceptual frameworks matters for political and social outcomes depends on deep philosophical questions about the relative roles of material and mental structures in transforming a society; those are topics well beyond our purview here. But surely it undermines the fixity of a racial order if people no longer agree on what the groups are that comprise that order. And if they move beyond disagreement to create a wholly new conception of race, that would contribute to turning instability into transformation.

How Should an Individual Be Classified?

Placing immigrants into American racial categories is an old problem. The many pages of instructions on racial classification given to census enumerators in 1890 included, for example, this paragraph: "In case the person speaks Polish, as Poland is not now a country, inquire whether the birthplace was what is now known as German Poland or Austrian Poland or Russian Poland and enter the answer accordingly as Poland (Ger.), Poland (Aust.), or Poland (Russ.)."[20]

As European boundaries settled down and immigration was drastically curtailed in the mid-twentieth century, individual classification receded as a problem. But it returned as immigration once again rose and as individuals began to identify themselves rather than be labeled by an enumerator. After all, a person's identity may be no more fixed than the border of Poland: "raised by white parents in a predominantly white town, I considered myself to be white. . . . In college new worlds of thought opened to me. Amid a boiling student struggle to create an Asian American studies program . . . , I began to see myself as an Asian American."[21]

Replacing census enumerators as the front line of people who must deal with unstable individual classifications are survey researchers:

> In Florida, . . . we had 1,400 of "others" who specified "Hispanic" for race. I blamed the subcontractor who did the fieldwork, and insisted we needed better training on race issues. . . . But when we repeated the survey in other states I was still getting a fair number of "other-Hispanic." And in reading the interviewers' notes, there were comments like "I know I'm not supposed to accept this, but he really insisted." These showed that the interviewer had indeed paid attention to the training, but still. I conclude that a lot of Hispanics genuinely see that as their race and either cannot or will not choose one or more of the "official" categories we offer. . . . I just can't see trying to force a respondent into a peg hole that they don't think fits them at all.

Health care officials are also frontline troops on the battlefield of individual classification; one study found that over two-thirds of the newborns identified as Hispanic by their mothers were recoded as White in North Carolina's 2002 live birth statistics, since "Hispanic" was an ethnic rather than a racial designation.[22]

As these examples suggest, the biggest problem of individual classification is that immigrants are unfamiliar with or dislike the categories offered to them in the United States. "In Brazil, I would be brown or mulatto, but as the term doesn't exist here, I will check 'black.' . . . Here I became even blacker; I'm a Brazilian black." Or, "we, Dominicans, do not want to look like Africans or embrace African culture; but it's also true that we do not want to embrace Spanish culture either. . . . We just want to be Dominicans, not Hispanics, or blacks, or whites." Somali refugees care much more about clan and religious identity than about American racial labels: as one student wrote, "the Somalis that live here in the U.S. won't talk to each other until they know your tribe. . . . so, [E]very time I meet someone the first thought that comes to me is, do they hate you [*sic*] tribe?"[23]

We can organize this complexity of individual classification along several dimensions. One is time. If a person has only one race and it is fixed at birth—as most Americans thought for most of the twentieth century— racial designations do not change except in unusual cases of "passing" or a mistake. But if a person's choice of a race is somewhat arbitrary, as it is for many immigrants to the United States, why not change it at some later point? In fact, some newcomers to the United States do just that. In a 2001 census bureau survey of about 133,000 respondents, just over seven-tenths of the people who identified as White Hispanics had been White Hispanics in the census a year earlier; only two-fifths of Black Hispanics in 2001 had called themselves Black Hispanics a year earlier. Even 6 percent of Asians in the 2001 survey had not identified as Asian in the 2000 census. In another national survey that recontacted earlier respondents, only two-thirds of people who had previously identified as Hispanic or Latino did so a second time. The surveyor concluded that "what this tells me is that ethnic/cultural identification is not as stable an attribute as many people (including many social scientists) think."[24] The proportion of Latinos identifying as White has ranged from 48 percent on the 2000 census to 63 percent in the 2009 American Community Survey (ACS) to 53 percent in the 2010 census.

For the same reasons, immigrants' racial classifications may be unstable across space. That is, if a person has only one race and it is fixed at birth, his or her racial designation will not vary from one community or social context to another. But if the person's choice of a race is somewhat arbitrary, as it is for many immigrants to the United States, why not change it in different locations? Thus in the 2000 census, two-fifths of Mexicans in California, but three-fifths in Texas, declared themselves to be White. Twenty percent of Dominicans in New York and New Jersey were White, while 46 percent were in Florida. Brazilians in Miami identify as Hispanic more than those in Boston; Brazilians in suburbs identify less with Hispanics than do those in the city. These variations appear to result not from distinct migration streams but rather from "a contextual . . . explanation." "The more rigid racial boundaries and 'racial frame' developed in the former Confederate states of Texas and Florida, and the severe stigma historically attached to those marked as nonwhite there, may shape defensive assertions of whiteness where racial status is ambiguous; in states like California and New York, the social dynamics have been more open to ethnic options and a rejection of rigid U.S. racial categories."[25]

Immigration status itself may be associated with one's choice of a race but apparently not in any consistent direction. Compare foreign-born to U.S.-born Americans with South or Central American ancestry in the 2000 census. In thirteen nationalities, the U.S.-born were more likely than the foreign-born to identify as White; in six nationalities, they were less likely to do so; and in four, there were no differences by location of birth. Conversely, more U.S.-born than foreign-born identified as Black among six nationalities; fewer did so in one case (Jamaica), and there was no difference in the remaining sixteen cases.[26] Heterogeneity of origin, nationality, and racial identity combine here into a mélange whose overriding characteristic is inconsistency.

If a person's racial classification is not fixed, he or she may be influenced by something as superficial as question wording or survey context. In one survey, 5 percent of Dominicans in two American cities defined themselves as Black when asked their race; 16 percent of the same respondents chose Black when offered a short list of races; and 36 percent thought that most Americans classified them as Black. That is almost inconceivable for American-born Blacks or Whites. A comparison of the self-administered 2000 census and the interviewer-administered 2000 Current Population Survey (CPS) conducted at essentially the same time found that only 88 percent of those who chose Asian in the census also chose Asian and Pacific Islander in the CPS.[27]

Immigrants' children may choose a different race or ethnicity from that of their parents—again, a phenomenon hard to imagine for native-born Americans. In the late 1990s, the Children of Immigrants Longitudinal Study (CILS) interviewed more than 5,200 seventeen- and eighteen-year-olds from seventy-seven nationalities living in South Florida or Southern California. Their immigrant parents were interviewed separately. In all nine Latino groups, only a few parents reported their race as Hispanic or Latino, whereas one-quarter to three-fifths of the children did. Conversely, in all groups, more parents than children identified as White. Parents sometimes were more likely to identify as multiracial or to identify with their nationality, and sometimes less likely to do so. Another study also found generational change but in the opposite direction: "rates of Mexican identification fall to 81 percent for second-generation children with only one Mexican-born parent, . . . [and] 58 percent for third-generation children with just one Mexican-born grandparent."[28]

Phenotypically black immigrants, who now comprise about 10 percent of the Black American population, face distinct issues with regard to individual classification. Some identify as African American while others prefer ethnic or nationality identities. Allegiances can be fraught: "I would identify with them [fellow residents of Harlem], but at the same time I wouldn't. They were like me, but at the same time they weren't." And self-identity may not resemble external identification: "from the inside we're Dominicans. From the outside, we're Black." Context matters: whether dark-skinned Puerto Ricans in New York identify as Hispanic or something else depends on their own socioeconomic status and that of their neighborhood as well as their appearance or preferences.[29]

Even for White immigrants, racial classifications are increasingly unstable in a way that is hardly imaginable to native-born Whites. A college student says she "never grew up around white people, only Turkish, Russian, U.S.-born Jews, Pakistanis, Blacks, Spanish, Christians, 'crazy' lesbians, Middle Eastern people." A journalist observed that a prize-winning high school math club had only one White student; the student corrected him with, "I'm not really white, I'm Albanian." A 2008 applicant to UCLA could not find the appropriate box in response to the question about race and ethnicity: "'I read it five times and was like, where is Middle Eastern? Is it on the other page, did it get cut off? I thought they forgot.' Her Lebanese-born mother told her that Arabs are considered white, but Salame didn't believe her. . . . 'It did not make sense to me, it's so far-fetched,' said Salame, who ended up checking 'Other.'"[30]

Aggregate data confirm anecdotes. About a sixth of the people who marked more than one race in the 2000 census chose White and Some Other Race—identified variously as "Greek, Italian, Irish, Russian, Ukrainian, Albanian, Egyptian, Iranian, and Arab." These respondents may be flagging "mixed parentage, an understanding of race at odds with census categories, or an ancestry that is nominally white but an experience in the society at large as only marginally white."[31] Whatever the reason, the fact is that as American groups become more internally heterogeneous and as more groups enter the United States, the assumption of the old racial order that a person can be readily and permanently classified in a given race is breaking down. At some point, instability in classification expands into transformation of a crucial component of the old racial order.

Relative Group Positions

Unstable individual classifications combine with disagreement about how to define a race to undermine any assumption that the given racial order is self-evident or natural. But until relative group positions change, the old order will retain much of its power. Immigration is, in fact, chang-ing relative group positions in the United States, to a greater or lesser degree depending on how immigrants are defined and how change is measured. At a minimum, the range of relative group positions is expand-ing at top and bottom: some immigrant groups understood as non-White are doing better than Whites, and some immigrants not understood as Black are doing worse than Blacks. At a maximum, immigrants are dis-rupting old hierarchies of wealth and poverty as well as old assumptions about who deserves to be included or warrants exclusion.

To show how and how much relative group positions are changing, we proceed in stages. First, consider immigration status.[32] Among American residents aged twenty-five and over, just over 9 percent of native-born citizens have less than a high school diploma, compared with 20 percent of naturalized citizens and 38 percent of noncitizens. At the other end of the schooling spectrum, 30 percent of adult native-born citizens have a bachelor's degree or higher—as do 34 percent of naturalized citizens and 24 percent of adult noncitizens. Thus immigrants as a group are both *less* well educated than and *better* educated than native-born citizens.

The same pattern holds, more weakly, for income. Again considering people aged twenty-five and older, about 14 percent of native-born citi-zens have an annual income of less than $20,000, compared with 15 percent of naturalized citizens and 24 percent of noncitizens. At the other end of the income spectrum, 20 percent of native-born Americans have an annual income of at least $100,000, compared with over 21 percent of naturalized citizens and just over 10 percent of noncitizens. Thus im-migrants as a group expand the bottom but not the top of the income distribution.

Second, consider the impact on relative group positions of immigration status combined with race or ethnicity. Table 2.1 shows relevant data on educational attainment and table 2.2 on household incomes. Compared with native-born Whites, White immigrants are more likely to have low levels of education and more likely to have completed college. So White immigrants *disperse* Whites' relative educational position, adding people at both the top and bottom ends of the distribution. Compared with native-born Blacks, Black immigrants have little impact on the poorly educated, but they increase the proportion that has completed college. Thus Black immigrants *raise* Blacks' relative educational standing.[33] Asian immigrants increase the proportion of Asians who have not com-pleted high school and boost the proportion of Asians who have com-pleted at least a bachelor's degree. Thus, like White immigrants do for Whites, Asian immigrants *disperse* Asians' relative educational position. Finally, compared with native-born Hispanics, Hispanic immigrants are much more likely to have low levels of education and a little less likely to

Table 2.1
Years of Schooling of U.S. Residents Aged 25 and over, by Race and Citizenship,
Current Population Survey 2009

	Native-born	Naturalized	Noncitizen
A. Less than high school			
Non-Hispanic White	7.9%	13.1%	11.7%
Black	16.7	11.9	16.8
Asian	6.3	13.6	13.6
Hispanic	19.8	34.4	55.2
B. Bachelor's degree or more			
Non-Hispanic White	32.4%	40.9%	44.7%
Black	19.6	34.2	27.0
Asian	46.9	46.3	55.5
Hispanic	17.6	17.1	8.0

have a college degree or more. Thus Latino immigrants *lower* Latinos' relative educational standing.

Overall, immigration moves Blacks up the schooling hierarchy, moves Latinos down, and spreads Whites and Asians out. Blacks are no longer the worst off educationally since Latinos, especially immigrants, have that dubious distinction; Whites are no longer the best off educationally since Asians, especially immigrants, occupy that position. More abstractly, due to immigration two groups—Asians and Whites—are more internally heterogeneous, and two groups—Asians and Latinos—have made the hierarchy itself more complex.

Table 2.2
Household Income of U.S. Residents Aged 25 and over, by Race and
Citizenship, Current Population Survey 2009

	Native-born	Naturalized	Noncitizen
A. Less than $20,000 annually			
Non-Hispanic White	12.1%	12.8%	14.3%
Black	30.1	20.6	26.8
Asian	7.4	11.5	15.5
Hispanic	20.2	18.1	29.7
B. $100,000 or more annually			
Non-Hispanic White	21.6%	26.4%	24.8%
Black	9.0	17.2	7.1
Asian	31.4	29.7	20.9
Hispanic	13.4	10.4	3.5

Immigrants' income does less than schooling to change groups' relative positions, as one would expect for a recently arrived population. Nevertheless, it also contributes to instability in this component of the racial order. White immigrants have about the same level of poverty and slightly higher incomes than native-born Whites; immigration thus marginally enhances Whites' relative economic position. Black immigrants are less likely to be poor and more likely to be well-off than native-born Blacks, so they contribute to raising Blacks' relative position. A higher proportion of Asian newcomers than Asian Americans are poor and a lower proportion are well-off, so they lower Asians' relative position (although as a whole that group still enjoys higher incomes than all other American groups). Finally, Hispanic immigrants increase the proportion of poor Latinos and decrease the proportion with high incomes, thus worsening their relative position. Thus immigration makes Blacks as a group (and Whites, to a lesser degree) better-off with regard to income; it reduces Asians' otherwise very strong position and lowers Hispanics' position to roughly that of African Americans. Asians show more internal economic heterogeneity as a consequence of immigration, but otherwise immigration changes relative income levels less than it changes relative levels of educational attainment. None of these changes implies that a given individual's situation or opportunities change, but over time they may undermine stereotypes about a given group's location in the social order.

Cross-sectional data on relative group positions tell us nothing about change over time; for that we need information on economic mobility across a lifetime and over generations. With the crucial exception of undocumented immigrants whom we discuss in chapter 6, the evidence consistently shows upward mobility. "After twenty years, cohorts post averages [on an occupational score based on average income for that job] that are three to four points higher than the initial levels. This occupational upgrading is roughly equivalent to a promotion from an unskilled laborer's position to that of an operative, or from an accountant's position to that of a mid-level manager. . . . These gains are . . . not necessarily inconsistent with the smaller increases found in the nineteenth-century data." Between 1994 and 2004, almost all cohorts of immigrants who arrived after 1970 closed at least a little of the gap between their own occupational scores and those of same-aged native-born citizens. Thus "the balance of evidence supports the view that immigrant workers become more like native workers, both male and female, with time in the American economy."[34]

Mobility is greater from immigrant parent to native-born child. First, "second generation immigrants exceed the educational attainment of the first generation by a considerable margin. In the case of advanced degrees . . . , they actually exceed the attainment of both first generation immigrants and non-immigrants." At the other end of the educational ladder, a fifth of immigrants but only 6 percent of their offspring—about the same as native-born Americans—have less than a ninth grade education. Second, immigrants' children on average earn more than both their parents and native-born workers. Finally, children who were brought to the United States before age five in recent decades have higher mean occupation scores than do native-borns, just as in 1900 and 1930.[35] In sum, immigrants and their families improve their relative positions as they or their children become incorporated into the American economic system; whether that does or must occur at the expense of the native-born is a subject for chapters 6 and 7.

Following Claire Kim's model of the racial order, we also consider relative group statuses along the horizontal dimension of insider to outsider. Some argue that "the recent anti-immigrant impulse in U.S. politics reflects a propensity to strengthen national identity and gain partisan advantage by excluding some from the body politic." Concerns about "the law-breaking nature of unauthorized status, terrorism and security threats, criminality among the unauthorized, the cost of social services, labor market competition with the native-born, dilution of American culture, and racial prejudice" combine to push immigrants, especially Hispanics, out of the American mainstream. Douglas Massey makes an even stronger argument: the United States is engaged in a "new politics of demonization," an era of "postmodern racialization" and "categorical stratification after 9/11":

> U.S. policies are moving Mexican Americans steadily away from their middle position in the economic hierarchy and toward formation as an underclass. Segregation levels are rising, discrimination is increasing, poverty is deepening, educational levels are stagnating, and the social safety net has been deliberately poked full of holes to allow immigrants to fall through. Whether or not Mexicans become a new urban underclass remains to be seen, but it is already clear that after occupying a middle socioeconomic position between whites and blacks for generations, the economic fortunes of Mexicans have now fallen to levels at or below those of African Americans.[36]

The balance of the evidence shows that this claim is too strong with regard to most Mexican Americans, especially across a lifetime or over generations, and only partially supported for even unauthorized migrants. Immigrants, Mexicans among them, are slowly but steadily improving their condition across their lifetime and across generations at roughly the same rate that immigrants did a century ago. They have more autonomy and capacity for action than Massey's portrayal allows for. In a later book, even Massey and his coauthor show that, despite very difficult lives, four times as many of their Latino immigrant interviewees are

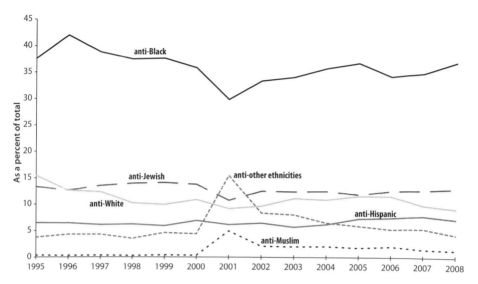

Figure 2.4. Hate crimes against groups, as percentage of total hate crimes, 1995–2008.
Source: Authors' analysis of FBI Uniform Crime Reports, annual Hate Crime Statistics

upwardly mobile as are downwardly mobile, and four-fifths believe that economic opportunities are greater in the United States than in their country of origin. As one person put it, "well, if we are realistic, we know that the opportunities are here. . . . No matter what kind of work you consider, there is employment."[37] Full-throated despair about the exclusion of newcomers seems unwarranted.

FBI data on reported hate crimes, shown in figure 2.4, similarly suggest that extreme hostility toward outgroups is not rising. Blacks represent a higher proportion of hate crimes than any other group, followed in all years except one by Jews and then Whites (tabulated separately). The exceptional year, not surprisingly, is 2001, in which the proportion of hate crimes reported against "other ethnicities" and Muslims spiked. Since 2001, hate crimes against Muslims and other ethnicities have declined as a share of the total, to almost but not quite the levels they had been before 2001. Similarly, anti-Hispanic hate crimes have risen a bit in the past few years but remain essentially flat. So unless one could show that underreporting of hate crimes has increased, and increased differentially by group, there is little evidence of rising levels of virulent hatred against new outgroups.

Nevertheless, setting aside extreme levels of hatred and maltreatment, American policies and practices are increasingly heterogeneous with regard to immigration and immigrants. This contradictory mix of policies, practices, and attitudes is best shown through consideration of the next two components of the racial order, to which we now turn.

Permitted, Required, and Prohibited Acts

Unlike in previous centuries, no American law excludes newcomers of specified nationalities or races, and no law sets a quota on the number of immigrants from a given country. No law prohibits particular groups of immigrants from becoming citizens or owning land. Those absences represent a huge transformation. In addition, federal laws and Supreme Court decisions require local public schools to serve immigrant children, including the undocumented, and to provide programs for students whose English-language proficiency is limited.[38] Even undocumented workers are covered by the Fair Labor Standards Act. These, too, are significant changes from earlier racial orders. But all of these steps toward inclusion occurred during the late twentieth century so are part of the current post-1960s racial order rather than part of a new transformative impetus. We focus instead on laws and policies that have emerged or become more important over the past decade.

Some government actions can be interpreted as hardening group-based prohibitions. Although appearance alone does not suffice to make a traffic stop legal, the Supreme Court ruled in 1975 that a presumption of Mexican ancestry is one of many factors that legalize traffic stops near the Mexican border in a search for unauthorized immigrants. As the Court explained, "because of the importance of the governmental interest at stake, the minimal intrusion of a brief stop, and the absence of practical alternatives for policing the border, we hold that, when an officer's observations lead him reasonably to suspect that a particular vehicle may contain aliens who are illegally in the country, he may stop the car briefly and investigate the circumstances that provoke suspicion." Among the list of circumstances that might provoke suspicion, "the Government also points out that trained officers can recognize the characteristic appearance of persons who live in Mexico, relying on such factors as the mode of dress and haircut."[39] Justice Douglas warned that "the suspicion test has indeed brought a state of affairs where the police may stop citizens on the highway on the flimsiest of justifications," but this decision remains in effect and may be increasingly brought into play.

Far from the Mexican border, problems can arise when localities become involved with federal immigration policies. Section 287(g) of the 1996 immigration law (IIRAIRA) "permit[s] designated . . . local law enforcement . . . officers to perform immigration law enforcement functions." The program has been strongly criticized by the American Civil Liberties Union, the Congressional Hispanic Caucus, and groups representing some police; even the institutionally cautious Government Accountability Office (GAO) titled a recent report on the use of Section 287(g), "Better Controls Needed over Program." It found that some local agencies have focused not on terrorism or serious crime as the program intended but instead "used 287(g) authority to process individuals for minor crimes, such as speeding." All local agencies lacked sufficient oversight, and most reported community concern that "use of program authority would lead to racial profiling and intimidation by law enforcement officers."[40]

Section 287(g) has had an impact well beyond the small number of communities or states (eleven states and about sixty communities, not including the biggest immigrant gateway states or cities) using it. By 2010, over three-fifths of respondents to a survey of Hispanics agreed that discrimination against Latinos was a major problem, up from less than half in 2002. Perceptions of bias varied with legal status: about 80 percent of unauthorized immigrants, compared with about 70 percent of legal residents, just over 60 percent of naturalized citizens, and about 50 percent of the native-born saw discrimination. Slightly over half of Latinos—a third of the native-born and seven-tenths of the foreign-born—worried that they or a close associate might be deported. A third claimed to know someone who had in fact been detained or deported within the past year.[41]

One set of responses in this survey, however, showed movement in the opposite direction. The proportion of Latinos who reported being stopped by the police and asked about their immigration status in the past year declined from 9 percent in 2008 to 5 percent in 2010. And a 2009 survey by a different organization also shows little police involvement; 5 percent of immigrants who have resided in the United States at least five years reported having been stopped by the police and questioned about their immigration status. But even in that survey over half of the long-term immigrant respondents agree that the "government is giving legal immigrants a harder time" since the attacks of September 11, 2001. They similarly concur that the government has become a lot (55 percent) or a little (21 percent) stricter in enforcing immigration laws.[42]

Dramatic cases make clear why intermittently tougher enforcement of immigration laws makes such a deep impression even on legal immigrants. In Maricopa County, Arizona, "America's Toughest Sheriff," Joseph Arpaio, uses traffic stops to arrest and detain immigrants. As of fall 2011, Sheriff Arpaio claimed over 42,800 "ICE 'Holds,'" as well as an additional 5,400 arrests of illegal immigrants under state and other federal laws. Since first being elected in 1992, he has been reelected four times by huge margins. Men caught up in Sheriff Arpaio's sweeps have been housed in stiflingly hot tents and dressed in pink underwear, clown-style striped pants, and pink sweatshirts reading "clean and sober." The intent to humiliate is not hard to see. In 2009, the Department of Homeland Security removed Sheriff Arpaio's authority to make immigration arrests in the field; he responded by claiming that he would continue to arrest illegal immigrants through state rather than federal law.[43]

Muslims and immigrants from Arab countries have been subject to different governmental restrictions, emerging from the attacks of September 11, 2001, rather than from unauthorized entry. Soon after the attacks, the FBI instituted a program called PENTTBOM (Pentagon/Twin Towers Bombing Investigation), during which it and the Immigration and Naturalization Service detained thousands of noncitizens. Unlike in previous practice, those detained were held without bail indefinitely until they could be cleared by the FBI; some were deported. Investigators also requested "voluntary interviews" from thousands of Muslim and Arab citizens. Based on a belief that another attack was imminent, the FBI conducted more interviews of Arab or Muslim men in 2004.[44] Measures to protect national security are undoubtedly essential, but these programs have been widely criticized as ill-judged and counterproductive. They arguably generated more anxiety and anger than useful information, as well as coming dangerously close to state-mandated discrimination and violation of the right to equal protection of the law.

Also in response to 9/11, immigration policies have been changed to provide the government with more tools to keep track of noncitizens. The Enhanced Border Security and Visa Entry Reform Program of 2002 requires fingerprint and digital image data for visitors to the United States, and the federal government now collects DNA samples from all immigration detainees and arrestees. The most stringent law was reserved for nationals or citizens from certain Muslim countries. During most of the 2000s, the National Security Entry-Exit Registration System (NSEERS) required adult male nonimmigrant alien visitors to the United States from twenty-five countries (twenty-four predominantly Muslim states plus North Korea) to register with the government at their port of entry. Their ports of entry and exit were restricted, and they had to notify the Department of Homeland Security of changes in address, employment, or school.[45] NSEERS was closed down, however, in 2011.

Finally, a Justice Department ruling holds that "Transportation Security Administration personnel, and other federal and state authorities, may subject them ["men . . . from a particular ethnic group"] to heightened scrutiny" if, for example, "U.S. intelligence sources report that terrorists from a particular ethnic group are planning to use commercial jetliners as weapons by hijacking them at an airport in California during the next week." In one blogger's colloquial interpretation, "while Public agencies condemn profiling, the message gets completely lost in translation for the common TSA federal agent or immigration officer. This is because there is no real Executive Imperative to stop it. Nor is there any efficacious cross cultural awareness training or a basic lesson in geography."[46]

It is unclear how frequently such travel restrictions occur. We know of no evidence on the relationship between occurrences and complaints, but for what it is worth, the Department of Transportation received eighty-seven complaints in 2008 alleging discrimination by airlines based on race, ethnicity, national origin, or color; four were security related. The Department of Homeland Security reported about eighty complaints in 2008 involving issues of discrimination, profiling, or the security-related watch list.[47] In short, under one hundred official complaints per year could be related to "flying while Arab," but we do not know whether that figure represents overreporting, underreporting, or neither.

The newest federal regulation of immigrants is the Secure Communities program, whose purpose is to "identify, detain and remove from the United States aliens who have been convicted of serious criminal offenses and are subject to removal," in the words of the Immigration and Customs Enforcement agency (ICE). Participating jurisdictions link the fingerprints of immigrants who are jailed with federal databases; if there is a match and evidence of an immigration violation, ICE may begin deportation proceedings. As of early 2011, thousands had been expelled through the program, of whom 13 percent were accused of serious crimes. Secure Communities is intended to be a nationwide program by 2013, but some communities and states are resisting it because it lacks legislative or regulatory guidelines and targets too wide a range of persons. In 2011, the governor of Illinois discontinued that state's participation on the grounds of "a conflict between the stated purpose of the Secure Communities program and the implementation of the program." New York and Massachusetts have also withdrawn; at this writing, other states and localities, including Colorado and California, are similarly considering withdrawal.

As the minimal participation in 287(g) and the growing controversy over Secure Communities imply, some laws or ordinances respond to immigration with permissions rather than prohibitions. The federal Department of Justice reminded all school districts in 2011 that "the undocumented or noncitizen status of a student (or his or her parent or guardian) is irrelevant to that student's entitlement to an elementary and secondary public school education." Despite being stalled at the federal level, laws permitting undocumented high school graduates to pay in-state tuition rates at state universities have been passed in twelve states since 2001; eighteen states have considered and rejected such legislation, and four explicitly prohibit it (one state, Oklahoma, straddles permission and prohibition)[48] Among the 1,059 immigration-related bills and resolutions introduced in all state legislatures in 2007, laws "expanding immigrants' rights were enacted at a higher rate (19 percent of 313 bills) than policies contracting immigrants' rights (11 percent of 263 bills)." Put another way, sixty bills to expand immigrants' rights passed, compared with twenty-eight that contracted them. As pluralist political theory would predict, states with the largest foreign-born population were most likely to promulgate laws to help or incorporate immigrants. And as some theories of racial threat would predict, states with few immigrants but large proportional increases were most likely to promulgate restrictive or punitive laws.[49]

Local governments are as heterogeneous as states are; as one headline put it, "US cities offer very different ways of dealing with illegal immigration." Some cities offer sanctuaries and some police departments work hard to develop trust and engagement with immigrant communities; New York City refused to participate in the 287(g) program. Other localities forbid landlords from renting to undocumented immigrants or report people to ICE. Almost three-fifths of the 129 immigration-related local ordinances that passed in the first half of 2007 reinforced immigrants' rights, while the remainder contracted them. As one set of experts puts it, "the uncertainty produced by conflict at multiple levels and the reluctance of many local governments and police executives to take positions ... [creates] a multilayered jurisdictional patchwork of enforcement authority: an emerging, confusing, and often contradictory geography of immigration enforcement in the United States."[50]

In sum, immigrants overall are no longer subject to governmental prohibitions and they have some legal protections, but immigrants with the wrong appearance in the wrong place and time, or visitors from the wrong countries, can face restrictions. The United States as a whole lacks a coherent policy to incorporate or help immigrants; some states and localities have taken steps to fill that void—or to do the opposite. This component of the American racial order is itself increasingly heterogeneous, which is an understandable if frustrating response to the heterogeneity produced by immigration.

Social Relations

"Social relations" is a catchall term, including everything from public opinion to political coalitions to incorporation in neighborhoods, schools, and jobs. It encompasses native-borns' views of immigrants and vice versa, direct interactions between immigrants and the native-born, and immigrants' social and political trajectories. Here, we can explore only a few of those issues; we have chosen those that most fully engage with the

grants are good for America split evenly over whether Hispanic immigrants are also. In 2006, respondents described Latinos and Asians similarly with regard to whether they "work very hard," "have strong family values," and "don't try to fit in," but they perceived Asians to do better in school and Latinos to be more likely to receive welfare or get involved in crime. Still, these results are more favorable than responses to similar questions in 1993 and 1997.[60] Twice as many agreed in 2009 that the annual number of Asian immigrants is "about right" as said the same about Latino immigrants (61 to 31 percent).[61]

Views of immigrants may vary in accord with the race of the survey respondent. Again to summarize a huge array of findings: in one study, native-born Whites living in a metropolitan area with a large proportion of Hispanics were more prejudiced against immigrants, while those living among Asians were less so. Whites living among Asians were more likely to agree that immigrants benefit the economy and enrich American culture, whereas Whites living in metropolitan areas with many Hispanics were more likely to believe that immigrants increase crime. Roughly speaking, native-born Blacks held the opposite views—they were more favorable to immigrants when living among Hispanics and less favorable to immigrants when living among Asians.[62]

As a further indication of heterogeneity of views, the topic at issue intersects with race in shaping attitudes toward immigrants. In a series of Gallup polls through the 2000s, Whites were a few percentage points less likely, and Latinos a few points more likely, than Blacks to say that immigration should be increased.[63] In the same series, Whites were similarly more likely and Latinos less likely than Blacks to agree that immigrants worsen the American crime situation and damage Americans' social and moral values. Blacks, however, were the most likely to see immigrants as harming the economy overall and worsening Americans' job situation. Whites appreciated immigrants' contributions to the United States' culture and food more than Blacks did (but less than Latinos). As if seeking to confuse the social dynamics even more, Americans are usually generous toward undocumented immigrants while remaining hostile to illegal immigration. Up to four-fifths agree that illegal immigrants "mostly take low-paying jobs Americans don't want."[64] In 2006, a slight majority agreed that illegal immigrants "mostly make a contribution to American society" instead of agreeing that they are "mostly a drain on American society." Not always, however: in May 2010, four out of five worried that illegal immigrants use too many government services such as schools and hospitals, and the same proportion thought illegal immigrants might drive down wages.[65]

Substantial majorities endorse border-hardening measures such as a literal or electronic wall on the Mexican border, using the National Guard

Table 2.3

Americans' Policy Preferences for Unauthorized Immigrants, 2006–7
"Which comes closest to your view about what the government policy should
be toward illegal immigrants currently residing in the United States?" (options
rotated)

Date	Leave U.S.[1]	Temporary[2]	Pathway[3]	Citizen[4]	Unsure
4/13–15/07	14%	6%	42%	36%	2%
3/2–4/07	24	15	–	59	2
6/8–25/06	16	17	–	66	1
5/5–7/06	21	15	–	61	3
4/7–9/06	18	17	–	63	2

Source: USA Today/Gallup Poll, in *Polling Report.* N = about 1,000 adults nationwide in each survey.
Note: Question wording is from the April 2007 survey, but the other surveys offer similar proposals for
three of the four options specified in April 2007.
[1]Require illegal immigrants to leave the U.S. and not allow them to return.
[2]Require illegal immigrants to leave the U.S. but allow them to return temporarily to work.
[3]Require illegal immigrants to leave the U.S. but allow them to return and become U.S. citizens if they
meet certain requirements over a period of time.
[4]Allow illegal immigrants to remain in the United States and become U.S. citizens if they meet certain
requirements over a period of time.

to patrol the border, enhancing the number of border police, and so on.[66]
But they also concur, usually in substantial majorities, with almost all
proposals for regularizing illegal immigrants' status, up to and including
pathways to eventual American citizenship. They endorse temporary
guest worker programs, point systems for high-skilled workers, the
"chance to keep their jobs and eventually apply for legal status," "the
right to live here legally if they pay a fine and meet other requirements,"
and so on.[67] Large majorities consistently oppose deportation of non-
criminal unauthorized immigrants. In a May 2010 poll, the same proportion, four out of five, that perceived great social costs of illegal immigration also worried that strict laws would cause severe hardship to
immigrant families or lead to harassment of Latinos. A complicated question asked several times while Congress was debating immigration reform in the mid-2000s is especially revealing since it required respondents to choose among several options (see table 2.3).

As this table suggests, throughout intense debates within and outside
of Congress over several years, Americans' policy preferences remained
fairly fixed; at least three-fifths wanted undocumented immigrants to be
able to become American citizens, and only one-fifth wanted to see them
deported. One-fifth is a large fraction given the massive disruption to
businesses, communities, and families that deporting about eleven million people would entail, but it is not clear whether proponents of depor-

tation (or of citizenship) have any idea of the number or location of illegal immigrants.

One survey nicely epitomizes the confused state of American views on immigration policy. In spring 2010, about three-fifths of voters endorsed a policy that would welcome all immigrants except security threats, criminals, or deadbeats; more Republicans than Democrats or Independents concurred. However, an even larger share of respondents, including those who endorsed a welcoming policy, said it is more important to get control of the borders than to regularize the status of unauthorized immigrants. Although it is not clear that they knew its terms, three-fifths of respondents, including those who would welcome more immigrants, endorsed Arizona's new stringent immigration law (discussed in chapter 6).[68]

The clearest conclusion from reams of survey data about immigrants and immigration is that no single conclusion is warranted. Americans are individually ambivalent and collectively incoherent about immigration policy, immigrants' behaviors, and immigrants' impact on the United States.[69]

Immigrants' own views are generally more consistent. Certainly they see problems and can point to flaws in the United States: anywhere from a tenth to a quarter of adult Hispanics report that regardless of their own legal status, increasing public attention to illegal immigration has made it more difficult for them to get or keep a job, find or keep housing, travel outside the United States, use public services, or go about their daily activities. Nevertheless, immigrants rate U.S. immigration services and officials highly, and more highly than their counterparts did a few years earlier. Between 2002 and 2009, positive ratings of immigration services rose from 48 to 58 percent, and negative ratings dropped from 12 to 7 percent; in 2009 only one-fifth disagreed that immigration officials are "respectful and do[ing] their best to help new immigrants." Immigrants who are not citizens but are legal residents gave government immigration services about the same positive ratings as citizens. Most surprisingly, even a majority of undocumented immigrants rated immigration services positively or neutrally. Only 2 percent of the newcomers in this survey rated immigration problems or policies as the most important problem in the United States, and another 2 percent identified discrimination or racism—whereas 62 percent noted the economy and unemployment. Those ratios varied little by legal status or recency of immigration.[70]

Not surprisingly, most newcomers do not think of themselves as Americans. But in 2006, many of their children reported a "very strong" identification with the United States, as did almost four-fifths of immigrants' grandchildren. Identity with the country of origin followed the opposite trajectory, although the two questions were distinct so it need not have done so.[71] A 2009 survey found that close to nine-tenths of immigrants are happy with life in the United States; seven-tenths would choose to come to the United States if they "could do it again."[72] Three-quarters accept the description of the United States as "a unique country that stands for something special in the world," and most endorse American job opportunities and the legal, health care, and education systems. Those not fluent in English are very eager to learn it, and almost all want their children to be taught in English even if they temporarily lag in substantive knowledge. Most important, fewer than five years were necessary for over three-quarters to "feel comfortable here and part of the community"; for nearly half, two years sufficed.[73] We suspect that the wording of this survey arguably encouraged assimilationist responses, but even with some discounting, it is not portraying a set of angry, alienated, disillusioned newcomers.

Many immigrants and their children are becoming not only emotionally incorporated but also physically less isolated. After decades of rising segregation, in the 1990s the ten largest metropolitan areas underwent a "profound transformation: . . . mixed-race neighborhoods replaced homogenous neighborhoods in large numbers." The number of predominantly White neighborhoods fell by almost a third, while mixed White-and-other and mixed Black-and-other neighborhoods increased proportionally. The trend continued and perhaps accelerated in the 2000s. Most broadly, "[i]mmigrant groups and their descendants are by and large becoming residentially assimilated in American metropolitan areas. . . . Immigrants who have been in the United States for a longer period of time are also generally less segregated from other groups than new arrivals. . . . In concert with broader political, economic, and cultural shifts, immigration has softened the black-white divide. . . . We may see racial and ethnic boundary blurring in the coming years."[74]

By 2010, journalists were reporting that "immigrants fanned out across the United States in the last decade, settling in greater numbers in small towns and suburbs rather than in the cities where they typically moved when they first came to this country." Despite the arrival of close to seven million people from Latin America during the 2000s and high birthrates among Hispanics, evidence is mixed on whether Hispanic-White segregation decreased more often than it increased. Consider one measure: of the fifty metropolitan areas with the highest levels of residential separation between Latinos and Whites in the late 2000s, thirty-five had a population that was more than 5 percent Hispanic in 2009. Among those thirty-five, eleven saw a rise and twenty-four saw a fall in segregation from the beginning to the end of the decade. Another measure, however, shows a

different pattern: "of the 100 largest metro areas only 38 showed Hispanic segregation declines since 2000, and 47 showed segregation
gains. . . . The new segregation of Hispanics is a consequence of recent
immigration and pioneering movement to new communities. It's uneven,
and will eventually decline as its members become established in these
new environs."[75] Metropolitan areas, in short, are becoming more
heterogeneous.

Social relations defined as political coalitions present a different face
of instability. Some coalitions or alliances between immigrants and the
native-born thrive; the prime example is the alliance of liberal Whites,
African Americans, Latinos, and Asian Americans that supported Tom
Bradley from his 1973 election as mayor of Los Angeles to his retirement
twenty years later. More common is cooperation on non-zero-sum substantive issues such as education policy. A united group of African Americans, Latinos, and poor and rural Whites was able to craft a new admissions policy for the University of Texas after race-conscious criteria were
ruled unconstitutional. Asian Americans and Latinos in Los Angeles
County similarly joined to fight discriminatory practices in schools.[76]
Labor unions, the Catholic Church, and even a new "conservative-
evangelical alliance" have joined with immigrant advocacy groups in
pursuit of laws to legalize the undocumented and solve border problems.[77] Even some politicians without large immigrant constituencies
pursue coalitional politics simply in order to deal with the impact of immigration on their community. As the former governor of Montana put
it, "by the circumstances we are involved in, we are obliged—you can't
avoid it—to be involved with and serve diverse populations."[78]

But coalitions are hard to create or sustain, perhaps especially among
non-Whites. African Americans may resent what they see as evidence
that immigrants are treated better than native-born Black Americans;
almost half of young Black adults in one survey, for example, agreed that
"the government treats most immigrants better than it treats most Black
people born in this country." Only three in ten Whites and one in five
Latinos agreed. Conversely, Hispanics may resent what they see as
Blacks' unfair grip on power; as we write, battles over ethnic succession
are brewing:

> Although Compton has gone from a predominantly African American com-
> munity to a city that is two-thirds Latino over the last two decades, no Latino
> candidate has ever been elected to the City Council or any other city office.
> Since 2000, six Latino candidates have waged unsuccessful campaigns. . . .
> Earlier this month, three Latina residents sued the city under the 2001 Califor-
> nia Voting Rights Act, contending that its at-large council elections violate
> Latinos' civil rights by diluting their voting power.

Groups that unite around a major event, such as the immigrants' rights marches of 2006, may fall apart once the moment has passed.[79]

In the end, economic forces may do more to change social relations than attitudes, living situations, political alliances, or governmental practice can. In Washington, D.C., the late 1990s saw "a turning point in the process of gentrification that *commodified* the ethnic diversity of the neighborhood, turning ethnic diversity into a feature that brought added symbolic value to living there and added economic value to real estate prices."[80] Once televisions switched to digital transmission in 2009 and opened new cable channels, one community saw forty-six new "multicultural" channels. Airlines and banks are right behind television and real estate agents. Cocktail napkins on United Airlines announce that "our flight attendants can speak over 30 languages and dialects. Chances are, they speak yours." HSBC Bank runs an advertisement showing a South Asian woman wearing a spectacular array of jewelry over the caption,

> With 173 nationalities, New Yorkers have some very different takes on bling. From multi-caret rings to Indian wedding finery, New Yorkers have a thousand different ways to shine. . . . We've built our business using the insights gained in 77 countries and territories worldwide to better serve our customers.

Cities are discovering the commercial appeal of incorporating immigrants. In 2011, Denver's marketing director worked to bring a Bolivian dance troupe honoring San Patricio into the Saint Patrick's Day parade. The 2011 Queen Colleen, Keriayn O'Donnell, is fluent in Spanish (learned from her grandparents) as well as adept in Irish step dancing. The goal is a "community-wide celebration, . . . a sign that . . . we're done with hibernation" and therefore out in public, says the marketing director, Steve Sander.[81] Even cartoonists capture the commercial appeal of transformative immigration, as seen in figure 2.5.

What unites all of these disparate social relations is that they are a response to and engagement with an increasingly heterogeneous American population. Demographic change through immigration is adding new groups to American society and making established groups internally differentiated; in consequence, the society, economy, and polity are all being transformed. In some cases the changes are painful, unwelcome, and met with punitive views and action. In other cases people are creating changes that are enriching, welcoming, and incorporative. But in all cases, institutions are changing along with attitudes and persons, which suggests that a new racial order is coming into being. The president of a community college speaks for many in describing her altered domain: "When you change in this diverse way, you have to fundamentally change your institution. You have to change the language skills of your frontline people in admissions, registration and records. You have to create international

3

Multiracialism

> O'Leary, O'Riley, O'Hare, and O'Hara
> There's no one as Irish as Barack O'Bama.
> His mam's daddy's grandaddy was one Fulmuth Kearney
> He's as Irish as any from the lakes of Killarney
> His mam's from a long line of great Irish mamas;
> There's no one as Irish as Barack O'Bama.
> — Hardy Drew and the Nancy Boys

> I did not have a problem until someone said, "Well, how can you consider yourself interracial? You are black!" . . . [The professor in my Black Awareness class said,] "You can't be both." So I said, "Well, I am both, you can't tell me I am not." So he said, "If there was a war, blacks are on one side and whites are on the other side, which side would you go on?" I said, "Probably neither, because I would have to choose between my father and mother and I don't have a favorite."
> — A student

> Our preference is to get a shelter dog, but most shelter dogs are mutts like me.
> — President-elect Barack Obama

SOON AFTER THE 1965 Hart-Celler immigration act was passed, the Supreme Court struck down laws forbidding interracial marriage in the 1967 decision *Loving v. Virginia*.[1] The demographic changes resulting from immigration combined over the next few decades with the new freedom of marital choice to produce a rise in interracial and interethnic marriage. The number of mixed-race children increased as a natural consequence, as did social and emotional commitments to the idea of racial mixture. Advocacy groups politicized these changes in the 1990s by seeking official recognition of mixed-race ancestry and identity. As we discussed in chapter 2, the OMB mandated a new classification system in 1997 for counting and analyzing the rapidly changing American population; the *Revisions to the Standards*, for the first time in American history, permitted individuals to define themselves in terms of more than one race. By 2000, eight states as well as the federal government recognized self-identified racial mixture, and almost seven million respondents chose more than one race in the 2000 census.[2] Multiracial advocacy organizations celebrated the beginning of a new era.

Recognition of multiracialism received its biggest subsequent boost in the person of Barack Obama. His White American mother was descended from a wig-maker who left Moneygall, Ireland, in 1850—thereby making possible the song, "There's no one as Irish as Barack O'Bama," which has been downloaded from YouTube by millions around the world. The irony of the song, as any sentient person knows, is that Obama's father was a Black Kenyan and Obama grew up as a mixed-race child trying to teach himself how to be an African American.

Obama's self-description as a "mutt" may be the wave of the future; multiracial identity and recognition could eventually dissolve extant groups into one grand cosmopolitan mélange, as in José Vasconcelos's "cosmic race."[3] As the O'Bama song puts it, "from Fenian to Kenyan, it's the American way." More likely, over the next few decades the number of people who identify as multiracial will remain small and racial mixture will remain an anomaly within the conventional racial structure. But the presence of even a few million mixed-race Americans will contribute to creating a new American racial order.

As we have noted, the Jim Crow racial order of the mid-twentieth century and the post–civil rights order of the late twentieth century share an assumption that race (and possibly ethnicity) is constituted by a few exclusive and exhaustive groups. Although advocates and experts insist that race is a social construction—that, as Omi and Winant put it, "concepts of race are created and changed, . . . racial identity is assigned and assumed"—both common discourse and scholarship overwhelmingly use terms such as "Black," "White," "Asian," or "Hispanic" as though they are meaningful, mutually intelligible, separate, and settled. Multiracial identity calls that usage into question. It opens the possibility that group identity, or identification by others, is optional and contextual rather than fixed, knowable, and singular.[4]

How much the recognition of racial mixture will alter American practice as well as understanding of race is an open question. Like the other three transformative forces, the degree to which increasing heterogeneity becomes undergirded by structural change and the degree to which it promotes a Madisonian order in which no faction is dominant are political questions to be solved by choices that Americans have not yet made. But multiracialism combines with immigration, genomic science, and cohort change to provide impetus to further transformation of the American racial order.

Recognizing Self-Identified Racial Mixture

Like immigration, multiracialism in the United States has a long and complicated history. Racial mixture was socially recognized, formalized

in public policies and laws, studied by scientists, and celebrated or de-
plored in cultural productions throughout most of American history.[5]
Americans, however, largely forgot this history of robust racial construction and deconstruction in the last half of the twentieth century. European immigrants of "mixed parentage" and many "mother tongues" were
consolidated into Whites; mulattoes, quadroons, octoroons, griffes, and
Melungeons all became Black; half-breeds were Indians; and Hindoos
and half-Hawaiians disappeared from official classification systems. As
we have seen, Hispanics remained ambiguously an ethnicity or a race but
are seldom referred to as an intrinsically mixed or mestizo population.
The struggle to defeat the Jim Crow racial order and replace it with a
racial order based on civil and social rights and immigration revolved
around replacing the structure of group hierarchy with a structure of
formal equality and opportunities, leaving untouched the assumption of
a small stable set of exhaustive and mutually exclusive races.

Toward the end of the twentieth century, some Americans began to
promote a public repudiation of that assumption. Many of these activists
identified with one race, typically White, but had spouses of a different
race and racially mixed children; a few were themselves racially mixed.
After congressional hearings in 1993 and 1997, reports from the National Academy of Sciences and other demography experts, experiments
in question wording by the census bureau, analyses by a federal inter-
agency review committee, and adoption of "select one or more" by several states, the federal government acted.[6]

The OMB's 1997 *Revisions to the Standards for the Classification of
Federal Data on Race and Ethnicity* required that "when self-identification is used, a method for reporting more than one race should be adopted." The *Revisions* also mandated that "other Federal programs
should adopt the standards . . . for use in household surveys, administrative forms and records, and other data collections." Census 2000 duly
included the instruction, "Mark one or more races to indicate what this
person considers himself/herself to be" in question 8, "What is Person 1's
race?"[7] With that, according to then census director Kenneth Prewitt,
"we turned a corner about how we think about race in this country."[8]

Implementing Multiracial Recognition

In 2001, in accord with the OMB's mandate, the Department of Justice
began to "include counts of persons who have identified themselves as
members of more than one racial category" in all of its new data collection efforts.[9] The Department of Commerce also brought its new surveys
into compliance, as did the Department of Agriculture and the Federal

Reserve Board in 2002. The Department of Health and Human Services and the Department of Defense followed suit the next year in all efforts that included a racial identifier.

Momentum picked up as the decade advanced. In 2005, the Centers for Disease Control and Prevention and Department of Labor required, and the Food and Drug Administration (FDA) recommended, that funded research include "Multiracial" in racial classification of experimental subjects or survey respondents. The Equal Employment Opportunity Commission (EEOC) published a new standard for employers' reports of employees' characteristics, requiring "two or more races" in order to "accommodate . . . the government-wide *Revisions*." The National Science Foundation now invites applicants to "select one or more" races on their application form. Most important was the 2007 "Final Guidance on Maintaining, Collecting, and Reporting Racial and Ethnic Data to the U.S. Department of Education." By 2010–11, all educational institutions were expected to collect information on "whether the respondent [generally, a student] is from one or more races" and to report the number choosing two or more races.[10]

Absent a mandate from an authority like the OMB, most states have not changed their classification systems. Even in California, where a quarter of the U.S. mixed-race population lives, legislators did not pass the proposed Ethnic Heritage Respect and Recognition Act, which would have required the use of "mark one or more" in state data collection. As an expert explained, "there was very little official opposition to the bill . . . , but a certain degree of indifference."[11] Nevertheless it seems plausible, though not certain, that most or all states will eventually follow the path of the federal government as their own demography changes and as it becomes increasingly costly and inefficient to be at odds with virtually all federal classification systems.

Until recently, most private actors also lacked a mandate or incentive to change their practices in this arena, and few did so. But that situation is changing. To comply with the 2007 Department of Education ruling, all educational institutions from prekindergarten through universities now permit students (or their parents) to choose more than one race.[12] High school students taking ACT's Scholastic Test have the option of "multiracial," and the College Board permits students taking the SAT to "check one or more of the following options that you identify with." As of 2009, the Common Application form used by almost 460 American colleges and universities and almost two million students instructs applicants to "select one or more of the following ethnicities." In short, institutionalization has moved from federal agencies to organizations with direct mandates to comply with, or indirect links to, the new classification policy.

Some private enterprises are also responding to the changed federal policy. In fall 2009, we examined the application form for entry-level white-collar jobs at *Fortune Magazine*'s hundred largest corporations. Fifty permitted applicants to specify two or more races, twenty permitted only one response, nineteen did not ask for racial and ethnic data, and we were unable to obtain the relevant information for the final eleven. As in the educational arena, changes in federal agencies' reporting requirements may provide further inducement to employers; the U.S. Chamber of Commerce endorsed the EEOC's 2003 ruling.[13]

After years of allowing respondents only a single-race option, some public opinion polls now permit multiple racial self-definitions. They include major long-running academic surveys—the American National Election Study (ANES), General Social Survey (GSS), Panel Study of Income Dynamics, Children of Immigrants Longitudinal Study (CILS), and UCLA's annual survey of first-year college students, among others. Important media polls, such as *Newsweek* and the *Washington Post*, sometimes permit more than one racial self-definition. So do other surveys heavily used by researchers such as the National Longitudinal Survey of Adolescent Health (Add Health), the National Longitudinal Survey of Freshmen (NLSF), the National Youth Risk Behavior Survey, the Early Childhood Longitudinal Study–Kindergarten Cohort, the National Health Interview Survey (NHIS), and the Early Childhood Longitudinal Study–Birth Cohort. The census bureau permits a "mark one or more" option not only in the decennial census but also in its annual ACS and monthly Current Population Survey (CPS). The American Political Science Association recently asked its members, "What is your race or ethnic origin? *Check all that apply*" (emphasis in original), and the Ford Foundation and other professional associations are following suit. The Implicit Association Test, downloaded by over 4.5 million users, allows a multiracial designation. If more organizations follow these leads, a classification system that includes the option of choosing more than one race may become an analytic, and then empirical, commonplace.

Demography and Social Context

As early as 1958, an analyst predicted that "once the colored race has become . . . the absolute equal of the white race, . . . then intermarriage will become frequent. . . . At first the fusion will be imperceptible; then it will be perceptible but slow; then it will move with a rush." He was precipitate, but a half-century later, intermarriage and its consequences have advanced from perceptible but slow to moving with a rush. As a result, as one school superintendent put it, "the [traditional] racial categories have lost their meaning."[14]

Interracial marriages rose by 65 percent from 1990 to 2000, and by 20 percent (from a higher base) over the next decade. Roughly 8 percent of all American marriages are across racial lines, and about 15 percent of new marriages in 2008 crossed group boundaries. Young adults are much more likely to marry across racial lines than are even the newly married among their elders. Thirteen percent of currently married people under twenty-five have a spouse of a different race; intermarriage rates drop steadily with increasing age, so that just 5 percent of married adults over age sixty have wed across group lines.[15]

Intermarriage varies not only with age but also by race, ethnicity, and immigration status. Comparatively few Blacks are married outside their race, but the proportion has tripled since 1980; in 2008, 16 percent of new marriages by Blacks were to non-Blacks. Albeit from a very low starting point, Mississippi was the state with the fastest growth in interracial marriages from 2000 to 2008. Proportionally few Whites also marry outside their race. In 2008, 9 percent did so, a rate that has more than doubled since 1980. Whites in what William Frey labels "melting pot" states are more likely to find spouses outside their group; in 2007, "nearly half of Anglo marriages in Hawaii and more than one in five in California fit the category. . . . Perhaps this is the wave of the future."[16]

People who are neither Black nor White are most likely to intermarry. Frey reports that two-fifths of Hispanics' new marriages involve a spouse outside the group, and all analysts concur that the proportion has been rising. Almost a third of Asians' marriages in 2008 were to non-Asians. Fully two-thirds of young American Indians married outside their race in 2007; by 2000, the proportion of self-defined Indians with non-Indian spouses had reached almost 60 percent.[17]

Marriage across racial lines is much higher among native-borns than among immigrants. In the mid-2000s, less than a fifth of immigrant Asian women and a tenth of Hispanic, Black, or White immigrant women married outside their group. Their daughters were more likely to marry exogenously and the rise continued into the third generation among Asians and Latinas (but not among Blacks and Whites). In contrast, by 2008 nearly three-fourths of new marriages by native-born Asians were outside that group; the comparable figure for Latinos was just over half. Both of these proportions have risen since 1990. Finally, nonmarital partnerships are especially likely to cross racial lines; about a quarter of Black cohabiters and close to half of Asians have a partner outside their group.[18]

The absolute numbers are impressive, but trajectory matters more in evaluating a trend. As figure 3.1 shows, there is no ambiguity here. One can readily see the clear inflection point in the 1970s, followed by a steep upward slope in intermarriage for two of the three groups. Asian Americans appear to be an exception, but despite the recent decline in intermarriage due to a rising number of Asian immigrants, the scale on the

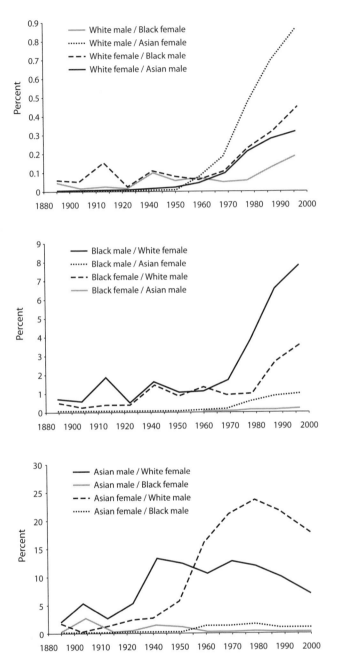

Figure 3.1. Interracial marriage rates as a percent of each group's marriages, 1880–2000.
Source: Adapted from Fryer 2007; see also Fryer 2005.

y axis shows that the absolute level of Asian intermarriage remains the highest.[19]

Given these trajectories, it is likely that outmarriage and interracial partnerships outside marriage will continue to increase. As one demographer puts it, once "a fifth to a quarter of children with a black grandparent . . . also have a non-black grandparent, . . . the history of outmarriage in other groups suggests it might well soar within a generation after 2010." Another projection shows that about a tenth of Whites and Blacks and over half of Asians and Latinos married outside their group by 2050.[20]

An unsurprising consequence of rising intermarriage is the increasing number and proportion of mixed-race children. Among children below age eighteen in married couple families, less than 1 percent had parents of different races in 1970, compared with 6.7 percent in 2000. (The number of mixed-race children born outside marriage is rising even more rapidly.) In 2009, 22 percent of Hispanics, 15 percent of Blacks, and 7 percent of Whites reported a mixed-race child; in households with children under age eighteen, the proportions rose to 27, 23, and 13 percent, respectively.[21] Looked at from the opposite direction, about half of the more than seven million people who marked more than one race in the 2009 ACS were under age eighteen.

Since families are not comprised only of parents and children, a single intermarriage or interracial child can have an impact well beyond the actual participants. The number of White and Black Americans with a family member or close kin of a different race is increasing exponentially, while the proportions among Asian Americans and American Indians are approaching or have reached the 100 percent ceiling. Table 3.1 shows the pattern. These calculations are conservative, since they exclude Latinos and people with multiracial ancestry who identify with one racial group. Even so, by 2000, "the fraction of whites with kinship networks that cross either racial or Hispanic ethnic lines is nearing one-half," using the less conservative estimate of 14.4 marriages over three generations. By some measures, then, at least half of Americans have a family member of a different group from their own. Americans recognize this change; by 2009, 35 percent reported an immediate family member or close relative who is married to someone of another race.[22]

How Does Multiracialism Transform the American Racial Order?

In one way, the answer to that question is obvious; by definition, people who straddle racial lines disrupt an order that is predicated on a few mutually exclusive and exhaustive categories. Their very existence creates

Table 3.1
Estimated Percentage of Americans in Mixed-Race Kinship Networks, by Race and Decade

	White	Black	Asian	American Indian
1960	1.9	9.2	81.1	89.6
1970	3.6	10.9	87.5	99.0
1980	9.8	21.9	91.5	99.9
1990	9.0	28.3	79.5	99.8
2000	22.4	49.8	83.9	100

Source: Joshua Goldstein, communication with the authors, January 29, 2009. See also Goldstein 1999. *Note:* Results are based on kinship network size of 10 marriages over 3 generations. With a less conservative estimate of 14.4 marriages over 3 generations, 30.5 percent of Whites, 62.9 percent of Blacks, and 92.8 percent of Asian Americans had kin of a different race in 2000.

a disruptive heterogeneity. But the full answers are more subtle and best revealed by examining each component of the racial order.

What Is a Race?

The key issue is whether multiracialism is best seen as a new race, analogous to the canonical five groups recognized by the OMB, or whether it should be understood differently. To some, racially mixed persons are similar in kind, though different in content, to monoracial persons. The self-trained social analyst Alfred Holt Stone articulated a biologically based version of that view a century ago:

> The mulatto is not a Negro, and neither written nor social law can make him one. . . . [W]e can no more make a Negro by such a process than we can alter the life traits and nationality of a Russian peasant by bestowing upon him an English name. . . . We must recognize the very simple and very patent fact that the intermixture of white and black races has given us a racial type that is neither the one nor the other.[23]

Few analysts conceive of racial types the same way today, but some do share the understanding of multiracials as in some sense a new, distinct group. The 1996 Olympic decathlon gold medalist Dan O'Brien, for example, was uncomfortable in a standard racial category: "I call myself a chameleon. . . . In college, people thought of me as African American, and I tried to fit in, but it didn't work out. I failed." Eventually, he found a new group: "over the last five years, I've become me. I feel a special connection to mixed-race kids. It's important for me to think I'm mixed-race. I found strength in others who are mixed-race." An activist echoed that sentiment; the first meeting with other multiracials "was like coming out of the closet. . . . The sense of belonging . . . [is] about . . . what you share in terms of feeling connected." To another, "it's not that just being biracial is like you're two parts. . . . There's a third part, a unique thing."[24]

Like those who see Latinos as a distinct race rather than a crosscutting ethnicity, advocates who see multiracials as a new group make claims on its behalf. They worry about bias: "sometimes people are discriminating against others just because they are multiracial—not because they are perceived to be one thing or another." They assert claims to rights: "we want choice in the matter of who we are, just like any other community has choice in the matter." They seek recognition: "despite this national mixed race baby boom, few people are aware of the unique needs of this rapidly growing community." They are "a racial group" with a "common characteristic."[25]

Specifying a new group with claims similar to those of the conventional races is itself disruptive of the extant racial order. But the old order is subverted even more if one rejects the image of multiracials as a new group and insists instead that "the fundamental concept—that you should be able to assign every American to one of three or four races reliably—is crazy."[26] Starting from that premise, multiracialism points the way to understanding race as fluid, contextual, and continuous rather than categorical and fixed.

The social construction of race is an old American concept. The 1870 census superintendent declared that "in the equilibrium produced by the equal division of blood, the habits, tastes, and associations of the half-breed are allowed to determine his gravitation to one class or the other." Thus "persons of part-Indian blood" who lived among Whites, "adopting their habits of life and methods of industry," should be enumerated as White, while the "opposite construction" applied to those "found in communities composed wholly or mainly of Indians." Soon after the turn of the twentieth century, a federal court asked, in something like official despair,

> Then, what is white? What degree of colorization . . . constitutes a white person as against a colored person, and is the court to take the responsibility by ocular inspection of determining the shades of different colorization where the dividing line comes between white and colored?
>
> The statute . . . is most uncertain, ambiguous, and difficult both of construction and application. . . . There have been a number of decisions in which the question has been treated, and the conclusions arrived at in them are as unsatisfactory as they are varying.

So multiracialism understood in terms of the fluidity of racial classifications is a rediscovery from the racial order that preceded Jim Crow segregation. But its current incarnation is nevertheless transformative. Kerry Rockquemore spells out just how: "(a) mixed-race people construct different racial identities based on various contextually specific logics, (b) there are no predictable stages of identity development because the process is not linear and there is no single optimal endpoint, and (c) privileging any one type of racial identity over another . . . only replicates the essentialist flaws of previous models, with a different outcome."[27] In short, if one does not "have" a race and if racial categories are continuous rather than dichotomous, then structures ranging from the use of blood quantum to determine who is a Native American to stringent conceptions of racial linked fate or group labeling are called into question.

How Are People Classified?

If people can change their racial identity as values or circumstances change, it is definitionally impossible to decide how many "are" multiracial. Before considering that possibility, however, let us begin with the politically and conceptually simpler idea that multiracialism adds a new group to the standard list of races. The latter framing permits an initial answer to the question of how many Americans identify as multiracial. Almost seven million respondents chose more than one race in the 2000 census. Figure 3.2 updates that result, using two sets of census calculations and another large, repeated survey, the NHIS. These data warrant caution for several reasons.[28] Nevertheless, these series provide the best available evidence (before the 2010 census data were released), and they all show the same basic facts: the number of people who define themselves in terms of two or more races is low, and the number is slowly rising. The 2010 census shows a further rise at the end of the decade; 9 million people—2.9 percent of the population, a 32 percent rise since 2000—chose more than one race.

Disaggregating these data provides reasons to expect self-definition as mixed race to continue rising. The category of Black + another race had a long history of being legally forbidden and remains emotionally fraught. Yet the proportion of Blacks choosing that combination rose from 4.8 percent in 2000 to 7.4 percent in the 2010 census. Black + White was the most common combination in census 2010, edging out even White + Some Other Race; the number of Black + White census respondents "soared by 134 percent since 2000." (Seven hundred and ninety-two census respondents chose all six races.) Other conventionally labeled groups also claimed more racial mixture. The proportion of White + another race rose from 2.5 percent in 2000 to 3.2 percent in

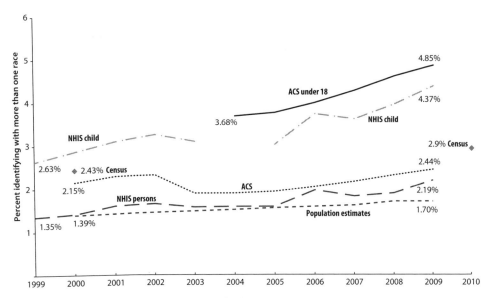

Figure 3.2. Identification with racial mixture in major surveys.
Sources: (1) U.S. Census 2000 and 2010; (2) ACS; (3) Population estimates: Bureau of the Census 2009; (4) NHIS: codebooks for National Center for Health Statistics (various years). In the NHIS and ACS, those under eighteen are a subset of the broader sample.

2010; the proportions choosing Asian + another race rose from 13.9 to 15.3 percent.[29]

Another reason to anticipate a rise in mixed-race self-definition is that people under age eighteen disproportionately call themselves (or are labeled by their parents as) multiracial. Barely 2 percent of adults identified with more than one race in the 2000 census, compared with twice as many under eighteen. In the 2008 ACS, the ratio was three to one. Put another way, just under a quarter of the American population was under eighteen in 2009, whereas almost half of the two-or-more-races population was. As figure 3.2 shows, the NHIS shows the same youthful over-representation. The 2010 census again showed a disproportion of young Americans among those who chose more than one race. If these young people retain mixed-race identity in adulthood and pass it on to their children, and given that future birth cohorts will have more demographically mixed-race children since interracial marriage is rising, the proportion of self-defined multiracials will increase. Furthermore, immigrants were three times as likely as the native-born to have marked more than one race on the 2000 census.[30] As a group, immigrants are relatively young, have a relatively high birthrate, and will probably remain a rising share of the American population. If they and their children continue to identify with more than one race, that is another reason to expect the multiracial share of the American population to grow.

Multiracial self-definition has already increased spectacularly in one group—American Indians. With the option to choose more than one race on the 2000 census, people no longer had to decide between their Indian and non-Indian ancestry. As a consequence the number of Indians increased over the 1990 census by 258 percent in Vermont, 216 percent in Pennsylvania, and 211 percent in South Carolina. Some view this increase skeptically: newly identified Indians merely "want to share an identity. There was a stigma attached to it through most of the 20th century. . . . [But with the movie] *Dances with Wolves*, and then, with the Indian Gaming Act in the 1980's, it's become profitable to be Indian." Others celebrate the rising commitment to American Indian identity among people who had moved away from tribal life: after the occupation of Alcatraz prison, "for the first time in my life I was proud to be an Indian. . . . I grew up in an all white area. It was very difficult. You were constantly struggling to maintain any kind of positive feeling, any kind of dignity."[31] Now this woman does not to have to choose between her parents (or ancestors), as the student in the epigraph to this chapter put it.

Other surveys show similarly idiosyncratic but significant movements toward an identity as racially mixed. In 2001, 17 percent of first-year students at selective colleges and universities who were identified by their institution as Black reported being of mixed race. Comparable figures for Latinos were 28 percent, for Asians 7 percent, and for Whites 2 percent. Also in 2001, 11 percent of CILS respondents in two highly diverse cities defined themselves as multiracial. Two years later, Taeku Lee investigated a more "fluid portrait of ethno-racial self-identification" by asking Californians to allocate ten points among racial or ethnic groups to indicate their own heritage. Just over a quarter gave at least one point to more than one group. Almost 8 percent of first-year law students identified with more than one race in 2004. In 2007, 8.3 percent of the roughly 48,000 students in thirty-one highly selective private American colleges and universities identified with more than one race.[32] In a 2009 *Newsweek* survey, 16 percent of the respondents considered themselves to "be of mixed race," and 11 percent reported a mixed-race child.

The annual UCLA survey of first-year college students has, uniquely, permitted respondents to choose more than one race since 1971. If we treat Hispanic as a race analogous to Black, White, Asian, and American Indian, the proportion of students identifying with more than one race has risen from just over 1 percent in 1971 to 8.4 percent in 2008. The proportion stayed between 1 and 2 percent until 1989, after which it rose steeply though not steadily. (There was a dip in the early 2000s, followed by an even steeper rise for the rest of the decade.) No evidence points to reversal.[33]

Finally, more people may come to identify with more than one race for the simple reason that the option is increasingly available. As people moving into adulthood are routinely offered "mark one or more" or multiracial when they register for high school, apply to college, get a driver's license, seek a job, join the military, fill out federal forms, answer surveys, register to vote, fill out a child's birth certificate, or go to a doctor, it could become merely an uncomplicatedly appropriate option. And familiarity may breed identity: "people have had an entire decade to think about this since it was first a choice in 2000. Some of these figures [showing a rise in multiracial identification] are not so much changes as corrections."[34]

The first and second components of the racial order thus reinforce one another; as multiracialism becomes more common in definitions of a race, more people will identify as multiracial. That interaction itself changes the extant racial order. But what if people disrupt the racial order more significantly by coming to understand race and their own racial identity as contextually specific, additive, and nonlinear? Maria Root provides one way to understand this new self-image:

I have the right . . .
Not to keep the races separate within me, . . .
Not to be responsible for people's discomfort with my physical or ethnic ambiguity, . . .
To identify myself differently than my brothers or sisters,
To identify myself differently in different situations, . . .
To change my identity over my lifetime—and more than once,
To have loyalties and identification with more than one group of people.[35]

This "Bill of Rights for People of Mixed Heritage" may never gain a wide following; traditional racial and ethnic identities are deeply rooted. Nevertheless, let us consider the evidence for Maria Root's paean to fluidity.

Self-definition may be unstable across contexts. Almost 21,000 teens in the 1995 Add Health survey responded to questions about their race or ethnicity in separate surveys at school and at home. The result: "54 percent of the home multiracial population are not multiracial in school data, and 75 percent of the school multiracial population are not multiracial in home data." A parallel analysis of Hispanics found the same pattern. As one student explained to an interviewer, "If I was with all Mexicans, I would be like '*I'm Mexican*, but I'm French and Italian too.' But I think that if I were with a group of White people, I would be like, 'I'm Mexican, *but I'm also French and Italian*.' I would emphasize that part to try and fit in a little more." More simply, "well, shit, it depends on what day it is and where I'm goin'."[36] In 2001, a tenth of those who con-

Table 3.2
Pathways of Racial Self-Definition among Teens, Add Health Survey,
1995 and 2001

	Weighted N
Nonswitching	10,972
Monoracial at both waves 1 and 3	10,821
Multiracial at both waves 1 and 3	151
Switching	699
Monoracial at wave 1 → multiracial at wave 3	305
Multiracial at wave 1 → monoracial at wave 3	280
Switching monoracial	93
Switching multiracial	21

Source: Hitlin, Brown, and Elder 2006.

sidered themselves to be of mixed race agreed that they "identify . . . [their] race differently in different situations" and another 7 percent volunteered that it "varies."[37]

Identities may be unstable across time as well as across contexts. In the repeated Add Health surveys, over five years "youth who ever report being multiracial are 4 times as likely to switch self-identification as to report consistent multiracial identities." Table 3.2 shows the various movements. Roughly an equal number of adolescents added and subtracted a racial category, and both choices were about twice as common as remaining consistently multiracial. These results are especially strong given that all Hispanics and all those who chose "other" race (available only in the first wave) were not included in the analysis. The authors conclude that for adolescents who might plausibly identify as multiracial, any situation requiring "forced-choice self-identification is a contested act in contrast to being a relatively uncontested cognitive process for monoracial individuals."[38]

Like Native Americans, immigrants or their children are especially likely to change their identity over time. In the CILS, 11 percent identified with more than one racial group in 1995 when they were aged 15–21 and about 12 percent did in 2001 when they had reached ages 22–27. However, this obfuscates the fluidity of identity choices across the surveys. Of multiracials in 1995, 57 percent (200) had switched to a single race identification by 2001, while 55 percent (183) of multiracials in 2001 had reversed the process, switching to that designation from a single race category in 1995. One woman explained the tensions behind these sorts of shifts:

I felt like I had to decide because the [Asian] Indian side is looking at me like, you don't even look like you are a relative to an Indian. . . . And then the Black side's looking at me like—we don't like you because you are too light-skinned or 'cause you have 'good hair.' . . . And that made me think I had to decide. I had to identify. When I finally gave it up was when I was just deciding that no one can make me [who I am] but me. So I'm gonna do whatever I want to do. . . . I'm just gonna do whatever makes me happy.[39]

Unlike this assertion of autonomy, some shifting self-definitions are strategic: "[My children] see themselves as Muslim Malaysian Americans. When it's convenient for them, they identify themselves as Malays with Javanese heritage. This morphing usually occurs when they desire certain Malay foods." Adults can be just as cunning: "I've also learned to manipulate the situation that I'm in. I know that if I say I'm 'biracial,' I will get certain things, and if I say I'm 'black' I will get certain things. So I know I probably play with that a little bit." In a convenience sample of forty self-defined multiracials, three-fourths similarly presented themselves as Black on applications for college, financial aid, or jobs. In a stunning understatement, the analysts point out that "the practice of passing as black, rather than white, suggests that blackness is arguably less stigmatized today than in earlier eras of American history—at least in certain contexts."[40]

Multiracialism may generate instability in racial identity across generations. One medical study, for example, tracked 205 babies among whom at least one parent was known to be racially mixed. Mothers identified only 93 of those babies as multiracial—and mothers varied unsystematically in whether they chose the father's, their own, or neither parent's race as the first race of their infants. An additional 70 babies were known to have parents of different races, but the mothers of only 45 of them identified their children as multiracial. Here, too, mothers varied in which parent's race, or neither's, was assigned to the child. As the senior author of this study put it, "the bottom line with respect to racial identification for multiracial infants is—there is no rhyme or reason."[41]

The 2000 census provides broader, though thinner, evidence that choice about multiracial identification across generations is not settled. Only half of the parents in racially mixed marriages reported their children as having two or more races. Whether a child ended up officially biracial was associated with the state of residence (western more than eastern or southern), sex of the non-White parent (more biracials if the mother is White), age (younger more than older), level of education (more schooling increased biracialism for Indians and Blacks but not for Asians and Whites), and the race of the non-White parent (Asian Whites more than Black Whites).[42] Even a tenth of the children with two multiracial parents were not reported as multiracial. There was only one fixed point in this mélange: children whose parents defined themselves as being in the same race were virtually always reported as a member of that race.

Another form of instability is internal—a disjunction between self-definition and ancestry. One young man, having grown up Black, took a DNA test that he expected would show about three-quarters African ancestry. The results "floored" him; they showed him to be almost three-fifths Indo-European, almost two-fifths Native American, and a small fraction East Asian: that is, no African ancestry at all. "For almost a year, Joseph searched his soul. . . . Before the test, 'I was unequivocally black. Now I'm a metaphor for America.'" He is in good company. For a PBS television show, Henry Louis Gates Jr. had his own DNA tested for ancestry. The result: "as for my mitochondrial DNA, my mother's mother's mother's lineage? Would it be Yoruba, as I fervently hoped? . . . A number of exact matches turned up, leading straight back to that African Kingdom called Northern Europe, to the genes of (among others) a female Ashkenazi Jew. . . . I have the blues. Can I still have the blues?"[43]

Finally, as with immigrants' race, simple contextual cues may be enough to induce a person to change his or her self-definition as multiracial. The apparently straightforward question in a public opinion survey "what is your race?" can wreak havoc with the data and therefore with subsequent analyses and interpretations. Consider one example, a 2001 *Washington Post* poll of 1,709 adult Americans.

- Asked, "Do you consider yourself to be of mixed race?" 317 respondents said yes, of whom 203 also said that their parents were of the same race;
- Asked how many "groups you consider yourself part of," 248 respondents said two or more;
- Asked their parents' race, 169 reported different races for their parents, of whom 58 said that they themselves were not multiracial;
- Asked if they had ancestors of different races, 163 said yes.

A more recent survey shows that self-definitions did not settle down over the succeeding decade. Asked their race, only 1 percent of a 2009 sample chose more than one. But asked later in the survey if they consider themselves to be mixed race, 16 percent said yes—8 percent of previously self-identified Whites, 20 percent of Blacks, and 37 percent of Hispanics.[44]

Who among these respondents is "really" multiracial? The question is unanswerable. Either these individuals are deeply confused—the appropriate interpretation if multiracialism is a race like all others—or they see their racial identity as fluid and variable, depending on some cue or context. That is not how Blacks, Whites, or Asians classify themselves.

Relative Group Positions

Immigration, as chapter 2 showed, blurs the third component of the American racial order by inserting groups into the stratification system above Whites or below Blacks, as well as by raising the status of Blacks or lowering that of Whites through greater heterogeneity within each group. Multiracialism changes relative group positions differently since in the aggregate, racially mixed people have a different status than do people who are monoracial in one or the other of their ancestral groups. That is, multiracial individuals or mixed-race families are better off than the median member of the lower-status race and worse off than the median member of the higher-status race. Figure 3.3 shows the patterns.

Asians have the highest levels of education and income of the monoracial groups (Hispanics are not included in this analysis), although the poverty of some Asian nationalities keeps that group from having the lowest poverty rates. On each measure Whites follow Asians, while African Americans and American Indians fall far behind. Among biracials, those with part-Asian ancestry are slightly worse off than monoracial Asians and slightly better off than Whites. In parallel fashion, those with Black or American Indian ancestry are slightly better off than monoracial Blacks or Indians and slightly worse off than monoracial Whites.[45]

The reasons for this pattern are not clear. Racially mixed people may be advantaged in the educational and labor markets compared with their lower-status forebears and simultaneously disadvantaged compared with their higher-status forebears. By that logic, racial mixture leads to changes in groups' relative positions. However, since ACS respondents define their own race(s), it may be that people who are strongly disadvantaged are especially likely to identify as African American or Indian even if they could identify as multiracial, while the best-off are disproportionately likely to define themselves as Asian or Asian + some other group. By that logic, relative position helps shape mixed-race identity—reversing the causal direction between multiracialism and relative position.

This causal conundrum is fascinating and socially important; sorting it out will be essential for determining whether multiracialism changes relative group positions. If marrying outside one's group changes one's own or one's children's status, intermarriage will improve the positions of racially mixed Blacks and Indians compared with monoracial members of those groups. By the same logic, intermarriage will worsen the positions of racially mixed Asians relative to monoracial Asians. The position of monoracial groups will not change as a consequence of multiracialism, but since young Americans are increasingly likely to intermarry, over time relatively fewer individuals will remain within the groups at the top and

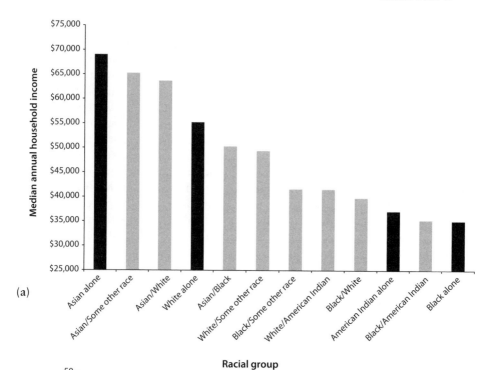

(a)

Racial group

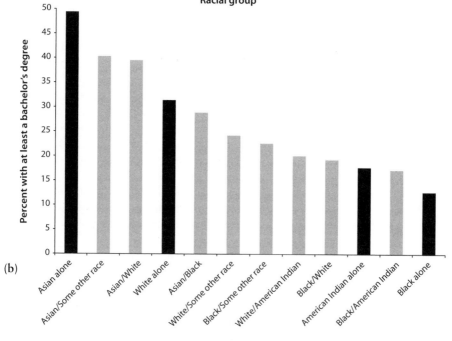

(b)

Racial group

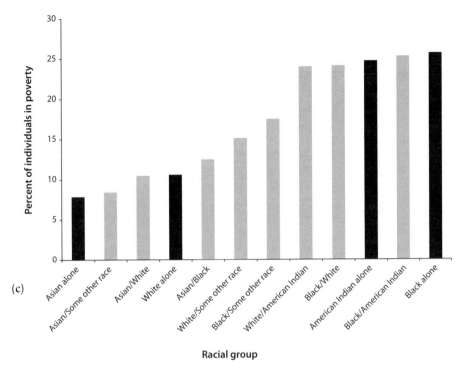

(c)

Figure 3.3. Comparison of self-identified biracials and monoracials, combined 2006–8 ACS.
(a) Median annual household income; (b) Proportion with bachelor's degree or higher; (c) Proportion of individuals below the poverty line.
Source: Authors' analyses of ACS, 2006–8.
Note that American Indian is actually American Indian and Alaska Native. Hispanics are not a separate race in the ACS, so any of these categories may include Hispanics.

the bottom of the status hierarchy. Thus if it continues to expand, multiracialism could destabilize the third component of the racial order by increasing heterogeneity in the middle of the socioeconomic spectrum and reducing the number of people in the extreme positions.[46]

Permitted, Required, or Forbidden Acts

To our knowledge, no federal law or public policy distinguishes people of mixed race, either positively or negatively, from other racial groups. In fact, the OMB's *Revisions to the Standards* mandated "mark one or more" for federal data collection rather than a catchall multiracial category precisely so that people with mixed ancestry could be statistically disaggregated into their component races for use in redistricting or civil rights monitoring and enforcement. A 2000 OMB ruling requires that when people are to be counted by group, individuals who chose one minority race + White be "allocated to the minority race," and responses with two or more minority races be "allocate[d] to the race that the complainant alleges the discrimination was based on." Alternatively, "if the enforcement action requires assessing disparate impact or discriminatory patterns, analyze the patterns based on alternative allocations to each of the minority groups."[47]

In other words, for legal and policy purposes multiracial individuals are to be treated as members of one or more minority races. That decision evoked mixed reactions. Civil rights advocacy groups were greatly relieved; an attorney for the NAACP Legal Defense and Educational Fund described the 2000 ruling as "an important first step to make sure that civil rights enforcement is not compromised by the implementation of these racial classification guidelines." Some multiracial advocacy groups were incensed; as the founder of MAVIN put it, "all of a sudden to finally be given the opportunity to choose more than one race, and then seemingly have that taken away, seems a little suspect." Some policy analysts began to worry about new problems—reincarnation of "one drop of blood" rules, violation of the principle of self-identification, and the fact that the allocation rule would bring people who think of themselves as primarily White under the umbrella of civil rights protection for non-Whites.[48]

From our perspective, however, the implementation ruling matters mainly as a statement that multiracials have no official standing as a group protected by civil rights laws and policies. Except for a few state laws or regulations, policies designed to compensate disadvantaged minorities for past injustices, such as affirmative action, majority-minority electoral districting, or small business set-asides, ignore racial mixture. Nor do universities or corporations include "multiracial" as an element of their desired diversity. So the fourth component of a racial order is largely irrelevant to multiracialism.

Social Relations among Groups

As with immigration, we can address only a few of the many activities encompassed by the concept of social relations. But unlike the case of immigration, most of these activities tend in the same direction—toward transformation of the current racial order in a way that expands individuals' array of choices.[49]

The starting point for analyzing social relations around multiracialism is recognition that interracial relationships are now the norm for young adults in many places. By the time they reached their senior year at a large public university, three-fifths of Latino students, almost half of the African Americans and Whites, and a third of the Asians had dated someone of another race. Two-thirds of young Californians have dated someone of another race and almost nine out of ten profess willingness to marry across racial lines. Fewer than a fifth of adult children of immigrants in New York City think endogamous marriages are important; up to three-fifths (depending on the interviewees' nationality) of those married or cohabiting have partners outside their group. In this young, urban sample, even three in ten native-born Whites and Blacks have partners outside their own race. "Feelings about intergroup dating sharply differentiated second generation youth from their immigrant parents," although the youth often claim that parents are coming around.[50] Even older adults are expanding their horizons; over a quarter of Hispanics, 30 percent of Asians, and 35 percent of African Americans have dated across racial lines.[51]

We lack the flood of survey items about multiracialism that was in evidence in the discussion of immigration. But also unlike that arena, what evidence exists is relatively consistent and shows a clear trajectory. Through much of the twentieth century and despite their involvement in producing such children, many Whites perceived racially mixed individuals as a detestable corruption of the natural order and "a scourge to both races," as the *New York Times* put it in 1904. Only 4 percent of American adults approved of interracial marriage in a 1958 Gallup Poll.[52] Despite behavior, the norm was not ambiguous.

Forty years later, the norm was equally unambiguous—but reversed. By 1999, more than three-fifths of respondents endorsed interracial marriages on the grounds that "they help break down racial barriers." In 2001, almost two-thirds agreed that it would be "good for the country . . . if more Americans think of themselves as multi-racial rather than belonging to a single race." And by 2007, the Gallup Poll found not 4 percent but 77 percent approval of interracial marriage. That result included 75 percent of Whites (86 percent under age fifty), 85 percent of Blacks, and 87 percent of Hispanics. More liberals than conservatives approved but almost as many Republicans as Democrats. In 2009, 88 percent of Whites, 85 percent of Blacks, and 81 percent of Hispanics aged eighteen to twenty-nine agreed that it would be "fine" with them if a family member married outside their group. Concurrence declined with age but only among Whites over age sixty-five did fewer than half endorse intermarriage within their family. Even this group opposed intermarriage solely with African Americans.[53]

Most Americans also used to fear for the future of racially mixed individuals. In 1971, seven in ten respondents to an unusually detailed survey agreed that "the children born of a racially mixed marriage would face a lifetime of harassment and prejudice"; majorities also thought interracial marriages would be stressful, unstable, and socially constrained. President Richard Nixon told an aide in 1973 that while he generally opposed greater access to abortion, "there are times when an abortion is necessary, I know that. When you have a black and a white. Or a rape." As recently as 2001, six in ten respondents agreed that "multi-racial children face more problems . . . growing up than children of a single race do" (a third said "a lot more"). Almost seven in ten perceived continuing discrimination against interracial couples. Blacks (77 percent) were most concerned, followed by Whites and Hispanics (67 and 64 percent), and finally Asians (48 percent).[54]

Marriages across group lines do show strains. In a 2001 survey of biracial couples, three-fourths perceived discrimination, three-tenths thought that crossing racial lines makes marriage more difficult (most of the rest said that it made no difference), and almost two-fifths perceived problems for the children of biracial couples (again, most of the rest saw no difference). Interracial couples have more difficult relationships or unstable marriages and are more likely to divorce than monoracial couples. Qualitative interviews or small-scale experimental studies sometimes, though not uniformly, show suspicion of or hostility toward multiracials or difficulty in daily interactions.[55]

Nevertheless, the situation has changed since the 1970s. As early as 1995, about two-fifths of both Blacks and Whites agreed that "the U.S. Census should add a 'multiracial' category to population surveys so some people aren't forced to deny part of a family member's heritage by having to choose a single racial category." After all, the same proportion agreed, "Black Americans today have such differing mixtures of African and European ancestry that it no longer makes sense to think of them as black and members of a single group." Multiracials themselves are also quite sanguine. In the 2001 survey, only 17 percent of those who defined themselves as mixed race reported actually having had "more problems . . . growing up than children of a single race" have, and only 8 percent reported a "harder . . . time succeeding at work." The same proportion (8 percent) reported an *easier* time at work.[56] In the 2001 *Washington Post* survey of racially intermarried couples, almost no one reported verbal or physical harassment of their mixed-race children and many more (44 percent) saw advantages to their children of having parents of different races than saw disadvantages (6 percent). Almost two-thirds reported that their marriages were perfect or nearly so. Compared with monoracial minority students, multiracial law students perceive less everyday discrimination, less larger-scale discrimination over their lifetimes, and fewer professional barriers due to race. And a longitudinal study shows that the more college students have dated outside their race or ethnicity, the less in-group bias and intergroup anxiety they show.[57]

The scant systematic evidence suggests that behaviors track these perceptions. Mixed-race teens "are as popular as non-white adolescents and have social networks that are as racially diverse as the single-race groups with the most diverse friendship networks. Biracial adolescents with black ancestry have an especially high rate of friendship bridging between black persons and persons of other races, relative to black or white adolescents."[58]

Multiracials may provide political as well as economic, social, and demographic bridges among groups. In the 1995 *Newsweek* survey, Blacks and Whites differed by 12 percentage points when asked if racial relations were poor in the United States; mixed-race respondents were exactly in between. They again fell between Blacks and Whites in the 2001 *Washington Post* survey in response to the questions of whether "too little attention is paid to race and racial issues" and whether there are "still major problems facing minorities in this country." In the NLSF, students who described themselves as Black + another race or Hispanic + another race were less likely than monoracial Blacks or Hispanics to express racial linked fate, more likely to see a promising racial future with less discrimination, and less likely to endorse voting for a co-racial candidate, shopping at co-racially owned stores, or having friends primarily in one's own group. People of mixed race show significantly less implicit racial bias on the Implicit Association Test than do Whites, though more than Blacks—again falling in between.[59] Multiracials' support for affirmative action, racial redistricting, and government intervention to ensure equality lies consistently between that of Blacks and Whites. So do their perceptions of racial tension and disenfranchisement. Only on survey items focusing on racial mixture, such as support for interracial dating or counting multiracials on the census, do multiracial respondents move away from their location between Whites and non-Whites.

The UCLA survey of first-year college students provides the longest-running comparisons between mono- and multiracial identifiers; it again consistently shows the latter's views falling between those of Blacks and Whites. Students in all groups are increasingly likely to agree that discrimination is no longer a problem in the United States (see chapter 5), and multiracial students are consistently in the center of that trend line. They are similarly positioned on whether "undocumented immigrants should be denied access to public education." First-year students' agreement with that claim declined and then rose from 1996 to 2008; in all five years that the question was asked, the combined sample of multiracials supported exclusion less than Whites, more than Blacks, Hispanics, and Asians, and less than the median respondent.[60]

If the results of these surveys hold up over time and if these views are manifested in politics, people who identify as multiracial may come to fill the middle ground between traditional racial and partisan poles. If they can also maintain connections with people on either side of them ideologically, that could help moderate—and possibly transform—the contemporary political rancor. Nothing is certain, but the conditions for change are in place.

Again as with immigration, economic forces may best indicate how multiracialism is changing American society. Such forces are also helping create that change. That is, marketers "draw on existing culturally resonant narratives of the meaning of racial mixedness for the purpose of selling. In so doing, they shape social perceptions that multiracials exist as such."[61] For example, after eliminating books that did not refer to individuals, we identified twenty-six new books in the 1990s on Amazon. com that included "multiracial," "biracial," "mixed race," "mulatto," or "racial mixture" in the titles. From 2000 through 2010, over one hundred such volumes were published; figure 3.4 shows two examples. Dozens more are being reprinted, especially from the era around the turn of the twentieth century in which racial mixture was salient socially, scientifically, and politically. Lexis-Nexis identified 1,041 usages of the same five keywords in magazines during the 1990s, and well over twice as many in the subsequent decade. The increase in the industry trade press was even greater: 91 Lexis-Nexis usages of the five keywords in the 1990s, and 535 in the 2000s.

The food and clothing industries are following the same path as the publishing industry. A spokesperson for American Apparel characterized multiracial models as "the face of America; . . . they deserve a prominent place in advertisements." For those who do not emulate supermodels, "to see the new face of the United States, . . . look at a box of Betty Crocker–brand food products. Betty's portrait is now in its eighth incarnation since the first composite painting debuted in 1936 with pale skin and blue eyes. Her new look is brown-eyed and dark-haired. She has a duskier complexion . . . , with features representing an amalgam of white, Hispanic, Indian, African and Asian ancestry. A computer created this new Betty in the mid-1990s by blending photos of 75 diverse women."[62] Headlines trumpet "The Changing Faces of America," "Generation E.A.: Ethnically Ambiguous," and "The New Face of Race." After all, "we live in a kind of multi-internetted world where you ought to be able to pick your own culture, frankly."[63]

Market research firms are at the pinnacle of "selling mixedness," as Kimberly DaCosta puts it. They aspire to clairvoyance with regard to emerging social trends, in part by "anticipat[ing] the enormous demographic shift already underway in the U.S." In this "new . . . market, it is essential to get beyond ethnic segmentation and understand that it is the very intermingling of cultures and ethnicities that defines the . . . [contem-

Figure 3.4. Books about racial mixture.
(a) Cover of *16 Extraordinary Multiracial Americans,* published by Walch Education, Portland, Maine, 2010. Reprinted by permission of the publisher. (b) Cover of *Mestizaje* by Rafael Pérez-Torres, published by the University of Minnesota Press, Minneapolis, Minnesota, 2006. Reprinted by permission of the publisher.

porary] sensibility." This firm concludes by demanding of its clients, "Will you be ready for this new, multi-colored, multi-cultural, multi-ethnic, and multi-lingual general market?"[64]

Not all is copacetic, even from the perspective of an advertiser who has found a new market. Two phenomena could derail multiracialism's capacity to transform the American racial order. First, others may continue to attribute a single racial identity to people who might plausibly be seen, or identify themselves, as multiracial. In a series of five laboratory experiments, in each case subjects were more likely to label a Black-White person, and somewhat more likely to label an Asian-White person, as monoracially non-White than as White. Even before Obama identified as Black on the 2010 census, 55 percent of Blacks reported that they mostly consider him to be Black rather than a person of mixed race; only a third described him as racially mixed (the others expressed no opinion). Half as many Whites and Hispanics concurred on Obama's Blackness.[65]

Multiracials know, of course, that identity and identification are different: "My mother told me . . . , 'Because your father is white, you may try to think that you're not black, or you'll get treated differently from other black people, but everyone who looks at you will see a black man, and you have to be prepared for that.' That's my earliest memory about race, and that is how I've thought about it ever since." Given that circumstance, they may opt to be "Black by Choice": Obama's census self-definition "did not deny his white parentage, but he acknowledged that in America, for those who also have African heritage, having a white parent has never meant becoming white."[66] Those options are posed too starkly; one need not become White in order to be not only Black. But if many people, including even those with non-Black ancestry, perceive that they have little or no choice in how to identify, multiracialism's contribution to creating a new racial order will be stunted or stalled.

The other potential derailment of multiracialism's transformative potential is linked to the first. Some people remain hostile to the idea of a status partaking of more than one race. In 2004, the *Philadelphia Tribune* portrayed a biracial person as "fighting for 'healing and self-acceptance' in a polarized world where 'blacks and whites are engaged in a vicious struggle that leaves no one unscarred.'" Others depict multiracialism as a stalking horse for "color blindness: an obstacle to racial justice." Most starkly, "the mixed-raced population functions as a neo-mulatto class that has been provided with access to what is termed 'whitespace,'" or "we ... know that our political future ... is at stake when we don't choose blackness."[67] If people of mixed race, especially but not only those with Black ancestry, respond to appeals to reject multiracialism, it will be hard for others to perceive multiracial identity as additive rather than embedded in a zero-sum game against racial purity. Whether Americans endorse boundary blurring and contextual identity or continue to prefer the twentieth century's small set of fixed categories will determine whether multiracialism contributes to creation of a new racial order.

4

Genomics

There is in biology . . . a sense of barely contained expectations reminiscent of the physical sciences at the beginning of the 20th century. It is a feeling of advancing into the unknown and [a recognition] that where this advance will lead is both exciting and mysterious.
—*The Economist*

What we've shown is the concept of race has no scientific basis.
—J. Craig Venter

The debate . . . should not be over the existence of population differences, but how to describe those differences with more precision. . . . Railing against what some claim are misguided efforts to use racial, ethnic, or geographic distinctions does not make the differences disappear.
—A supporter of BiDil

We got to have a re-vote. This ain't right.
—Snoop Dogg, on discovering through DNA ancestry testing that he has more European ancestry than Charles Barkley

IMMIGRATION AND RACIAL mixture are very old topics in American history; indeed, they *are* American history. Genomics is a new topic, whose eventual scientific and social import may rival that of immigration and mixture. The *Economist*, normally sober and cautious, breathlessly describes "the sense of barely contained expectations, . . . advancing into the unknown, . . . [that is] both exciting and mysterious." Its clichéd prediction that the impact of twenty-first century biology will be "for both good and ill" captures well the mix of dire warnings and excited revelations one finds in the encounter between race and genomics.

A genome, briefly, is "an organism's complete set of deoxyribonucleic acid (DNA), a chemical compound that contains the genetic instructions needed to develop and direct the activities of every organism. DNA molecules are made of two twisting, paired strands. Each strand is made of four chemical units, called nucleotide bases. . . . The human genome contains approximately 3 billion of these base pairs, which reside in the 23 pairs of chromosomes within the nucleus of all our cells. Each chromosome contains hundreds to thousands of genes, which carry the instructions for making proteins." Genomics is "the branch of genetics that studies organisms in terms of their genomes (their full DNA sequences)."[1]

A broader philosophical definition of genomics suggests what is at stake as biology moves into the social arena. In this formulation, the older genetic science is a mechanistic, even deterministic, study of how and how much a given gene causes a given trait: "In the context of the nature-nurture controversy, 'nature' became more or less identical with 'genes.'" But with the discovery that humans have merely 22,500 or so genes rather than the 100,000 or 200,000 initially posited—"'only about twice as many as in worm or fly'"—scientists began to focus on the tremendous complexity and plasticity of genomic functioning and on the mutual causation between "nature" and "nurture." Genomics must be studied as an interactive system in which the whole cannot be reduced to the aggregation of its component parts; there are too many interactions and contingencies for an additive logic to make sense. The new science of genomics is thus "involved in governance of novel forms of information."[2]

Whether understood in the more technical or more philosophical way, genomics will affect the American racial order because it reopens the old question of whether racial or ethnic groups are in any way biologically distinct rather than being merely social inventions. As genomic science filters into U.S. society through medicine, schools, the legal system, commerce, and perhaps religion and politics, Americans may come to understand racial heritage and composition differently. Genomics may also contribute to changes in groups' relative medical and judicial positions. Whatever the exact impact of this new science turns out to be, as in the early twentieth century with physics, we are only beginning to glimpse how it will contribute to creating a new racial order.

Genomic Science and Race or Ethnicity

The study of genetic inheritance became a serious science in the mid-nineteenth century with the research of Gregor Mendel and Charles Darwin. A steady sequence of discoveries over the next century made it possible for the study of genetic inheritance to become the study of the genome. The first sequenced human genomes were published in 2001, after more than a decade of work and at a cost of almost $3 billion for the publicly funded Human Genome Project.[3]

Less than a decade later, "Singularity Hub predicts the cost to sequence an entire individual human genome will plummet to an astonishing $1,000 by the end of 2009 and the time required for sequencing will require less than one week. The ability to sequence entire genomes for $100 in a matter of days or hours is not far behind, probably only two to three years away." This claim proved overly ambitious, but most scientists agree that "genotyping cost is asymptoting to free"; within a generation "it will be easier to know someone's genome than their name." Thus "every baby born a decade from now will have its genetic code mapped at birth. . . . A complete DNA read-out for every newborn will be technically feasible and affordable in less than five years, promising a revolution in healthcare, says Jay Flatley, the chief executive of Illumina [a major genome sequencing company]. Only social and legal issues are likely to delay the era of 'genome sequences,' or genetic profiles, for all."[4]

Other than the straightforward but encompassing goal of basic scientific knowledge, the main purpose of genomic research is medical. Scientists hope to identify genes and genomic interactions that cause or contribute to susceptibility to diseases ranging from depression and schizophrenia to many varieties of cancer and heart failure. Diabetes, Parkinson's disease, arthritis, sickle cell disease, Crohn's disease, combined immunodeficiency, Huntington's disease, Tay-Sach's disease, adrenoleukodystrophy (ALD), HIV, depression, and others all have been or are being investigated for their genetic factors. The goal, of course, is to design effective drugs and to target medications to a patient's specific version of a disease, as well as to prevent genetic defects from becoming a disease or disability.

Genomic medicine has not yet fulfilled the fervent hopes that emerged after completion of the Human Genome Project; the *New York Times* reported in 2009 that "the era of personal genomic medicine may have to wait. The genetic analysis of common disease is turning out to be a lot more complex than expected." The genetic bases for almost all illnesses, as for human development more generally, are much less direct than scientists had expected, and interactions among genes, environment, and behavior are subtle and perhaps variable. So it will be decades, if ever, before genomic medicine lives up to the heady promises of the early 2000s; in the meantime, gene therapy is showing the greatest success in rare diseases that are genetically relatively simple. Nevertheless, the major financial services firm PricewaterhouseCoopers estimates that the commercial market for "a more personalized approach to health and wellness will grow to as much as $452 billion by 2015."[5]

DNA profiling is also growing in the legal arena. Courts use DNA evidence to reopen unsolved criminal cases, exonerate those wrongfully convicted, and determine verdicts in new cases. Dispute over the use and validity of genomic evidence is now common in criminal trials. Forensics investigators have used genetic information to identify victims of political events such as the Srebrenica massacre and tragedies such as the felled Air France Flight 447. It was used to identify victims of genocide in Rwanda and "disappearances" in Argentina, usually but not always with the support of local relatives.[6] DNA tests confirmed the death of Osama bin Laden.

Genomic science has other uses, variously deemed consumer, social,

races, since every level of clustering would determine a different partition and there is no biological reason to prefer a particular one. . . . Minor changes in the genes or methods used shift some populations from one cluster to the other.

Cavalli-Sforza and his coauthors demonstrated the intrinsic and irreducible incoherence of conventional racial boundaries in a series of magnificent illustrations showing how group lines swirled and merged within and across continents. They also pointed out, following Richard Lewontin and many others, that "the difference between groups is . . . small when compared with that within the major groups, or even within a single population." Furthermore, "whatever genetic boundaries may have developed, given the strong mobility of human individuals and populations, there probably never were any sharp ones, or if there were, they were blurred by later movements."[11]

Later analysts reinforced this conclusion by determining, as the National Human Genome Research Institute (NHGRI) puts it, that "all human beings are 99.9 percent identical in their genetic makeup." By the end of the 1990s, the American Anthropological Association was able to base its statement that the concept of race is merely "a worldview, a body of prejudgments that distorts our ideas about human differences and group behavior," on evidence from genomic science. As the association put it in the first paragraph of its Statement on Race: "Evidence from the analysis of genetics (e.g., DNA) indicates that most physical variation, about 94%, lies *within* so-called racial groups. . . . In neighboring populations there is much overlapping of genes and their phenotypic (physical) expressions. . . . The continued sharing of genetic materials has maintained all of humankind as a single species."[12]

A flood of scholarly writings has reinforced the pioneers' assertion that genomic science destroyed any claim about biological distinctions among races. A tiny sample includes a special issue of *Nature Genetics* titled "Human Genome Variation and 'Race'—The State of the Science" in 2004, a Web forum called "Is Race Real?" organized by the Social Science Research Council, Howard University's National Human Genome Center's position statement titled "State of the Science on Human Genome Variation and 'Race,'" and the discovery published in *Nature* that the genetic structures of indigenous hunter-gatherer peoples of Southern Africa "seem to be, on average, more different from each other than, for example, a European and an Asian." The current director of the National Institutes of Health, Francis Collins, wrote in 2001 that "those who wish to draw precise racial boundaries around certain groups will not be able to use science as a legitimate justification."[13] At the 2001 White House celebration of sequencing the human genome, J. Craig Venter observed that "what we've shown is the concept of race has no scientific basis."

This simple, clear conclusion is not, however, quite the end of the story. Many researchers find that they need some sort of concept like race and are reaching for terms such as "ethnicity," "biogeographic ancestry," or "region of the world." However labeled, the idea of a reasonably coherent group does real work. A good illustration is the 2008 genetic map of Europe produced by the Erasmus University Medical Center in Rotterdam (see figure 4.2).

Commentators have noted a few flaws and anomalies in this map. Finns perhaps appear so isolated because no Estonians were in the study; there is so much ethnic variation in France that a group only from Lyon is inadequate to represent the French; and so on.[14] Nevertheless, it enables three observations. First, this genetic map has an eerie resemblance to old maps of Europe that divided the population into Nordic, Noric, Alpine, Mediterranean, and other "races"—not in the empirical bases for boundaries within the continent but rather in the assertion of biologically based subgroups among "White" Europeans. Second, this form of racial boundary blurring differs from that articulated by Cavalli-Sforza and the American Anthropological Association. The mapmakers do not claim that one group blurs indistinguishably into another so that categorization is arbitrary and meaningless. Their point instead is that meaningfully distinct groups—which they call ethnicities—overlap with one another. This is indeed boundary blurring but of a different type than the smooth clinal argument.[15] Third, despite overlap, most of the named ethnicities remain distinguishable. Finns and Italians are the most distinct, Irish and Austrians the least, but as one commentator put it perhaps too baldly, "what the study shows is that autosomal aspects of DNA can be used to discover ethnicity."[16]

Latin America and Africa look much like Europe. Using thirteen mestizo populations from seven Latin American countries, and analyzing autosomal and X-chromosome microsatellites, another set of analysts distinguished the proportion of African, Native American, and European ancestry in each population (see figure 4.3). Again we can draw three conclusions. First, group boundaries are thoroughly blurred, since members of all thirteen populations combine all three of the conventionally understood races. Second, group boundaries blur differently across the continent due to different histories of colonization and intermarriage. Southern Brazilians (RGS) have the most European ancestry, and northern Argentines (Salta) the least. Finally, the analysts did not find a way to discuss boundary blurring without starting from and using the language of conventionally defined nominal races.[17]

That irony is common in the study of race through genomics. On the one hand, most social scientists writing in this arena endorse Venter's and other scientists' insistence that "the concept of race has no scientific

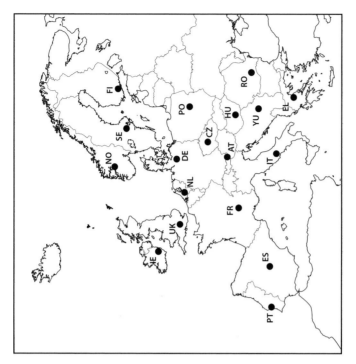

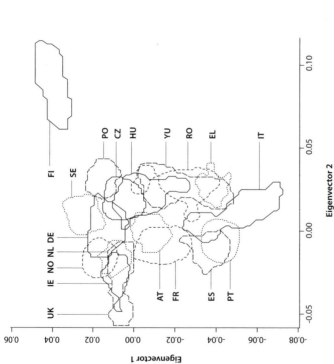

Figure 4.2. Genetic map of Europe.
Source: Lao et al. 2008. The right-hand map locates the populations from which autosomal DNA was retrieved. The left-hand map locates the populations in relation to each other according to the similarity of their autosomal DNA; the larger the area assigned, the larger the genetic variation in that population. *Note:* Some population groups have been deleted from the original image for purposes of visual clarity. Published with permission from Elsevier.

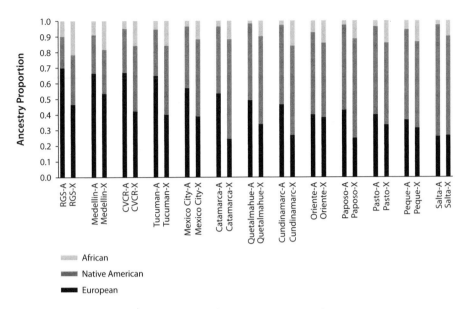

Figure 4.3. Ancestry proportions in thirteen mestizo populations.
Source: Wang et al. 2008. "A" represents the autosomal markers, and "X" represents the X-chromosome markers.

basis." Passions on this point can be intense: "the category of race is still powerful and dangerous, especially in scientific work. . . . This tendency [to treat "racial categories . . . as biological 'givens'"] must be resisted and vigorously contested." Or "race as a biologically rooted idea is supposedly in the dustbin of history with no scientific utility, but it keeps raising its ugly head."[18]

On the other hand, as the latter quotation suggests, it turns out to be very difficult to report analyses of genomic material at the level of populations without using conventional nominal racial categories in ways that imply their meaningfulness. Thus in the Latin American study, even heterogeneity is demonstrated by showing how much of each conventionally defined race appears in each population. A parallel study shows not only the uniquely wide genetic variation and mixture across Africa but also the fact that "using this color scheme virtually the whole of East Asia is a virtually undifferentiated sea of pink, Europe a block of blue, and even the diversity of India is reduced to a mix of just two colours."[19] That is, East Asians and Europeans each comprise a fairly homogenous "race," and despite its genetic diversity, parts of Africa have a sufficiently similar genetic inheritance that the language of race is hard to avoid.

Even Cavalli-Sforza and his colleagues write that "the color map of the world [on the cover of *The History and Geography of Human Genes*] shows very distinctly the differences that we know exist among the continents: Africans (yellow), Caucasoids (green), Mongoloids, including American Indians (purple), and Australian Aborigines (red). The map does not show well the strong Caucasoid component in northern Africa, but it does show the unity of the other Caucasoids from Europe, and in West, South, and much of Central Asia." This does not quite contradict their assertion that "classification into races has proved to be a futile exercise," but it does tend in the opposite direction. As Duana Fullwiley observes, "habits and ways of reading socially understood racial difference [are leading to a system in which] ... DNA molecules ... are increasingly made to carry the self-reported US racial descriptor of their donor as they leave his or her body and enter the laboratory. The DNA is then analyzed with the racial label attached for the duration of its life in the lab and beyond."[20]

In short, genomic scientists' insistence that racial boundaries are irreducibly blurred is not the same thing as social scientists' insistence that race is a purely social invention. Researchers in medical genomics both reject bright-line boundaries between nominal racial categories and cannot or will not abandon the terminology of race in the study of human variation. As the pharmacogenetics researcher Esteban Burchard reflected, "How distinct are these categories? I don't think they're distinct at all, and that's part of the reason why we measure ancestry. Race is a complex construct. It includes social factors, it includes self-identity factors, it includes third party factors of 'how do you view me?' But it also includes biological factors."[21]

Some researchers in population or medical genomics go a step further, simply taking for granted the existence of biologically intelligible racial or ethnic categories. Titles and summaries of an essentially random selection of recent articles convey the point:

- Whole Genome Distribution and Ethnic Differentiation of Copy Number Variation in Caucasian and Asian Populations: Our findings of ethnic differentiation of CNVs ... may furnish a basis for understanding the genomic differentiation of complex traits across ethnic groups.
- Racial Clues in Bowell Cancer Find: UK scientists found one of the genes increased risk in people of European descent, but not Japanese people. ... Professor Malcolm Dunlop ... who led the research, said: 'This is the first time that a race-specific effect has been found for a genetic marker.' ... Dr. Lesley Walker, from Cancer Research UK, said: 'We can now begin to explain some of the difference in rates of the disease between populations through specific genes.'

- Genome-wide Patterns of Population Structure and Admixture in West Africans and African Americans: Quantifying patterns of population structure in Africans and African Americans illuminates the history of human populations and is critical for undertaking medical genomics studies on a global scale."[22]

So genomic research answers the question "what is a race?" ambiguously. It undermines both a straightforward conception of a few biologically distinct and internally homogeneous groups *and* the claim that race is an arbitrary verbal invention.[23] Over the next few decades, Americans are likely to absorb some version of this mixed message. However they receive and interpret it, the newly invigorated discussion of race, biology, and boundaries will transform current assumptions. The nominal groups that persisted in common discourse from the Jim Crow and nativist racial order through the post–civil rights and immigration-based racial order may come to be understood as too simplistic, while the social constructivist view may come to be understood as too shallow. Although Americans may bring some conception of biology back into the language of race without starting down the slippery slope of eugenics and measuring skull sizes, we disagree among ourselves as to whether such conceptions are possible or potentially useful.

How Are Individuals Classified in a Race?

If races are simultaneously real, arbitrary, heterogeneous, and blurred, it is not surprising that individual classification is intricate and contested. Genomic analysts in medicine, law, and genealogy sharply disagree among themselves on how much and how best to classify individuals.

The issue of race-specific medication has generated the most visible classification debate. In 2005, the FDA approved the drug BiDil for use in treating congestive heart failure—but only for self-identified African Americans. Its supporters' reasoning was simple: "The African American community is affected at a greater rate by heart failure than that of the corresponding Caucasian population," and clinical trials apparently showed that BiDil provides effective treatment for them, though not for Whites. Some argued that the reason is genetic; Blacks' congestive heart failure differs genetically from that of other groups in ways that affect response to medication. Thus "the approval was widely declared to be a significant step toward a new era of personalized medicine, an era in which pharmaceuticals would be specifically designed to work with an individual's particular genetic makeup." BiDil was not unique; the FDA cautioned in 2007 against giving the anti-seizure medication carbamazepine to Asian patients since the genetic variant that contraindicates it

sonalized medicine may be near for a few ailments; "cancer doctors at Massachusetts General Hospital plan within a year to read the genetic fingerprints of nearly all new patients' tumors, a novel strategy designed to customize treatment."[32] One can buy an iPhone application to download genomes from the University of California at Santa Cruz's Genome Browser, and another that enables one to "interactively monitor your sequencing runs" from Illumina's sequencers. For most patients and most diseases, however, personalized genomic medicine is not near; the issue of racial classification of individuals, and its uses and harms, will remain salient for a long time.

The use of genomics in the legal system generates the same controversies because it may also transform classification systems and their uses. As in the medical arena, in the abstract few dispute the use of genomics to solve crimes and free those wrongly convicted, but people vigorously contest the legitimacy of current and possible uses of the new technologies.

Forensic DNA phenotyping generates the fiercest arguments with regard to classification. The issues are basically the same as in population studies and medical research: is it scientifically valid and socially acceptable to focus on the tiny proportion of the human genome that purportedly differentiates population groups into something resembling "races"? Or should research and practice focus entirely on the vast majority of the genome that is the same across groups or variable only at the level of individuals? A company named DNAPrint Genomics claimed that its test DNAWitness™ "will provide the percentage of genetic makeup amongst the four possible groups of Sub-Saharan African, Native American, East Asian, and European. When appropriate, DNAWitness™ allows for a breakdown of the European ancestry into four components: Northwestern European, Southeastern European, Middle Eastern, and South Asian." DNAPrint Genomics observed that "the names of the components/groups is [sic] meaningful but not exact, since they are cast in modern-day terminology but the assay is an anthropological one that reports affiliation with populations who share common ancestry extending back many thousands of years. The real value of the percentages reported are [sic] as population (rather than individual) bar-codes." Despite this caveat, "DNAPrint® is the first forensic product that provides predictive capability," and the ancestral percentages it provides "are very useful for inferring certain elements of physical appearance."[33]

Forensic phenotyping became publicly visible in a 2002 case involving serial rapes and murders in Louisiana. Police relied on eyewitness accounts and an FBI profile to search for a White man and collected DNA samples from hundreds. Sent a DNA specimen from one crime scene, however, a molecular biologist using DNAWitness™ concluded that "your guy could be African-American or Afro-Caribbean, but there is no chance that this is a Caucasian." The police shifted their focus, eventually arrested a Black man, and found that his DNA matched crime scene samples. He was convicted. The biologist was not surprised; by examining DNA from 176 locations on the genome, he says, he "can predict ancestry with a tiny margin of error."[34]

Forensic phenotyping has been used in dozens of cases in several countries, and DNAPrint Genomics claimed that it has been correct (that is, "consistent with phenotype and self-held notions of ancestry") in thousands of blind tests. It is still used only rarely, due to both the cost of the test and police concerns about the appearance of racial profiling. Nevertheless, if forensic phenotyping is accurate, it suggests that race, or at least racial appearance, has a biologically specifiable component. Research in this arena is expanding, with recent publications claiming to have identified the genetic determinants of eye, skin, or hair color.[35] These scientists avoid the term "race," but they might see DNAPrint Genomics' claim of accuracy as plausible.

Other analysts, not surprisingly, challenge the test's accuracy as well as the legitimacy of its use. Some focus directly on the difficulty of classifying individuals in a society with a great deal of racial boundary blurring and internal group heterogeneity: "In . . . [some] localities, the populace will contain many people of recently mixed ancestry and many people whose phenotypic characteristics make them racially ambiguous. Localities with large populations of Latin American, Middle Eastern, or South Asian descent . . . might be regions of the country in which attempts to draw inferences about a person's race on the basis of her or his ancestry would not prove useful." Furthermore, as we discussed in chapter 3, "genetic information about ancestry can be at odds with a person's self-identified or attributed race. . . . Some percentage of people who look White will possess genetic markers indicating that a significant majority of their recent ancestors were African. Some percentage of people who look Black will possess genetic markers indicating that the majority of their recent ancestors were European. Native Americans may be genetically indistinguishable from Hispanics (Mexican Americans) or African Americans. Inferring race from genetic ancestry may mislead police rather than illuminate their search for a suspect."[36]

Another analyst argues similarly that DNAWitness™ is creating rather than finding clearly defined races. The company chose the DNA markers for the reference populations by focusing only on specific alleles (gene variants) that were most distinct for a given continental group (a.k.a. "race") and most different from the alleles of other continental groups. "Such purified, or *artificially* homogenized, samples came to serve as 'parental populations'" for the tested samples. Not only does that methodology construct pure "races" out of populations that are in fact mixed, but "problems arise when social context and historical accounts meet with sampling limits." Some ancestral populations, such as the vast majority of indigenous Americans, no longer exist. Or the person whose DNA is sampled may actually have a closer genetic link to ancestors from parts of the globe that were not included in the reference populations than to those that were included.[37] In this view, anything like a pure race does not exist, and any effort to classify individuals in terms of a race is fallacious and potentially dangerous. Where this new method for classifying individuals will come to rest remains unclear because it is at least as much a political as a scientific question.

In contrast to the medical and legal arenas, in recreational or genealogical genomics, individual racial classification is the goal rather than incidental knowledge on the way to some other goal. For some people, ancestral DNA testing stabilizes the meaning of race and their own racial identity. Mika Stump grew up in foster homes, knowing nothing of her roots except that she is Black. "But a DNA test she took recently showed strong similarities between Stump's genetic code and the Mende and Temne people of Sierra Leone, in Africa. Now, 'I have a place where I can go back and say, "This is who I am; this is my home." That's something I never, ever expected to say.'" The Reverend Al Simpson traveled from Chicago to Sierra Leone to give tribal elders of the village of Lunsar documentation of his Temne lineage. He remembers saying, "'Five hundred years ago my DNA was removed from here by slave traders and taken to America, so I'm coming back for my seat. My seat's been vacant.'" He asked for a Temne name in order "'to reclaim what was taken away from me.'"[38]

Others find that genetic ancestry testing destroys any possibility of racial solidity. (Journalists find these stories almost as irresistible as those about finding one's roots.) The red-haired, freckled, apparently Scottish Jack Hitt "carr[ies] the DNA marker found in great abundance among the Fulbe tribe of contemporary Nigeria." Danny Villarreal, a Hispanic Texan who believed himself to be of pure Spanish blood, found through DNA testing that he was closely related to Jewish populations in Hungary, Belarus, and Poland. Genetically, he is an Ashkenazi Jew. (His reaction: "I was kinda surprised. . . . I'm a good ol' Catholic boy.") One enthusiast points out that DNA ancestry testing could even enable a person to reject his or her inherited identity in favor of a preferred one: "it might give enough data to identify with somebody else that they feel more comfortable with."[39]

African Americans may be especially likely to use DNA ancestry tests as an aide to self-definition, since for them the drastic disruptions of enslavement curtail the value of more conventional genealogical tools. As Gates puts it, "for the first time since the seventeenth century, we are able, symbolically at least, to reverse the Middle Passage. Our ancestors brought something with them that not even the slave trade could take away: their own distinctive strands of DNA. . . . A match . . . reveals a shared ancestor, and possibly a shared ethnic identity, that has been lost for centuries." A Lexis-Nexis search found 717 articles through 2010 reporting on individuals who have done DNA ancestry tests. Two-thirds of the 132 persons discussed in these articles were Black.[40]

Nevertheless, people from other groups, especially those with disrupted genealogical records such as the Irish, Native Americans, and Jews, can be equally excited.[41] The enterprising director of the Centre for Forensic Investigation at Glasgow Caledonian University intends "to have DNA swabbing kits in all the tourist information offices and hotel lobbies across the UK, so people can go and pick up a kit for a few pounds then post it off to us and we will do the DNA tests for them." For the researchers, that will "contribute to a DNA database of Scottish and Irish clan groups." For the Scottish tourist industry, "DNA testing will be a draw for ancestral tourists who might want to 'walk in the footsteps of their ancestors.'"[42]

If genetic ancestry testing becomes widespread, and if people choose to test maternal as well as paternal lines, awareness of ancestral mixture is likely to rise. A study of 365 African Americans found the median proportion of European ancestry to be about one-fifth; the tested individuals ranged from more than 99 percent West African ancestry to less than 1 percent.[43] Unlike those who embrace multiracialism, some—such as Snoop Dogg in one of the epigraphs to this chapter—may be disturbed at losing the clarity of a single racial ancestry. Genetic genealogy "is 'not for the faint-hearted,' says Melvyn Gillette, a member of the African American Genealogical Society of Northern California and a longtime family researcher. 'Before you go opening any door, you need to ask, "Am I really ready for what might be behind it?" Not everyone is.'" Lisa Lee, formerly active in the Black Power movement, found no African ancestry on her father's side: "What does this mean; who am I then? For me to have a whole half of my identity to come back and say, 'Sorry, no African here,' it doesn't even matter what the other half says. It just negates it all. . . . It doesn't fit, it doesn't feel right." Another put it more crisply: "I was expecting Kunta Kinte, but I got Lord De La Warr."[44]

Others find this type of racial boundary blurring exciting, even faintly transgressive. A sociology professor reports that "everyone wants to take the test, even students who think they are 100 percent one race or another, and almost every one of them wants to discover something, that they're 1 percent Asian or something. It's a badge in this multicultural world." All of his White students said, "'Oh man, I hope I'm part black,' because it would upset their parents. That's this generation. People want to identify with this pop multiracial culture. They don't want to live next to it, but they want to be part of it. It's cool." He has a serious purpose, however, beyond shocking his students' parents:

> I try to demonstrate to students how complex race and ethnicity are. My secondary goal is to improve race relations, and when people discover that what they thought about themselves is not true—"I thought I was black, but I'm also Asian and white"—it leads them to have a different kind of conversation about race. It leads them to be less bigoted, to ask the deeper questions, to be more open to differences.[45]

We rely heavily on journalists' stories here both because they reveal the emotional substrate of DNA ancestry testing and because there is not yet a robust body of scholarly research on its impact. "Commercial DNA testing is in its infancy and so are research efforts . . . which seek to explore the potential impact on personal perceptions of ethnic identity."[46] Two pioneers of this field warn repeatedly that test results are inevitably partial and subject to error, and they point to a "potential negative consequence" when reports of ancestral categories are "misinterpreted as indications of 'real' racial divisions, even if they are explicitly acknowledged as being continuous and, to some extent, arbitrary groups." They nonetheless assert that a personalized genetic history "has the potential to affect ethnic, religious, racial, and family identities." At this point, research is unsettled about the impact of DNA testing on group identity. One study found clients of DNA testing firms engaging in "affiliative self-fashioning"—accepting or rejecting the test results in accord with their prior self-definition, genealogical knowledge, and chance occurrences. But another warns of commercial firms' "appeal to 'genetic essentialism'—the view that our genomes do intrinsically define our personal identities, as secular substitutes for the 'soul.'"[47]

We know of no accurate count of the number of people who have engaged in genetic ancestry testing, never mind a comprehensive survey of their motivations or the consequences. (One expert estimates about half a million people worldwide.) Current users may not, in any case, be good predictors of future users. This arena will surely grow as tests become cheaper, more accurate, and more widely disseminated. Probably "the technology will show how mixed we are";[48] unless knowledge is walled off from emotions, the new science is thus likely to contribute further to the growing heterogeneity within and across groups.

Relative Group Positions

Scientists, research organizations, and direct-to-consumer firms are generally careful to state explicitly their opposition to any use of genomics that would contribute to relative group positioning. The history of eugenics and its collapse into American sterilization programs and the Nazis' search for racial purity through genocide is widely known; no one in a position of public responsibility proposes to re-create that racial order. Thus scientists typically insist that most genetic diseases and all behaviors with a genetic component are expressed only through interaction with environmental and personal factors. To choose only two among hundreds of examples: the first paragraph of a general interest book developed from the American Museum of Natural History's exhibition "The Genomic Revolution" observes that "it is . . . increasingly evident that gene-environment reactions are of seminal importance. Scientists now recognize that our genetic composition does not represent predestination or predetermination, but rather sets the stage for the interaction between genes and an array of factors in our individual and shared environments." The second paragraph of a scholarly book from the authoritative Institute of Medicine of the National Academies of Science similarly points out that "examining interactions among genetic and social-environmental factors could greatly enhance understanding of health and illness. . . . The socioeconomic status of communities is associated with variations in central nervous system serotonergic responsivity, which may have implications for the prevalence of psychological disorders and behaviors such as depression, impulsive aggression, and suicide."[49]

Nevertheless, some research does investigate the possible genetic bases of intelligence, moral faculties, tendency toward aggression, or other traits, and it could move in the direction of searching for heritable group differences. An early meta-analysis of twenty-four studies found "a strong overall genetic effect that may account for up to 50% of the variance in aggression"; it said nothing about racial or ethnic groups. A decade later, genomic science permitted greater precision: "three genetic polymorphisms . . . are significant predictors of serious and violent delinquency when added to a social-control model of delinquency." With controls for environment, socioeconomic status, and age, this study found no statistically significant effect of race on young men's serious or violent delinquency. Adding genetic propensities to the model of social control did not change the lack of statistical impact of race on delinquency. Hispanicity was, however, sometimes weakly associated with delinquency in both models that did and did not include genetic propensities among the independent variables.[50]

Other lines of research argue more boldly that certain attributes are genetically more prominent in particular groups. Scientists at the University of Utah have "proposed that the unusual pattern of genetic diseases seen among Jews of central or northern European origin . . . is the result of natural selection for enhanced intellectual ability." Their article was published in a peer-reviewed journal, despite Steven Pinker's observation

be junk), the Offender Index may raise more privacy concerns than norms or laws permit or than the designers of the system intended. Some worry about "surreptitious sampling"—police collection of DNA samples inadvertently left in a public space through loss of hairs, discarding a cigarette butt, or generating other "trash for public consumption." Laboratories and police departments may mishandle DNA samples; expert witnesses may, intentionally or not, convey misleading information. Like all human endeavors, in short, the science of DNA matching is replete with uncertainty and opportunities for error.[58]

But proponents point to safeguards. Courts permit challenges to improper handling and storage procedures. DNA samples from arrestees who are acquitted or never charged, and from felons whose convictions are overturned, must (or may, depending on the source) be expunged from official databases. The legal system has well-developed practices for responding to misleading experts. Courts have consistently found the use of convicts' and crime scene DNA samples to be constitutionally permissible under Fourth Amendment provisions for search and seizure,[59] and Congress and state legislatures have appropriated funds to develop databases and eliminate the backlog of unprocessed DNA samples. DNA samples are especially valuable in cases involving rape or sexual assault, so there is a gendered component to grounds for support and opposition. More generally, the "potential value" of DNA databases includes

(1) the number of cases in which likely suspects have been excluded (saving both the potential suspect some distress and the police investigative resources); (2) investigative resources saved because of the shortened investigations resulting from cold hits; (3) society's costs from additional crimes committed by perpetrators who either would not otherwise have been caught or would have been caught later; and (4) the deterrent effects of a DNA database.

Proponents' ultimate argument is—as President Obama put it after reminding his audience that he is the father of two young girls—"it's so important to every family across America and there are just too many horror stories that remind us that we're not doing enough. . . . We insist on justice."[60]

It is not that simple. Justice for some can produce injustice for others; this is the point where amassing DNA samples intersects with the fourth component of the American racial order. The legal system's collection of genetic material is asymmetric across population groups due to disproportions in arrests, immigrant detentions, felony convictions, or simply family size. That is, forensic biological evidence comes disproportionately from non-Anglo populations. Once partial matches and familial searching come into play, non-White family members are more likely to be subjects of investigation than are White family members—what some call "guilt by genetic association." African Americans (mostly men) comprise about two-fifths of the CODIS Offender Index, since roughly 40 percent of the people convicted of felonies in a given year are Black. According to one calculation in 2006, assuming that the average person in the database has five living first degree relatives, using partial matches to identify offenders' relevant family members means that about 17 percent of the Black population, compared with only 4 percent of non-Blacks, could be under surveillance. (The disproportion would be even greater if Hispanics were separated from Whites, which this calculation did not do.)[61]

This is problematic in itself. It becomes even more so given that the rate of false positives—that is, the likelihood of many partial matches to people who have no link to the matched offender or crime scene—rises as the size of the DNA database increases. Eventually, according to one attorney, "what you're gonna end up seeing is nearly the majority of the African American population being under genetic surveillance. If you do the math, that's where you end up."[62] To a lesser degree, Hispanic men are also disproportionately likely to be arrested and convicted and thus especially subject to DNA-based investigations. Hispanics are further disadvantaged by family size: "as the demographic group with the highest rate of natural population growth, each profile input from a Hispanic defendant is likely, on average, to lead investigators relying on familial testing to a higher number of genetic relatives than if the profile had been obtained from a non-Hispanic person. Disproportionate distribution of privacy violations is nearly inevitable in such a system." By this analyst's arithmetic, Hispanic offenders' relatives will soon be even more likely than Black offenders' relatives to be subject to DNA-based surveillance.[63]

Disproportionate impact of familial matching will not be "the result of any unstated racially discriminatory purpose or intent in the use of family forensic DNA." CODIS is not high-tech Jim Crow; it does not mandate state-sponsored segregation. The courts are therefore likely to permit partial matches and perhaps familial searches. Nevertheless, "like racial profiling, it does seem fundamentally unfair, in a way that has systemic implications broader than those affecting random families that include convicted felons."[64] In our terms, forensic genomics may tend toward a new group-based prohibition, or at least new grounds for the old group-based stigma.

It is possible, however, that forensic genomics will transform the racial order in a more profound way in the opposite direction—by helping more than harming disadvantaged groups. After all, Blacks and Hispanics are disproportionately victimized by crime as well as by overpolicing; the Grim Sleeper's alleged victims were Black. So a more effective criminal justice system could in the end help those groups—whether more than the new high-tech profiling will harm them remains to be seen.

Forensic genomics could even offset some of the current racial bias in the criminal justice system. Genetic samples are not themselves racially biased, whereas other phenomena that can lead to conviction—arrests, eyewitness reports, police treatment and reports, legal counsel, judges' rulings, juries' verdicts, drug laws—often are. As the authoritative National Academy of Sciences report *Strengthening Forensic Science* puts it, "among existing forensic methods, only nuclear DNA analysis has been rigorously shown to have the capacity to consistently, and with a high degree of certainty, demonstrate a connection between an evidentiary sample and a specific individual or source." The Innocence Project argued unsuccessfully in 2009 before the Supreme Court for a prisoner's right to DNA testing, and it has worked to ensure that states preserve biological evidence and guarantee the right of testing to prisoners. Forty-four states do provide access to DNA testing for prisoners, although with a variety of conditions; the Supreme Court ruled in 2011 that convicted prisoners may sue states under a civil rights law to obtain potentially exonerating DNA evidence rather than only being able to use more restrictive habeas corpus suits.[65] So genomics may be a substantial part of the solution as well as a contributor to the problem of racial bias in the criminal justice system.

Innocence Project lawyers certainly think so. As of 2011, more than 270 prisoners have been exonerated through DNA tests, with "staggering numbers of innocent people" remaining incarcerated, according to the organization's Web site. An earlier study provided more detail: from 1989 through 2003, DNA evidence enabled convictions of 144 people to be overturned. Hispanic and especially Black men are "greatly overrepresented among those defendants who were falsely convicted of rape and then exonerated, mostly by DNA." An even greater proportion of freed juvenile than adult convicts were Black. Based on this and similar evidence, these advocates argue that most of "the thousands, perhaps tens of thousands" of people imprisoned through "miscarriages of justice" are Black or Hispanic.[66]

Genomic science also contributes to government-sponsored permissions or prohibitions in a very different arena—determining the opportunities available to members of certain Indian tribes. In the early 2000s, several tribes voted to exclude Freedmen, the term for descendants of Blacks who joined them in the nineteenth century through some combination of enslavement, marriage, adoption, federal mandate, and presence on the Dawes Rolls. The tribes asserted the right as sovereign nations to set their own citizenship requirements, deciding that descent from an Indian on the Dawes Rolls was essential: "what it boils down to is the Cherokee Nation has determined that to be a member of our Indian nation, you need to be at least part Indian," in the words of one spokesperson. In a suit for reinstatement to tribal membership, some Freedmen have taken a DNA ancestry test in order to "establish that we are Indian people, not just African people who were adopted into the tribe."[67]

As of this writing, courts' and federal agencies' decisions on reinstatement have rested on legal, moral, and political considerations, not on genetic testing. Nevertheless, as a contributor to a listserv discussion of this issue pointed out,

> what we cannot do is dismiss the impact these studies will have on issues of indigenous identity and sovereignty. . . . When nations depend on blood quantum or other genetic factors as a standard to determine citizenship, then I think they must be prepared to respond, consider and perhaps even change some enrollment policies as our knowledge and understanding of genetic identity increases. . . . To ignore what knowledge this science will produce and dismiss the conclusions set[s] a dangerous precedent.[68]

Once again, Americans have a new set of tools to use in creating a new racial order. Whether these tools will be used to exacerbate or ameliorate inequalities among groups are political choices not yet made.

Social Relations

Americans remain largely ignorant of genomics research. Asked what DNA is, only 40 percent of respondents had even a vaguely appropriate answer in 1988; in the 1990s, fewer than one in ten survey respondents claimed to have read or heard a great deal about "new genetic tests." But public awareness and knowledge are growing. By the 2000s, the proportion who claimed to have read or heard a great deal about new genetic tests had doubled, and about 75 percent gave a plausible answer in 2001 when asked to explain DNA. In 2006, four out of five respondents said that they were very or somewhat interested in the human genome. Two years later, 80 percent of American adults and even more eighth-grade students knew that traits are transferred across generations through both egg and sperm. Roughly two-thirds of adults know (or guess correctly) that the father's gene determines the sex of a baby.[69]

Nonetheless, genomics research is still being done in something close to a societal vacuum. That permits a wide range of predictions about its impact on social relations, from deeply pessimistic to broadly optimistic. On the pessimistic side, some ethicists see the use of in-vitro fertilization and genetic testing by well-off parents as the first steps toward favorable genetic selection. Even if morally acceptable, which many doubt, at least for the foreseeable future genetic selection will be available only to privileged classes, potentially exacerbating social and racial inequalities. Fetal genetic testing also raises a deeper concern: although we know of no efforts to use genomic science to prevent reproduction among people with presumedly less desirable traits, some fear a possible reincarnation of eugenicist thinking through efforts to clone or create ideal humans without disability, disadvantaged race, or other purported flaws.[70]

Also on the pessimistic side, some worry that insurance providers and employers will try to use genetic information to deny coverage or jobs to certain individuals in order to avoid expensive health care costs for people genetically predisposed to illness, obesity, or other conditions. The Genetic Information Non-Discrimination Act (GINA) of 2008 is intended to address these concerns by prohibiting discrimination by health insurers and employers on the basis of genetic differences. It was the United States' first preemptive law against discrimination. But GINA does not protect against discrimination for life, disability, or long-term care insurance; it does not apply to settings beyond one's workplace; and it only applies to asymptomatic individuals.[71] So the pessimists still have plenty to worry about.

Another set of anxieties: will potential marriage or reproductive partners spurn individuals with less desirable genetic profiles? Will actuaries place lower value on the lives of people with "defective genes," or will juries award lower damages to people with genetic illnesses because of a lower life expectancy? And will the definition of less desirable profiles or genetic illnesses itself be racially implicated? At this point, these questions are speculative. GINA's impact is unknown since it has only recently been implemented. No one has brought a case of genetic discrimination to federal or state courts, and the EEOC has ruled on only one, in 2001.[72] Surveys consistently show that the public wants protection against genetic discrimination, but GINA is too new to have received much public response.

Rather than technology pessimism, an alternative way to fill the societal vacuum around genomics is technology optimism.[73] Americans tend to trust scientists to act in the public interest and to know what they are doing. Four out of five consistently agree that medical genetic testing should be readily available "to all who want it."[74] Generally before and always after 2000, many more respondents agree than disagree that the benefits of genetic testing outweigh its harms. Despite substantially different question wordings, table 4.1 shows the pattern clearly.

The pattern of general support for genomic science is unambiguous, but it remains completely unknown whether ordinary Americans share experts' fear of new forms of genetically based social relations among groups. As of this writing, of the 823 questions in the Roper Center for Public Opinion's compendium of survey items that include the word "DNA," "gene," "genetic," "genomic," or their variants, none addresses issues of race, eugenics, or group attributes.[75] The scant evidence does not

Table 4.1
Weighing the Harms and Benefits of Genomic Science, 1985–2009

Year and survey organization	Positive effects	Negative effects	Combination, "It depends"	No effect	DK, NA, or refused
Louis Harris & Associates, 1983	67	16	–	–	17
Cambridge Reports, 1985	29	15	16	–	41
Roper Organization, 1985	22	28	29	–	21
Louis Harris & Associates, 1986	68	22	–	2	11
Roper Organization, 1987	38	26	11	–	25
GSS 1990	48	21	11	–	21
GSS 1996	51	24	–	–	25
U.S. News and World Report, 1997	61	5	–	23	12
NPR/Kaiser/Harvard 1999	50	21	–	18	11
Time/CNN/Yankelovich 2000	40	46	–	–	14
Pew Research Center, 2000	29	61	–	–	10
Pew Research Center, 2000	80	20	–	–	1
Los Angeles Times, 2000	59	17	–	–	24
Virginia Commonwealth University, 2001	57	27	–	–	16
Harris Interactive, 2002	81	11	–	–	8
GSS 2004	71	29	–	–	–
Virginia Commonwealth University, 2004	58	27	–	–	15
Virginia Commonwealth University, 2008	54	25	–	–	21
Pew Research Center, 2009	72	19	–	–	9
Pew Research Center, 2009	53	13	–	22	13

Note: All surveys are of a randomly selected national U.S. adult sample of at least 1,000 respondents. Question wording and further information is on iPOLL. Questions from the same survey organization usually have similar or identical wording and answer categories. None of these questions specifies any substantive arena (such as medicine, cloning, genetically modified food, fetal genetic testing, and so on).

show non-Whites to be more fearful of genomic science than Whites; one survey, in fact, found both Blacks and Latinos to be more eager than Whites to use prenatal and adult genetic tests.[76]

Nor is it clear that one group is more inclined toward genetic explanations for various traits than another. One 2000 study found Whites to be significantly more likely than Blacks to accept genetic explanations for "athleticism, math performance, drive to succeed, tendency toward violence, intelligence, and sexual orientation." But in another survey at about the same time, with a variety of controls, "disadvantaged respondents, whether in terms of education or race/ethnicity, regard genetics as *more* important to the determination of life outcomes than members of advantaged groups. Moreover, the most disadvantaged respondents, in terms of education and ethnicity, regard genetics as most important." Blacks and Latinos were significantly more likely than Whites to agree that "every person should be required to have a genetic screening test before he or she can get married," and Blacks were significantly more likely also to agree that before marrying, one should find out "whether the person has a history of mental illness in the family." The three groups did not differ significantly on whether "the Human Genome Project and other research on human genetics [are] likely to be helpful or harmful."[77] In the 2004 GSS, a higher proportion of Whites than Blacks or "other" respondents agreed that genetic testing will do more good than harm, but a substantial majority of all groups (three-fifths of non-Whites and over seven-tenths of Whites) concurred.

Whether social scientists are excessively concerned, or the general public is naïve, is one more feature of genomics that remains to be seen—or rather, to be shaped—over the next few decades. We *can* predict that Americans' knowledge, or at least awareness, of genomic science will grow as its recreational uses are disseminated and as the phenomenon seeps into popular culture (see figure 4.4). An issue of *Vanity Fair* focused on Africa—which included an article by Spencer Wells on the genomic inheritance of people with African ancestors, that is, everyone in the world—identified the haplotype of almost all persons named on its masthead. They were color coded to indicate the gender of the line of descent, and presented an arresting variation on the usual boilerplate of a magazine's masthead page. One of Google's logos is the iconic twisted double strand of DNA, substituting for the "oo" in the middle of the search engine's name. Visual media as well as print media are popularizing the genomics revolution; in 2008, the three major television networks devoted twenty-nine minutes of leading nightly news stories to the use of genetic testing to predict disease, second in amount of coverage only to research on cancer in the list of science and technology items tracked by the National Science Foundation. From 1969 through 2009, American

"*I got my DNA analysis back. Guess what—I'm a Hapsburg.*"

"*We think it has something to do with your genome.*"

Figure 4.4. Genomics in society.
Top: David Sipress, *The New Yorker*, 2008; © David Sipress/The New Yorker
Collection/www.cartoonbank.com
Bottom: Robert Mankoff, *The New Yorker*, 2000. © Robert Mankoff/The New
Yorker Collection/www.cartoonbank.com

newspapers ran almost six thousand articles that addressed both genetics or genomics and race, ethnicity, or heredity. The number has grown steadily over time, from roughly fifty per year in the early 1990s to a peak of eight hundred per year in 2008.[78]

Most consequential for the long-term social impact of genomics is the momentum of the research itself. *Science* magazine observes "a great deal of excitement, because everyone realizes the field is changing so fast." The postdoctoral fellows in genetics researcher Mary-Claire King's lab are "banging down the door at 7 A.M., they are so excited" about their work.[79] Others place American society "in the midst of a revolution, . . . an explosion in ability to analyze the entire dna sequence of individuals. . . . The medical and technological breakthroughs that will accompany widespread, cheap, and fast human genome sequencing will be far reaching and stunning." *Genome Technology* features a scientist describing genome function as "a very exciting field. Almost every week a new paper appears which makes you say 'Wow,' and a new brick is added to the building that we are trying to build." To one philosopher, genomic science is about nothing less than "the equitable and intelligent use of complex information."[80]

An endeavor that generates this set of exclamations from normally sedate scholars and scientists is likely to have a transformative impact, especially when backed by billions of dollars of research funds from the federal government, universities and research organizations, and pharmaceutical companies. It will, for better or worse, bring biology back into discussions of race and keep race in the criminal justice arena; it may also finally explode conventional racial categories and teach people how their environment—including their racial identification, with all that implies—interacts with their genetic inheritance. Once all of those lessons are learned, the life sciences could indeed have as much of an impact on the twenty-first century as physics had on the twentieth.

5

Cohort Change

I don't want to say it's in the cultural DNA, but a lot of us who are older than 30 have some memory of disappointment or humiliation related to banks. The white guy in the suit with the same income gets a loan and you don't. So you turn to local brokers, even if they don't offer the best rates.
   —Colvin Grannum, explaining why middle-class Blacks frequently
   obtain subprime mortgages

[Ayanna] Pressley, [candidate for Boston City Council], sees her generation as "coalition builders" able to "talk to and relate to other people" from different backgrounds. . . . "I think the successes of our parents' generation have better positioned us—by being exposed to different opportunities, you're exposed to different people, different cultures, different perspectives."
   —a journalist

Even if a few conventions are accepted by one generation, it does not follow that the next will observe them too, for in a democracy each generation is a new people.
   —Alexis de Tocqueville

Black America, as we knew it, is history.
   —Eugene Robinson

DURING A HISTORICAL era with a stable racial order, participants share a few key collective memories that help explain its origins and lineaments. Opinions about these events and the racial order itself will differ, but many people will note the same moments—in the current racial order, the Selma march, Watts riot, grape boycott, fall of Saigon—as meaningful markers of their political period.[1] When a collective memory fades or fragments, the moral force of the associated racial order is weakened, although behaviors may not change until something impels them into a new channel. Thus a *collective racial memory*—distinct from but linked to the passage of time and the process of aging—is central to a society's racial structure.[2]
   Starting at least with de Tocqueville, thinkers have linked the idea of collective memory to generational transitions. Adolescence and young adulthood "are constitutive of world views and political perspectives that, though not inflexible, tend to be carried forward as individuals age. . . . One's sense of self is . . . stamped by the historically significant

A few of the many possible illustrations suggest the tone of political transformation. The novelist Darryl Pinckney observed a panel including Jesse Jackson Jr., Al Sharpton, and Cornel West, all of whom emphasized Blacks' "alternate understanding of American history. . . . And yet I got a sense from the students around me that although they were saying thank you to the older style of black politics, it was for them very much a new day." San Francisco's then district attorney, Kamala Harris, concurs: "our civil rights heroes fought so that we could be free to be anything we wanted." In an epigraph to this chapter, a young Black city council candidate describes her generation as "coalition builders," able to "talk to and relate to other people. . . . I think the successes of our parents' generation have better positioned us—by being exposed to different opportunities, you're exposed to different people, different cultures, different perspectives."[24] The experienced political operative Gwen Ifill insists that "the Obama generation is just beginning its run. South Carolina state representative Bakari Sellers is so young that when the picture on his office wall of him posing with Jesse Jackson was taken in 1988, Sellers was just 4 years old." Tim Scott, then a conservative candidate whom a reporter described as "poised to become the first black Republican elected to Congress from the Deep South in more than a century," was ambivalent about that distinction: "the historic part of this is nice to have—maybe." But it is also a "distraction. . . . I don't spend much time on history." Mr. Scott was in crowded company; an unprecedented thirty-two Blacks ran for Congress in the 2010 Republican primaries. (Unlike most, however, he won his primary and then the election.) Says the new Black mayor of ill-famed Philadelphia, Mississippi, election of a Black in that city is "an atomic bomb of change."[25]

More systematic evidence supports the assertions of these politicians, at least about growing Black political impact. The sheer number of Black elected officials is rising at a faster rate than the number of officials is. In the two decades after 1990, the number of African American members of Congress rose from 26 to 42; comparable figures for statewide elected officials are 14 to 37. For state senators, the rise was from 96 to 160, and for state representatives from 340 to 470.[26] In 1990, 317 towns had Black mayors, whereas in 2010, 506 did. Also in 2010, 43 cities with more than 50,000 residents had Black mayors, compared to 33 in 1990.[27]

Non-White Americans increasingly have descriptive representation, since most of these politicians are elected in majority Black districts or districts in which Blacks and Latinos combine to form a majority. The trajectory of Blacks' election from districts in which a majority of voters are not Black shows a more complicated picture. Overall, Black elected officials are now more likely to represent majority Black, or majority-minority, districts than they were a few decades ago. Combining all Black members of Congress, statewide officials, and state representatives and senators, we find that 37 percent represented non-majority Black districts in 1991, declining to 33 percent in 2009.

Looking at each level of office separately, one sees that the proportion of Black members of Congress representing districts with populations less than half Black has increased slightly, moving from 35 percent in 1991 to 38 percent in 2009. Proportionally more state senators also now serve districts that are not majority Black; 37 percent represented such districts in 2009 compared to 28 percent two decades earlier. However, the proportions of Black state representatives and mayors representing non-majority Black districts have gone in the other direction over this period (from 43 to 34 percent for the former and from 28 to 24 percent for the latter).[28]

Nothing here indicates that American politics are being deracialized. But racial politics is nonetheless changing, in part due to younger Black candidates with new programs and new orientations to race. Half of the black mayors in 1977 were first elected when they were at least sixty years old, compared with only 18 percent in 1999. As one set of experts concludes,

> age is becoming . . . important . . . given the generational changes in voting we have been seeing. The African American leaders and the leaders of the women's movement that we are most familiar with are all in their sixties and seventies and are fading out. For the new generation of voters, many of the categories pollsters commonly look at no longer mean what they do to people who were raised in my generation. A genuine generational change is occurring.[29]

If young Black political activists are gaining political ground, that may be partly due to American voters' increasing willingness—again led by young adults—to cede some power to a formerly despised group. Although he points to continued racial tensions, a middle-aged White southern judge observes that "my children have a different view of racial makeup than I had. From my father's generation—extremely prejudiced—to mine—we're working through it—to my children, race is a nonissue."[30] In 2008, 55 percent of young adults agreed that Whites have too much influence over government policies, compared with fewer than 40 percent of those over age fifty. Almost twice as many young as older adults thought that Blacks had too little influence. The pattern was similar though weaker with regard to Hispanics' influence.[31]

President Obama is the best proof of Blacks' growing political power. Regardless of whether his presidency succeeds or fails, Americans have shown that "a Black candidate can win in the majority-white constituency that is the national presidential electorate." Obama won for reasons that indicate the impact of even partial changes in relative group political positions. First, he received a higher percentage of White support (43 percent) than had all but two of the eleven Democratic candidates since 1968. He received more support from suburbanites, first-time voters, and Whites in battleground states than their counterparts had previously given Democrats.[32]

Young voters were especially enthusiastic. Between 1980 and 2000, eighteen- to twenty-nine-year-olds were only marginally more Democratic than all voters. But there was a 6 percentage point gap in 2004 and a large 13 percentage point gap in 2008 between young and all voters' support for Democrats. Obama carried 95 percent of young Black voters, three-fourths of young Hispanic voters, and 54 percent of young White voters. Even controlling for education, race, party identification, and views about the economy and equity, age was significantly related to support for Obama's candidacy. Despite continuing high scores on a racial resentment scale, young Whites relied less on racial views in deciding how to vote in 2008 than did older Whites.[33] Racial attitudes were still a significant predictor of voting for Obama, and studies disagree on whether Obama's margin of victory was smaller than it would have been had he been a White candidate. Still, despite the caveats, he won, something few thought feasible even when his candidacy began. Obama's coattails may be long; if, as scholars have consistently found, a person's early political experiences tend to shape their later commitments and actions,[34] then now-young White voters may be more willing over the next few decades to support non-White candidates than their counterparts used to be.

In any case, a winning candidate needs fewer White voters than in the past because of the increasing importance of non-White voters; that is a second reason for Obama's victory. Through 1972, Whites represented over 90 percent of the electorate, but by 2008 they comprised less than three quarters. In fact, far from being a victory for post-racial America—whatever that might be—"Obama won *because of* race—because of his particular appeal among black voters, because of the changing political allegiances of Hispanics, and because he did not provoke a backlash among white voters. . . . His victory [was] built upon the highest degree of racial polarization seen in many years." Despite polarization, the combination of Black, Hispanic, and White supporters led nine states, including three from the former Confederate South, to switch from Republican in 2004 to Democratic in 2008.[35]

Given demographic changes, the combination of younger voters being more willing to vote for non-Whites and voters being increasingly non-White may well intensify transformation in the political arena. In the 2010 election (as in 2008), a higher proportion of younger than older voters were racial or ethnic minorities: 65 percent of 2010 voters under age thirty were White, compared with 80 percent of those over thirty. Compared with older voters, young adults favored Democratic candidates for the House of Representatives much more, were much more likely to approve of Barack Obama's activities and policies, and were more likely to describe themselves as liberal Democrats and opponents of the Tea Party. The latter results held within each racial group as well as generally.[36] It is too soon to say if this mixture of changing voters and changing voters' attitudes will persist, but so far it suggests that relative group positions will shift politically faster than economically.

Political transformation remains incomplete and potentially reversible. One need only look at the Senate or the set of governors to be reminded that being Black or Hispanic remains a disadvantage in political contests. Whites are still more reluctant to vote for a non-Anglo candidate than vice versa; few large cities with a White majority have a Black mayor whereas most large cities with a non-White majority have a White mayor. Black legislators continue to have less success than Whites in getting their bills passed. Many young Blacks and Hispanics, especially in large cities, exhibit high levels of political alienation and frustration.[37] Nevertheless, once Blacks win mayoralties, Whites are becoming more willing to vote on the basis of their quality as incumbents rather than on their race; that logic may hold for other offices as well. Even Al Sharpton, despite concern about the Tea Party, permitted himself a moment of gratified reflection—and who should know better?: "You don't get control of the White House and two governors and the Justice Department, and then start arguing with people carrying signs."[38]

Permitted, Required, and Forbidden Acts

No law or policy distinguishes among racial or ethnic groups within a given age range. That achievement was part of the transformation of the racial order during the late twentieth century. Nevertheless, some argue that state actions still at times uphold the pre–civil rights racial order. For example, the following scenario, included in the Department of Justice's explication of permissible racial profiling, seems an invitation to disparate treatment:

> The victim of an assault at a local university describes her assailant as a young male of a particular race with a cut on his right hand. The investigation focuses on whether any students at the university fit the victim's description. Here investigators are properly relying on a description given by the victim, part of which included the assailant's race. Although the ensuing investigation

affects students of a particular race, that investigation is not undertaken with a discriminatory purpose. Thus use of race as a factor in the investigation, in this instance, is permissible.

Police do, in fact, stop young Black men more often than others. As one student puts it, "they'll pull me aside sometimes because they say I fit the description. Yeah. Young black male. I always 'fit the description.'" Controlling for delinquency, Black teens are twice as likely as Whites to have experienced a police intervention by the tenth grade. A study of Chicago found that 20 percent of all sampled residents, but fully 70 percent of young Black men, recalled being stopped by police in the past year. Among the 31,000 Black men aged eighteen or nineteen in New York City in 2006, there were 29,000 stops by police—that is, a 93 percent probability of being stopped. The comparable probability for Hispanic men was 50 percent and for White men it was 20 percent. These disparities persisted even after a variety of controls were introduced into the analysis to measure neighborhood disadvantage, disorder, and crime risk.[39]

Young Black men are not alone in being singled out. In 2008, a third of Hispanics under thirty compared with a fifth of those over thirty reported being questioned by the police in the previous five years. They were four times more likely than those over age fifty-five to have been arrested or had someone in their family arrested. Young Hispanics are also more likely to have been in prison or jail, or on probation or parole.[40]

Reactions to the criminal justice system are complex, not to say muddled. In one survey, more younger Mexicans (and to a lesser extent, younger Dominicans and Puerto Ricans) than older ones agreed that the police treat Latinos fairly. Two years later, however, fewer young than older Latinos expected police officers to "do a good job enforcing the law." Blacks express similarly mixed views. Given that they are more likely to be victims of crime,[41] Blacks of all ages fear underpolicing. From 1973 to 2010, the GSS has asked respondents twenty-three times if there are areas "right around here" where they are "afraid to walk alone at night." Overall, more Blacks than Whites aged eighteen to twenty-nine have responded yes—45 percent of the former and 38 percent of the latter. Blacks' fear matched or was greater than Whites' fear in all but four of the twenty-three years.[42] Nevertheless, Blacks may be wary of calling the police to aid them. They are concerned about surveillance and overpolicing in their communities, and young men in particular are likely to experience bad personal treatment from police.[43]

As with immigration, this component of the American racial order is the hardest to evaluate, the most internally contradictory, and the most politically controversial of the five components. Compared with American history until a few decades ago, when government prohibitions were easy to see and caused barely any concern among Whites, that is an accomplishment. But if Americans hope to create a genuinely new and improved racial order, structures and practices must change enough so that people do not feel singled out for official maltreatment because of their race, age, or legal status. That has not (yet?) happened.

Social Relations

Stereotypes

Like their votes, the attitudes of young Whites are becoming more liberal at a faster rate than those of older Whites. Young non-Whites are sometimes more conservative than older ones, and the views of young adults of all groups are moving closer together. Although surveys do not always show these patterns, they appear in a wide range of polls and on a variety of issues.

Expressions of negative stereotypes show clearly White liberalization, some Black movement toward conservatism, and young adult convergence. Repeated questions on the GSS enable us to distinguish cohort change from aging or broad changes over time, as the results in figure 5.3 demonstrate. There is a clear age effect; in both periods, younger Whites see fewer differences between Blacks and Whites than older Whites do. There is also an effect of time: all four White age groups offer fewer negative stereotypes of Blacks in the 2000s than their counterparts had done in the 1990s.[44] Finally, there is a cohort effect: because of both liberalization among young Whites and increasing conservatism among young Blacks, young adults differ little in the 2000s in their evaluations of each race's work ethic. That was not the case in the earlier decade and is not now the case for any other age group. The same patterns hold, though less strongly, for GSS results on questions about Blacks' and Whites' level of intelligence. Through the same set of movements, by 2004–8 Blacks and Whites under age thirty held fairly similar views. That had not been the case for young adults in 1990–98, nor was it the case for older adults in either period.

Roughly the same dynamic obtains in another longstanding set of questions that ask why the races are economically unequal. Two of the standard four response options—"less in-born ability" and "lack of motivation or willpower"—clearly make negative attributions to Blacks. Every time the GSS asked that question from 1977 through 2008, there is an age effect for both response options: younger White respondents were less likely than older ones to blame Blacks for their lower status.[45] One also sees change over time; within each age group of Whites, the proportion explaining Blacks' poverty pejoratively declined. Most inter-

sponses give texture to the idea of a new racial order in a way that surveys can never do:

> For my major. I want to go into Chemistry or Physics. . . . I want to attend a major research university that is reknown for its success in the sciences. This cancels many of them out. . . . My guidance counselor also says that many of these schools wouldn't suit my intrest in undergraduate research.

> I come form a very diverse hs and I dont want to give that up. I love being around Black ppl, but I also value having people around me who are completely different. . . . I really want a diverse school where I can experience ppl of all ethnicities, cultures, religions, etc. I want a school where I can have my group of blk friends, but where most people are different.

> It doesn't reflect the real world. Being around all Black ppl is great, but many come out not accustomed to interacting w/ ppl of every background. . . . Also, you need a strong network base that includes ppl pf all backgrounds.[49]

Substantive interests and ambitions, the appeal of widely varying peers, the desire for networks that reflect "the real world"—these are goals and considerations that reflect a new understanding of the role of race in students' lives. As the president of Ohio University put it, "civil rights have come, and students know they have choices."[50]

Young adults are also exercising new options in choosing friends and making connections. "Sociologists have long maintained that race is the strongest predictor of whether two Americans will socialize. But . . . whom you get to know in your everyday life, where you live, and your country of origin or social class can provide stronger grounds for forging friendships than a shared racial background." This conclusion is drawn from a study of first-year students at a private college who posted photos of classmates and tagged them on Facebook. Students of the same race did indeed befriend one another in this fashion at high rates, but other variables did more to shape who posted images of whom. Reciprocity (returning an overture of friendship), triangulation (becoming the friend of a friend), being a roommate or having the same major, coming from the same state or home country, or having also attended an elite private high school—these characteristics mattered at least as much and in most cases more than did race per se in determining links on this increasingly ubiquitous social network.[51]

Attitudes

Stereotypes, perceptions, and options become meaningful beyond the individual when they affect actions, or at least intentions to act. Another series of GSS questions, based on the Bogardus social distance scale,[52]

enables us to sort out age, change over time, and cohort effects with regard to preferred social relations. There is an age effect: each time the
questions have been asked, young adults were much more likely than
their elders to endorse "liv[ing] in a neighborhood where half of your
neighbors" are of a different race or ethnicity or "hav[ing] a close relative
marry" someone of a different race or ethnicity. We also see change over
time: with occasional small exceptions, opposition to integrated neighborhoods or to intergroup marriage declined over the 2000s in all age
groups and with regard to all target groups. The decline in Blacks' and
Whites' opposition to intermarriage was proportionally greater among
younger than older adults, even though the younger expressed much less
opposition to begin with.

Most important, we see convergence in views among young, but not
older, adults. Younger and older Black and Hispanic respondents have
changed places in their preferences for living in racially integrated neighborhoods; in 2000 and 2004, young non-Whites showed greater hostility
to such communities, but by 2008, older ones did. As a result of this shift
in views, the responses of young adults from all groups became increasingly similar, while the responses of older adults did not.[53]

This willingness to interact will be reinforced if non-Whites become
more persuaded that they will not meet with discriminatory actions in
integrated environments. It could also be reinforced by a more subtle
change: young non-Whites continue to see discrimination but perceive it
to be less debilitating, prevalent, or determinative of life chances than
older ones do, while young Whites are increasingly willing to recognize
discriminatory practices by their own race. That is, interactions across
groups will increase if non-Whites' perceptions of discrimination decrease, if Whites' realization of discrimination increases, or if groups'
perceptions of the depth and impact of discrimination converge.

Some, though not all, recent surveys do indeed show one or another of
these patterns. On convergence: in 2007, young Black adults agreed more
than older ones that "blacks who can't get ahead in this country are
mostly responsible for their own condition," while young Whites agreed
more than older ones that "racial discrimination is the main reason why
many Black people can't get ahead these days." As a result, despite wide
racial divergence among older adults, about two-thirds of those under
age twenty-four concurred in choosing personal responsibility over discrimination. A year later, younger Whites saw racial discrimination
against Blacks as more serious than did their elders while younger Blacks
saw it as less serious than did their elders—again, a move toward convergence among the young.[54] Blacks of all ages are consistently more likely
to disagree than are Whites of all ages with the repeated GSS item on
whether Blacks should "work their way up without special favors." But

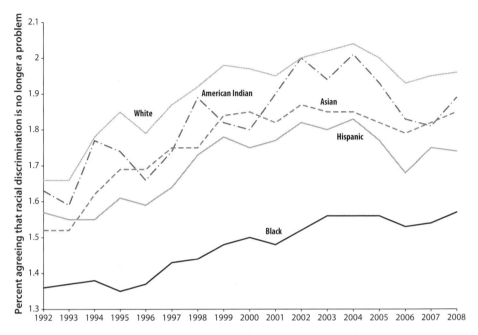

Figure 5.5. "Racial discrimination is no longer a major problem in America," first-year college students, 1992–2008 (mean levels of agreement by race).
Source: Analyses for authors, by staff of Cooperative Institutional Research Program (various years). Response categories ran from 1 (disagree strongly) through 4 (agree strongly). The graph excludes data for 1990 and 1991, since the results appear to be anomalous. Self-defined multiracials are not included, and Hispanics are analyzed separately from non-Hispanic Whites.

by the mid-2000s, the youngest White adults had shifted toward more disagreement while the youngest Black adults moved toward more agreement. They thereby moved closer to one another's outlook.

On decreasing perceptions of bias, especially among Blacks, most young adults would not agree with one Asian American's touchingly optimistic assertion that "not like the previous generations, we teens have eliminated prejudice."[55] But the longstanding survey of first-year college students does show movement in that direction. Black students always see the most discrimination, Whites see the least, and the other groups are arrayed in between. Views are not converging, so this survey does not support one of our contentions about changing social relations. It does, however, support another: an increasing proportion of well-educated young Americans believe racial discrimination is declining. Possibly young people are becoming less aware of discrimination or perceive increasing costs of "playing the race card," but the fact that Black students show the steadiest rise in agreement about its decline suggests a deeper attitudinal change than merely rising cluelessness or social caution (see figure 5.5).[56]

Not all surveys or all questions show liberalization of Whites' views, easing of concern about discrimination among non-Whites, or convergence among young adults around immigration or other race-related issues. Most strikingly, the ANES shows convergence much less often than do the other repeated cross-sectional surveys; instead, it generally depicts liberalization of views over time in roughly equal proportions for Blacks and Whites, or for older and younger adults. Occasional survey items even contradict our argument for transformation by showing more despair or stronger perceptions of discrimination among younger than older non-Whites. (To our knowledge, no survey item contradicts our argument about changes in young Whites' views compared with those of older Whites.)[57] There are several plausible explanations for these varied results, ranging from what surveyors call house effects, to influence on respondents of cues in the immediate environment, to the impact of different political or social contexts and recent experiences. In our judgment, our claims about cohort change rest on a firm empirical foundation, but whether young adults' new attitudes are strong enough to overcome blockages (see chapter 6) or contradictory forces within the current racial order remains to be seen. Nothing is certain, though much is possible.

Demographic Change, Interaction, and Collective Racial Memories

One reason that changing views are likely to persist is that young adults live in a different world than their elders and will do so even more as they grow older. Barely half of those under age fifteen are non-Hispanic Whites, compared with four-fifths of those over sixty-five. Whites are already a minority of residents under eighteen in thirty-one metropolitan areas, even though in roughly half of those areas the majority of adults are White. About 40 percent of New York's public school students live in a home in which a language other than English is spoken. The school system translates documents for parents into Spanish, French, German, Chinese, Japanese, Urdu, Persian, Hindi, Russian, Bengali, Haitian Creole, Korean, and Arabic. It teaches students who speak 167 languages—no surprise given that they come from 192 countries. Montgomery County, Maryland, teaches students from 164 countries, speaking 184 languages. Whatever those figures mean for school personnel and the immigrants themselves, it means that native-born American students cannot help but encounter a linguistically and culturally complex environment. Brooklyn "is gaining on Queens for the title of most diverse county in the nation, and possibly the world"; one store advertises "Asian, Mexican, and Russian groceries."[58]

Increasing heterogeneity need not be, but in fact is, associated with increasing group interactions in neighborhoods and schools. We described in chapter 2 the decline in neighborhood separation between Latinos and other groups, or more generally between immigrants and native-born Americans. Starting from a higher base, residential segregation between Blacks and Whites fell more in the 2000s. Of the fifty metropolitan areas with the highest levels of Black-White residential separation in the late 2000s, forty-seven had a population that was more than 5 percent Black in 2009. Among those forty-seven, only two saw a rise in segregation from the beginning to the end of the decade and forty-five saw a decline. Put another way, sixty-one of the one hundred largest metropolitan areas showed a decrease in the level of Black-White segregation in the 2000s.[59]

Declining residential segregation affects people of all ages, although the young may be especially susceptible to interactions with peers. Schools, in contrast, are the special province of the young and the recently young, so patterns of segregation there may be especially important for the future American racial order. Despite Supreme Court decisions making it increasingly difficult for districts to desegregate even voluntarily, students are somewhat more likely to attend schools with people outside their race in the late 2000s than they had been in the 1990s. Figure 5.6 shows the evidence.

In 1995, about three-fourths of White students attended schools in which at least three-fourths of their classmates were also White; by 2007, that proportion had dropped to just over three-fifths. Proportionally many fewer Black students attended schools where at least three-quarters of the students were also Black but there was no decline over time; the figure was one-third in 1995 and just under one-third in 2007. Slightly more Black students, however, attended schools with fewer than half Black classmates in 2007 than in 1995, thus lowering segregation levels for that group a little. The overall number of Hispanic students rose dramatically during this period and new immigrants tended to cluster in a few gateway cities, so it is surprising that school isolation did not rise much for Latinos. But it did not: three-tenths attended schools in which three-fourths or more of their peers were also Latino in 1995, and a third did so in 2007. About 70 percent of Asians attended schools with fewer than one-quarter of Asian students in both decades, as did about 60 percent of American Indians and Alaska Natives. The largest change, in short, was among White students, who were less racially isolated in 2007

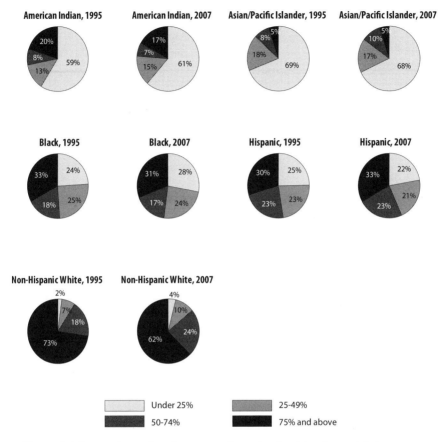

Figure 5.6. Proportions of students attending schools with others of their race or ethnicity, 1995 and 2007.
Source: National Center for Education Statistics 1995–96, 2000–2001, 2007–8. Our thanks to Susan Aud of the Department of Education for helping us locate these data.

than in 1995. Whether that change becomes associated with an improvement in the quality of schooling for all, or at least for those non-Whites in the same schools and classrooms as Whites, is one of the next decade's urgent policy issues.

William Frey and others worry about a cultural generation gap in which political views, policy goals, and group identities are all structured by age. We discuss that possibility in chapter 7; what is important to emphasize here is how many young adults seem comfortable with the new and growing racial and ethnic mix. In Implicit Association Tests measuring unconscious responses to various stimuli, young adults are less likely than older ones to distinguish between European and Asian Americans when asked to identify Americans or foreigners, or to associate Arab Muslims with "bad" and "other people" with "good." More explicitly, as a young New Yorker observes, "I work in a stockroom, and my best workers are people who don't really speak English. It's cool to get to know them. My stepdad says, 'why do I have to press 1 for English?' I think that's ridiculous. It's not that big a deal. Quit crying about it. Press the button."[60]

This stance might not last. Under the pressure of high unemployment levels in a stagnant economy, rising tension over immigration, fear of Muslim terrorists, or stubbornly high levels of segregation and poor education, young adults might retreat into the tensions of past generations. In that case, creation of a new American racial order will be stalled if not halted. But the bulk of the evidence suggests that James McBride speaks for many when he reflects that "my parents have completely different ways of being in the company of White folk than when they are in the exclusive company of Black folk. . . . My sister and I—and certainly my nephews—adhere far less to such divisions. . . . I can only dream that . . . the generational politics shaping my nephews' perceptions of themselves in the world will allow them to soar in ways that I cannot yet fully comprehend." For that to happen, the collective memories of the racial order created by civil rights struggles, the Great Society, and the opening of immigration need to fade and be replaced by new ones. That is occurring, as those with memories of the construction of the current racial order move to the end of their public careers and as immigrants with no memory of any American racial order join the society. (As Eugene Robinson puts it, "the immigrants are anything but ignorant about America's racial history, but they arrive at the theater in the middle of the third act.")[61] Groups are becoming more internally heterogeneous, led by improved education for some young adults. Genomics is on the verge of changing how young adults conceive of and practice race. Young Americans remember not the Edmund Pettis bridge but September 11, Hurricane Katrina, and President Obama. They inevitably engage with members of different groups whether in friendships and marriage or through jobs, school, and simply walking down the street. The impact of all of this change will play out over the next few decades.

6

Blockages to Racial Transformation

Since America's racial disparities remain as deep-rooted after Barack Obama's election as they were before, it was only a matter of time until the myth of postracism exploded in our collective national face.
   —Peniel Joseph

All I need to know about Islam I learned on 9/11.
   —Sign at protest over constructing a Muslim community center near the former World Trade Center

Some of my classmates are all hyped because a black man wants to be president and my teacher says we should be excited because a woman's running. I mean it's cool for them, or whatever, but at the end of the day what difference does it really make? Don't neither one of those people care about what's going on in my neighborhood and nobody knows the kind of stuff we deal with. . . . I just wanna be heard. To feel like I matter and the people around me matter.
   —Lamont, a high school student

IMMIGRATION, MULTIRACIALISM, GENOMICS, AND COHORT CHANGE are separately and cumulatively challenging the racial order of the late twentieth century. But nothing is certain. We have already discussed countervailing evidence, events, and laws that inhibit transformation and ways in which transformation may be successful but unappealing. However, we have not yet considered deeper structural conditions that could halt creation of a new American racial order or distort it almost beyond recognition.

We see four main impediments to the creation of a new order. First, some people will be harmed by or feel great loss as a consequence of change that weakens racial boundaries, even if—or perhaps because—such a change benefits many members of their group. Second, concentrated poverty, unemployment, poor education, and incarceration may prevent residents of some communities, especially Blacks, from benefiting from the changes occurring elsewhere. Third, wealth disparities among groups contribute to the maintenance of traditional relative group positions even though education and income gaps have narrowed over time. Finally, along the horizontal dimension of inclusion-exclusion, the United States may be inventing new pariah groups; unauthorized immigrants, and possibly Arabs and Muslims, are taking over the status of unwanted outsiders.

Like the four forces promoting transformation, these four blockages operate both separately and interactively. And unlike the impediments to transformation already discussed, they are deeply institutionalized in American society and politics. Breaking them down is a matter not of punishing individual miscreants, adjusting social norms, or changing specific laws and policies. It is a matter of reinventing important political, social, and economic structures. The question for the next few decades is whether Americans will embark on that restructuring in ways that reinforce the positive and minimize the negative momentum of transformation.

Costs of Racial Transformation

The Need and Desire for Group Identity

Scholarship, politics, and literature all make clear just how important are shared identities, even if they are artificially constructed and even if each writer means something slightly different by "identity." As Horace Kallen wrote in 1915, each *natio* has "its emotional and involuntary life, . . . its own individual . . . esthetic and intellectual forms." Michael Walzer points out that "ethnic identification gives meaning to the lives of many men and women." In Michael Sandel's terms, we are not "bound only by the ends and roles we choose for ourselves. . . . [We can] sometimes be obligated to fulfill certain ends we have not chosen—ends given . . . by our identities as members of families, peoples, cultures, or traditions."[1]

A transformation that undermines people's conventional definition of a race and classification of individuals blurs Walzer's "ethnic identification." If it further encourages people to move outside their group for spouses, friends, coworkers, neighbors, and fellow worshipers, it blurs Sandel's "identities as members of families, peoples, cultures, or traditions." Neither change was central to the transformation of the Jim Crow era into the civil rights and immigration-dominated era of the late twentieth century. But both are central to the current creation of a new order—and for some Americans, those changes mean loss rather than liberation.

Consider, for example, people for whom racial inequality and discrimination still constrain their economic prospects and social valuation. To them, dissolving strong group boundaries, particularly if that involves closer association with Whites or acknowledgment of White ancestry, may seem mainly a license for the dominant group to indulge in an unjustified fantasy of a post-racial society. In this view, celebration of racial transformation simply lets Whites off the hook despite weak affirmative action policies, no reparations for centuries of exploitation, continued or novel forms of racial injustice, persistent economic inequality or exploitation—that is, racism of all sorts. Thus the more some people celebrate transformation of the racial order, the more others feel that they must fight for group cohesion.

David Roediger holds this view; although "race is today a far more fluid category, both popularly and at law," nevertheless "fluidity and choice . . . exist within the very structures of deep contemporary inequality. Such inequality especially afflicts those readily identifiable as Black and poor, or as Latino, poor, and 'illegal,' or as American Indians on or off reservations." We must not lose sight of "the tenacity of old racial divisions, and the force of new ones." Peniel Joseph is even more explicit, continuing the sentence quoted in the first epigraph to this chapter by pointing out that "for all of America's racial progress, . . . race retains stubborn political and social bonds among black people that require shared affinity, identification, and sacrifices. . . . The struggle for racial and economic justice remains fraught."[2]

By distinguishing identity from solidarity, Tommie Shelby offers the most nuanced and persuasive version of this concern. He argues that Black (or perhaps any group) identity is no longer feasible or desirable in the United States given large and increasing heterogeneity in class position, political and social views, and life choices. That is probably progress toward racial equity. But racial solidarity remains both feasible and necessary, since progress is not and may never be complete. Shelby prescribes "pragmatic nationalism": "Blacks should unite and work together because they suffer a common oppression; and given the current political climate they can make progress in overcoming or ameliorating their shared conditions only if they embrace black solidarity. . . . Black unity is . . . a contingent strategy for creating greater freedom and equality for blacks."[3]

The view that post-racial hopes are folly in the face of continued racism is especially salient, though not unique, to Blacks. To cite only one of the many possible demonstrations of this point, consider a 2005 survey of young adults that oversampled residents of large cities. Over half of young Blacks agreed that "the leaders in government care very little about people like me" and that "on average, black youths receive a poorer education than white youths." Three-fifths agreed that "it is hard for young black people to get ahead because they face so much discrimination" and that blacks are treated poorly in the health care system. Four-fifths perceived police discrimination against Black youth. In each case, fewer Latinos concurred and even fewer Whites (although in some cases a majority of those two groups shared the views of young Blacks). Questions framed in the opposite direction sometimes showed less optimism among Blacks than among Latinos and Whites: although three-fifths of young

Blacks agreed both that "generally, I feel like a full and equal citizen in this country with all the rights and protections that other people have" and that all Americans have "an equal chance to succeed," more Latinos and many more Whites concurred with the first claim (there was no group difference on the second).[4]

Another concern about blurring racial boundaries *is* specific to African Americans: is promoting transformation really a strategy for non-Black minorities to become "honorary Whites" and thereby escape the group at the bottom? This is an old dynamic. Chinese sharecroppers in the post–Civil War Mississippi Delta region struggled ruthlessly and successfully to change their legal and social status from "like Blacks" to "almost Whites." They moved to new towns, became small entrepreneurs, broke ties with Chinese who had married ex-slaves, and rejected the children of such marriages. More generally, argues Andrew Hacker among others, "if most Asians are not literally 'white,' they have the technical and organizational skills expected by any 'Western' or European-based culture." In the United States, grandchildren of people in Asian-White marriages "will undoubtedly be regarded as a new variant of white. Much the same process can be observed among Hispanics. . . . Members of all these 'intermediate' groups have been allowed to put a visible distance between themselves and black Americans."[5]

Multiracialism, in this view, is a variant of the same phenomenon: allowing people to identify with more than one race "can result in the 'whitening' of a racial minority background through the removal of non-white racial distinction." Even more pointedly, "exponents of a new multiracial ideology who laud increasing rates of intermarriage as proof of the abolition of racial and sexual taboos also harbor deep antipathy toward expressions of black pride and liberation as tantamount to racism."[6]

If, in fact, transformation of the current racial order is just an updated version of the old phenomenon of requiring immigrants to become literally or metaphorically White in order to become American, then what appear to some as gains in equality and freedom of choice will be understood by others as losses. In our view, this anxiety is important but overdrawn; many people of mixed race, for example, move back and forth between monoracial and multiracial identities. Many non-Whites continue to battle racism and discrimination while seeking upward mobility and legitimacy as full Americans; many Whites who are included and well-off are committed to the same battles. Nevertheless, if the fear is widespread that creating a new order implies a dangerous loss of group identity, that view could retard, if not stall outright, changes in the American racial order.

People might want to retain group identity not only to protect against denigration but to preserve cherished values. As Kallen, Walzer, Sandel, and others have argued, close association with people like oneself can enrich daily life, deepen one's sense of historical rootedness, and provide children with a bridge to the future. In the face of millennia of anti-Semitic attacks, Jews have clung to their faith, household rituals, endogenous marriages, and self-contained communities. So have Shiite Muslims in Sunni-dominated states. Examples abound. Pawnee Curly Chief recounted a tribesman's rejection of gifts from White officials seeking land and a treaty:

> You see, my brother, that the Ruler has given us all that we need: the buffalo for food and clothing; the corn to eat with our dried meat; bow, arrows, knives and hoes; all the implements which we need for killing meat, or for cultivating the ground. Now go back to the country from whence you came. We do not want your presents, and we do not want you to come into our country.

Less poignantly but just as clearly, Sean O'Brien informed Mary Waters "in no uncertain terms" of the importance of his ethnic identity. Despite being "born and raised in New York City, . . . I'm Irish. That's it. And when I die, I told Christine, on my tombstone I want her to put, 'This Irish S.O.B. had a good time while he was here.' That is going to be on my tombstone. I am not saying this American-Irish, or this American, but this Irishman." In the 2000 GSS, three-tenths of Whites and two-fifths of Blacks agreed that it is "better for America if different racial and ethnic groups maintain their distinct cultures." (Equal proportions of the two races agreed with the alternative proposition that groups should "blend into the larger society as in the idea of a melting pot.")[7]

To people who cherish ascriptive group identity, transforming the meaning of race and blurring individual classifications may feel like a serious loss, regardless of its impact on racism or discrimination. As we discussed in chapter 3, some people may retain a strong sense of racial solidarity while endorsing a more blurred, fluid, multiracial future. But others will see that as an impossibility; being committed to the group implies endorsement, even celebration, of bright line distinctions. It remains to be seen whether, in a new American racial order, enough people will still value their group identity so much that those who want to will be able to continue feeling part of a robust and sharply etched community.

Benefits to Some May Be Costs to Others

As we and many others have shown, Blacks and Latinos are more likely to be politically powerless, economically immobile, and maltreated than are Whites and Asian Americans. If, at the same time, they are losing the language and practice of group solidarity or identity, some will share

Lamont's view (in the third epigraph to this chapter) that their already narrow pathway for escape from dismal circumstances is being squeezed shut: "Increasingly, between the Abandoned and the rest of black America, there is a failure to communicate, much less comprehend." That is, as more and more people move away from the old racial order, those inadvertently remaining in it will feel, and will be, more disadvantaged, part of a shrinking minority, and less well equipped to understand and contend with racial dynamics. That is not a good position to be in; as Lamont says, "sometimes I just want to scream, 'We here too!' But what good does it do to scream if no one's listening?"[8]

The inverse relationship between the size of a group and its degree of disadvantage has several facets. To begin with, as a group becomes smaller and more homogeneous, its members can become more isolated. The Amish and some communities of orthodox Jews embrace that trade-off, preferring the purity of a religiously sanctioned way of life to the heterodoxy of mainstream society. But other groups, such as many residents of inner cities, do not choose their isolation and are harmed by it. Destructive separation can deepen if the better-off of all groups begin to distinguish the few "undeserving" or "incapable" non-Whites from the many "deserving" or "capable" ones. The dynamic intensifies: as mainstream society becomes more and more broadly heterogeneous and inclusive, minority group members who are left out become ever more sharply isolated and poor.

Furthermore, as many people attain some degree of success and come to believe that racial barriers no longer explain inequality—a view that becomes more plausible as an increasing share of minority group members succeed in the mainstream and themselves come to believe that discrimination is not the main cause of poverty—it becomes harder and harder to find a language with which to understand persistent racially inflected disadvantage. Commentators have long observed the opaqueness of the American class structure; as steel worker Mike LeFevre queried Studs Terkel about his dying industry, "Who you gonna sock? You can't sock General Motors, you can't sock anybody in Washington, you can't sock a system."[9] Similarly, as the American racial structure becomes more heterogeneous and in many ways looser, it also becomes more opaque to those who cannot benefit from its changes. Once Asian or African immigrants are known to be better-off than many Whites, or once a Black candidate is elected president, the persistent impact of racial bias on the life chances of those left out gets hidden behind the diminishing impact of racial bias on the life chances of the others. The concepts, even the language, of institutional racism or structural bias become more abstract, more purely rhetorical, more detached from how people can make sense of their lives. What is left is individual blame; the few lose without quite understanding why while, or because, the many gain.

Incarceration

One group especially likely to be left out of, or actually harmed by, transformation of the American racial order is incarcerated young Black and Hispanic men, their families, and their communities.[10] Everyone reading this book knows of the rise in the number of those imprisoned in the United States over the past few decades. By 2008, the United States held in prisons or jail 762 people per 100,000; the next highest Western country was the United Kingdom, at 149 per 100,000 in 2007. If incarceration rates remain unchanged from those in 2001, over 11 percent of American men can expect to be in prison at some time during their life.[11]

Some groups are incarcerated at much higher rates than others. Fewer than 1 percent of White men, compared with 1.8 percent of Latinos and 4.7 percent of Blacks, were in prison or jail in 2009. That disproportion multiplies among the most disadvantaged: among male high school dropouts aged twenty to thirty-four in 2008, 7 percent of Latinos, 12 percent of Whites, and fully 37 percent of African Americans were in prison or jail.[12]

Figure 6.1 shows the rise in the number of incarcerated people and their racial or ethnic distribution over the past five decades. The rising trend lines over time in figure 6.1 suggest that we should look not only at the incidence of imprisonment at a given moment but also at its prevalence—that is, the proportion of people who have ever been involved with the criminal justice system. The most recent data show that in 2004, 17 percent of Black men had been incarcerated at some point in their lives and over a third had a felony conviction (compared to 5.5 and 13 percent, respectively, for all men). This is a substantial increase in absolute numbers and a widening of the racial disparity from the late 1960s, when only 7 percent of Black adult men had been to prison and 15 percent had a felony conviction (compared to 2.2 and 5.5 percent, respectively, for all men).[13] And even these data underestimate the degree of involvement with the criminal justice system; while Blacks account for 38 percent of the general prison population, almost half of those with life sentences and 56 percent of those serving life without parole are Black.[14]

Imprisonment worsens a person's job prospects, especially if the person is not White. Controlling for a variety of factors associated with jobholding, formerly incarcerated Black men are especially penalized with regard to job attainment, and Hispanic men with regard to hourly wages.

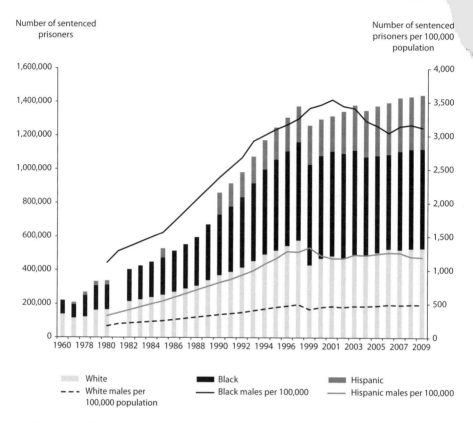

Number of sentenced
prisoners

Number of sentenced
prisoners per 100,000
population

White

Black

Hispanic

White males per
100,000 population

Black males per 100,000

Hispanic males per 100,000

Figure 6.1. Sentenced prisoners in state and federal prisons by race or ethnicity, 1960–2008.
Source: Bureau of Justice Statistics, "Publications and Products: Prisoners," various years.
Note: The graph includes only those sentenced to a year or more, and only those in prison (not in local jails). Beginning in 1999, Whites and Blacks exclude Hispanics. Data are missing for 1960 (Hispanics only), 1981, 1981–84 (Hispanics only), 1986–89 (Hispanics only), and 1998. The number of prisoners per 100,000 population is not available for all three groups in 1960, 1970, 1978–79, 1982–84, and 1986–89.

On average, the wages of never-incarcerated young adult men rise over time (for Whites and Hispanics more than for Blacks), while the wages for formerly incarcerated men remain almost flat. Black male dropouts aged twenty to thirty-four have, at best, poor chances of getting a job; by 2008 just over 40 percent were employed. But adding in imprisonment reduced that group's employment level to barely a quarter.[15]

Imprisonment also harms ex-felons' social lives and their families. It lessens Black men's already low rates of marriage and increases Hispanic and White men's probability of divorce. Imprisonment "has a lasting and significant impact on health" in mid-life, both directly and indirectly through its association with poverty, marital status, and labor force participation. It also explains a large part of the racial disparity in the proportion of men suffering from HIV/AIDS. Children with incarcerated parents, especially boys, may be more likely than otherwise similarly situated children to experience developmental delays and behavior problems, and they are at a higher risk than other children of eventually being incarcerated themselves. By 2008, however, about 11 percent of Black children (along with under 2 percent of White and under 4 percent of Latino children) had a parent in prison or jail.[16]

The people who end up incarcerated are concentrated in a few communities. Almost three-quarters of New York State's prisoners, for example, came from just seven out of the fifty community board districts in New York City; a few neighborhoods of Detroit, Richmond, Houston, and Boston are similarly affected. In Chicago, "the basic pattern of concentration is stark . . . [with] an extremely high level of persistence."[17] Given all of the psychological, economic, and social difficulties experienced by ex-felons, this concentration harms whole neighborhoods that are already badly off. It creates "a mutually reinforcing social process: disadvantage and crime work together to drive up the incarceration rate. This combined influence in turn deepens the spatial concentration of disadvantage, even if at the same time it reduces crime through incapacitation." In another harmful feedback loop, at low levels incarceration helps reduce crime, but at high levels it leads to future increases in crime. Absent significant social and policy changes, people in such "imprisoned communities" will find it very difficult to partake in any positive transformation, never mind be able to help create a new racial order.[18]

Incarceration has undermined political as much as economic and social capacity. As of 2010, just over five million American citizens (1 in 41 adults) had lost the franchise as a result of being incarcerated or having a felony conviction. Because they are more likely both to be convicted and to live in states with restrictive laws, Black men are seven times as likely to be disenfranchised as the national average; 13 percent of Black men could not cast a vote in the 2008 presidential election. Data are less complete for Latinos, but one study found substantial overrepresentation of Latinos in the disenfranchised population in six of the ten states studied (with evidence too scanty to use in two of the remaining four states). Perhaps not surprisingly, these include the states—California, Arizona, New York, and Texas—in which a large majority of Hispanics reside.[19]

Some describe the permanent disenfranchisement of felons as the sole institutional remnant of the Jim Crow racial order, persisting for decades after the Supreme Court struck down other racially disproportionate laws such as poll taxes and literacy tests.[20] Felony disenfranchisement laws are, however, being reversed in some places. Since 1997, twenty-three states have repealed or altered their laws, easing the restrictiveness of statutes and expanding vote eligibility for an additional eight hundred thousand citizens. Both Republican and Democratic governors have supported these changes. As of this writing, only two states (Virginia and Kentucky) bar felons from voting for life, and one of those two has a smaller than average proportion of Blacks.[21]

Groups' disparity in incarceration results partly from disparities in the commission of crime.[22] But it also results from selective enforcement of laws or selective laws. Even with controls for actual crime levels, police are more likely to make drug arrests in open-air markets and to focus resources in Black neighborhoods. Until 2010, the federal mandatory minimum for crack cocaine trafficking was ten years in prison; possession of five grams of crack cocaine incurred a five-year sentence. In contrast, one needed to possess five hundred grams of powder cocaine to trigger the five-year mandatory minimum. Federal legislation has reduced the crack-powder disparity considerably, however, and some of those imprisoned under the old law may be freed. Still, since 1970 arrests for drug trafficking and possession have risen exponentially, so that now almost two million drug arrests take place each year. In federal court where penalties are most severe, people convicted of drug and weapons offenses are disproportionately Black and Hispanic, despite the absence of statistically significant differences in reported drug use among Blacks, Whites, and Hispanics in the wider population.[23]

In chapter 5, we noted the racially inflected disparities in police stops and arrests for young Black and Hispanic men. Young men are not unique in this regard; an analysis of 125,000 New York City police stops of pedestrians over fifteen months found that, even controlling for variation in crime levels in particular neighborhoods and for race-specific estimates of crime participation, Whites were stopped less frequently than non-Whites. Compared with the number of arrests of each group in the previous year, Blacks were stopped 23 percent more often than Whites and Hispanics 30 percent more. Controlling for precinct increased the disparities. This "finding . . . does not require inferring that police engaged in disparate treatment. . . . [H]owever, it does provide evidence that whatever criteria the police used produced an unjustified disparate impact."[24]

A final reason for dramatically different levels of imprisonment is that, once stopped, arrested, and convicted, Blacks (and Latinos to a degree) receive longer sentences than do Whites even when legally relevant characteristics such as the defendant's prior record and offense severity are taken into account. This finding holds across all types of crimes, and holds at the state as well as federal level.[25]

For this book, the crucial issue is less the causes of disproportionate incarceration than its consequences for the American racial order. Black mass imprisonment is a relatively recent development, worsening in the racial order of the late twentieth century. Unless the trajectory is reversed and the consequences of incarceration dealt with, the development does not bode well for transformation among important segments of the American population.

Differences in Wealth Holding

Unlike incarceration, which mainly involves poor neighborhoods and poor individuals, differential distributions of wealth affect people at every income level. The American economic system simply froze out non-Whites in the Jim Crow racial order; in 1962 race was "such a powerful variable that even the more modest of the class effects that stratified whites were cancelled by the skin color of blacks." Blacks "experienced a perverse sort of egalitarianism"—neither high nor low earnings made much difference in what African Americans could hope to accumulate over a lifetime or across generations.[26] That perverse egalitarianism no longer obtains—a major accomplishment of the post–civil rights racial order. The Levy Institute Measure of Economic Well-Being (LIMEW), a more comprehensive measure than the census bureau's measure of "extended income," shows that in 1959 (the first year with data), the mean value of non-White households' economic well-being was 0.64 that of Whites; it rose to 0.76 by 2004 and remained at that level through 2007. Median values followed the same path, rising from 0.61 to 0.85 in 2004.[27] This is some, but not a lot of, change for a half century since the Jim Crow racial order was abolished.

Despite this move toward greater equality, a huge wealth gap remains between Whites and other Americans. Since the distribution of wealth, like that of income, is more uneven among non-Whites than among Whites, non-Whites' mean net worth is higher than their median net worth. But measured either way, non-Whites hold little wealth and their share is not rising. The Survey of Consumer Finances has measured families' net worth, separately for Whites and for non-Whites and Hispanics, every three years from 1989 through 2007 inclusive. The ratio of non-Whites' to Whites' mean net worth has fluctuated from a high of 35

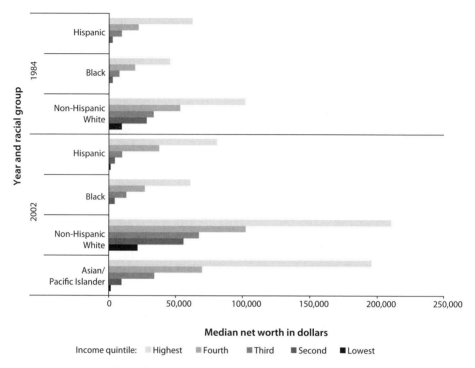

Figure 6.2. Median net worth, by monthly household income quintile and race or ethnicity, 1984 and 2002.
Source: Authors' calculations based on the Study of Income and Program Participation.

percent in 1992 to a low of 24 percent in 2001 and back up to about 33 percent in 2007. The comparable ratios for median net worth have varied from a low of 9 percent in 1989 to a high of 21 percent in 1995; as of 2007, the median non-White family had no more than 17 percent of the net worth of the median White family.[28]

Even African Americans with high incomes have much less wealth than Whites with similar incomes. Figure 6.2 shows the pattern. In 2002 Whites in the highest income quintile have at least four times the net worth of Blacks in the highest income quintile, and almost the same disproportion with regard to high-income Hispanics. That is a larger disproportionality than existed in 1984, when the Whites with the highest incomes had just over twice as much net worth as Blacks and just under twice as much as Hispanics. At the other end of the scale, Whites in the bottom income quintile have some net worth and Hispanics and Asians have a trace; the lowest-income Blacks have none. That was also the case in 1984 (data are not available for Asians in 1984). It is possible that these proportions have changed over the past eight years, but figure 6.2 suggests not very much.[29]

At this writing, it is too early to be sure how much more the economic crash of 2008 hurt non-Whites' wealth holding proportionally to Whites', though most observers believe it was a lot. At a given level of wealth, Whites have always been more likely to own stocks and other high-risk assets, and their housing is usually assessed at a higher value. So the average White probably lost more in absolute terms from a higher starting point. And one demographer suggests that on average the gains to non-Whites seeking to buy their first house may offset the losses to non-Whites who saw the value of their homes plummet in the debacle.[30]

Furthermore, despite strong claims by advocacy groups, analysts have not reached consensus on how much non-Whites were disproportionately targeted for costly subprime mortgages in the mid-2000s. Most agree that homebuyers in predominantly Black or Latino neighborhoods were more likely to have subprime mortgages than were buyers in predominantly White neighborhoods, even controlling for median income of the neighborhood or economic situation of the buyers. But individual-level analyses show more mixed results. On the one hand, by one calculation, well-off Hispanics were at least as likely as poorer Hispanics to receive a higher-priced home mortgage loan in 2006 and 2007. High-income Blacks were slightly less likely than low-income Blacks to receive unfavorable mortgage terms in both years, while high-income Whites were only half as likely as low-income Whites to do so.[31] The most statistically sophisticated analysis used data on millions of 2006 loans collected pursuant to the Home Mortgage Disclosure Act to match borrowers on multiple dimensions. It found that Blacks were 6 percent more likely than similar White borrowers to receive high-cost loans. Hispanics were slightly more likely, and Asians were less likely, to be offered a subprime mortgage than similarly situated Whites. The results varied by state.[32]

On the other hand, a Federal Reserve staff report examining over seventy-five thousand variable-rate mortgages found "no evidence of adverse pricing by race, ethnicity, or gender of the borrower in either the initial rate or the reset margin" of subprime mortgages granted in 2004–6. "If any pricing differential exists, minority borrowers appear to pay slightly lower rates. We also find that borrowers in zip codes with a higher percentage of black or Hispanic residents or a higher unemployment rate actually pay slightly lower mortgage rates." In another study, the proportion of Blacks or Hispanics in a community had no statistically significant association with the pattern of foreclosures, once levels of poverty, "high-cost lending activity," and other factors were taken into account. Neither

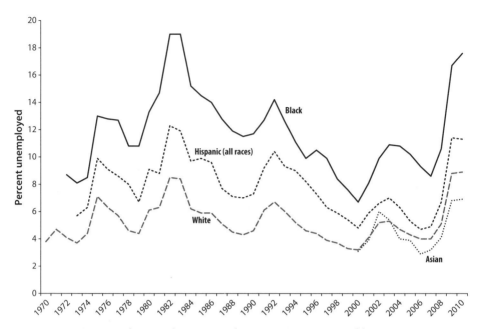

Figure 6.3. Unemployment by race or ethnicity, 25- to 34-year-olds, 1970–2010. *Source*: Bureau of Labor Statistics 2010.

we nor anyone else to our knowledge can explain these discrepant findings—as Haughwout and his coauthors put it, "these results suggest appreciable scope for further research."[33] But they do suggest caution in assuming that non-Whites were discriminated against in the housing bubble.

But non-Whites have certainly suffered as a consequence of the crash. Young Black and Latino adults are consistently employed at much lower rates than Whites, as figure 6.3 shows, and recent years have been no exception. Over the first six months of 2010, fully 41 percent of Black sixteen- to nineteen-year-olds were unemployed, compared with 24 percent of young Whites.[34]

The job situation for all non-Anglo adults shows the same pattern as that for young adults, although with slightly less dramatic swings and slightly lower levels of unemployment. While the poverty rate rose for all Americans between 2007 and 2009, it rose twice as much (from a high base) for Latinos as for non-Hispanic Whites or Blacks. Similarly, while median household income fell for all Americans over the same period, it fell almost twice as much (from a low base) for Blacks as for Whites or Asians.[35] Thus most evidence suggests, though the SFC does not yet confirm, that non-Whites' net worth will fall relative to that of Whites as a result of the economic disasters of the late 2000s. Even if that does not occur, nothing suggests that policy or economic changes to reduce wealth disparities are in the offing—an important blockage to transformation of the American racial order.[36]

Inserting New Groups at the Bottom

Focusing on the horizontal dimension of insider and outsider raises a different set of concerns from the vertical dimension of material well-being. Unauthorized immigrants and Muslims risk being slotted into the status of "unwanted outsider" that Pacific-rim Asians used to occupy (and still do in some arenas).[37] Some Americans have never been particularly well disposed toward either group, but over the past decade lines of exclusion have arguably hardened with regard to the undocumented and developed with regard to Muslims.

Muslims

Surveys show mixed views of Muslims. Most Americans are not interested in creating a new governmental regime of legal group-based discrimination. Even soon after the terrorist attacks of September 11, 2001, at least three-quarters and as many as nine-tenths of Americans were very or somewhat concerned that "Arab Americans, Muslims, and immigrants from the Middle East will be singled out unfairly by people in this country."[38] Poll respondents agreed that Arab or Muslim naturalized citizens should have the same legal rights as native-born citizens if arrested, whether for car theft or for suspected terrorism. Immediately after the September 11 attacks, half of the respondents in one survey were asked about "closely monitoring the whereabouts of legal immigrants to the United States" in order to "improve security and protect against terrorism," while the other half were asked about monitoring immigrants "from Arab and Muslim countries." The level of support was almost the same in both cases. Over three-fourths rejected the idea of "scrutiniz[ing] more closely" applications for immigration from Arab countries than from other countries. In 2007, only one-quarter (still a high number) would favor "mass detentions of U.S. Muslims" if there were another major terrorist attack, while three-fifths would oppose detentions.[39] Although civil libertarians will not be satisfied with these findings (nor are we), the surveys show no general inclination to reinstate legal, Jim Crow–style discrimination.[40]

Furthermore, Americans are generally sympathetic to native-born or naturalized Muslims (or Arabs—the two groups are usually treated as synonymous). Soon after the attacks, a majority of respondents strongly or overwhelmingly agreed that "most Arab-Americans and immigrants from the Middle East" are "loyal to the United States and opposed to terrorism." Even in a Fox News survey, a plurality agreed a few years later that "Muslim immigrants really want to become a part of this country and support American traditions and culture."[41] Large majorities would permit students to wear headscarves in classes, would not object if their child dated a Muslim, and agree that American Muslims do not condone violence. Over half think that American Muslims are more peaceable than those living outside the United States, compared with only 7 percent who think the reverse. In 2009, six out of ten Americans agreed that Muslims face discrimination—much more than adherents to any other religion, more than Blacks or Hispanics, and just a little less than gays and lesbians.[42]

Immigrant or foreign Muslims, however, may be a different matter. In 2006, just over a fifth of Americans did not want Muslim neighbors (the figure is about the same for immigrant neighbors and lower for homosexual neighbors). But acceptance of gay neighbors is rising, while acceptance of Muslim or immigrant neighbors is declining.[43] And when questions focus on religion, support or ambivalence sometimes gives way to hostility. In 2007, only 8 percent of Americans agreed that "the teachings of Christianity . . . generally tend to promote violence" and only 13 percent said the same about Judaism, while 39 percent concurred about Islam. Asked in the same survey "which religion is most likely to have followers who would use violence in an attempt to spread their religion," only 4 percent chose Judaism, 11 percent chose Christianity, and a huge 69 percent chose Islam.[44] Asked in a different survey for the word that "best describes your impression of Islam," twice as many respondents (30 to 16 percent) chose a negative term (for example, "fanatic," "dogmatic," "wrong," "killers," "violent," "confused," "crazy") as chose a positive term ("acceptable," "faithful," "peaceful," "strong," "misunderstood").[45]

Examining trajectories shows mixed results. In surveys since 2002, unfavorable views of Muslim Americans have doubled in two series—from 17 to 38 percent in one[46] and from 24 to 49 percent in another.[47] But young adults are consistently more favorable toward Islam than are older adults, as well as being more knowledgeable, more likely to see Islam as peaceful rather than violent, and more likely to say that it teaches respect. Only half as many under as over age thirty admit to some hostile feelings about Arabs or Muslims. Young adults are much more likely to know a Muslim personally and much less likely to endorse profiling air travelers.[48] They are twice as likely as older adults to say that news coverage of Muslims is too negative. This association between more advanced age and more negative views of Muslims holds up with a variety of controls. In one study of the 2004 ANES and five Pew surveys since 2000, younger Whites held more favorable views of Muslims or Muslim Americans than older Whites in all of them. In four of the six and even with a variety of controls, the relationship was statistically highly significant and substantively important.[49] Whether young adults remain relatively supportive of Islam and Muslims as they age remains to be seen.

Over a series of polls in the 2000s, Americans remained evenly split on whether they would vote for a Muslim for president if their party nominated a qualified person. That compares with over 90 percent reporting willingness to vote for a Black and generally over 85 percent willing to vote for a woman, Jew, Catholic, or Hispanic. More would support a Mormon than a Muslim, slightly more would support a homosexual than a Muslim, but fewer would support an atheist. One cannot tell until an election, of course, whether these claims reveal actual choices, but the best analysis of electoral results argues that voters do not overclaim their support for women and no longer do so for Blacks.[50] At most, however, the surveys indicate only lukewarm acceptance of the idea of politically powerful Muslims at the national level.

American Muslims are relatively well-off, so status as quasi-outsiders does not in their case go along with a position at the bottom of the group hierarchy. About half have attended college; many have non-Muslim friends; and the distribution of family incomes resembles that of the American population as a whole. A higher proportion agrees that hard work is the path to success than do White, Black, or Hispanic Americans. American Arabs (not necessarily Muslims) hold elective as well as appointed positions in local governments and perceive a clear path to further empowerment.[51]

Muslims' own views about their position in the United States vary widely. Some shrug off "unexpectedly intense opposition to their plans for opening mosques: 'We are newcomers, and newcomers in America have always had to prove their loyalty. It's an old story. You have to have thick skin.'" In 2009, only a fifth of Muslim immigrants, compared with close to half of other immigrants, perceived discrimination against "immigrants from [their] home country," and almost twice as many Muslim as other immigrants (61 to 33 percent) reported being "extremely happy" in the United States. A focus group with Middle Eastern immigrants, a majority of whom were Muslim, was "by far the most overtly patriotic."[52]

Nevertheless, some Muslims report heightened scrutiny, rejection, and even attacks: "We are not comfortable. . . . We feel that if anything bad happens overseas, in the U.S., in England, we are going to be treated badly. You get scared to be a Muslim. People treat you bad, look at you bad. We are scared for our safety. I get scared that if something happens they will come attack us here in our home." Three-fifths report that their biggest problem as Muslims is some combination of discrimination, being viewed as terrorists, Americans' ignorance about Islam, and stereotyping—and many of the rest offer some variant of this list. More Muslims complained of religious bias to the EEOC in 2009 than had done so in 2002 (after a drop in the middle of the 2000s); how much that represents a change in discriminatory behavior rather than a change in willingness to report cannot be determined. Young adults have the most disparate experiences; they describe both more discriminatory or insulting treatment, and more support or positive encounters based on their faith or ethnicity, than do their elders.[53]

Most public officials do not promote the exclusion of Muslims. President George Bush made a point of going to a mosque soon after the attacks of September 11, 2001, observed that people of all religions "pray to the same God," and described Islam as "a great religion that preaches peace." Two members of the House of Representatives are Muslim. A Muslim chaplain has opened a House session, and the House passed a "symbolic but deeply moving" tribute "to Muslims and Ramadan" in 2007. New York Mayor Michael Bloomberg and New Jersey Governor Chris Christie have vigorously and repeatedly defended Muslims' right to build a mosque and community center near the site of the World Trade Center attack. Barack Obama is, of course, the descendant of Muslims, lived in Indonesia, and has a distinctly Muslim name; he somewhat lukewarmly endorsed Muslims' right to build a mosque where they wish. With little to no publicity, Obama's "administration has reached out to this politically isolated constituency in a sustained and widening effort that has left even skeptics surprised." The Los Angeles police department has made considerable effort to develop effective relations with the city's Muslim community.[54]

But some public actors evince barely disguised hostility. One member of Congress observed in 2007 that "those . . . changes" (invocations by Muslims, Buddhists, and representatives of other religions on the House floor) are "not what was envisioned by the Founding Fathers. The principles that this country was built on, that have made it great over these centuries, were Christian principles derived from Scripture." (Pressed to apologize or resign, Representative William Sali insisted that he "meant no offense.") A leader of one branch of the Tea Party urged voters to "retire" Representative Keith Ellison in the elections of November 2010. "He is the only [sic] Muslim member of congress. He supports the Council for American Islamic Relations, HAMAS, and has helped congress send millions of tax dollars to terrorists in Gaza." Ellison responded with a "call to civility."[55] He was reelected.

History does not repeat itself, and the United States is not re-creating for Muslims a racial order of legal segregation, economic exploitation, and social opprobrium. Most non-Muslims do not want such a society, and Muslims have enough resources and allies to effectively resist it if an attempt were made. Muslims are overall enthusiastic and successful Americans. Nevertheless, under the pressure of fear of terrorism, ignorance about Islam, the strain of radicalism that runs through adherents of some versions of Islam, and perhaps a general rise in xenophobia, some Americans seek to push Muslims into the status of unwelcome outsiders. That view may be broadening and hardening.

Once again, political choices are crucial. The impulse to push Muslims out can be reversed if Muslim immigrants and their children continue to abjure terrorism, if the United States is not subjected to another Arab-led terrorist attack, and if American society makes it easier to be both devoutly Muslim and fully incorporated. But none of those are certainties; until they are, the post-1960s racial order's clear boundaries among groups is receiving an unanticipated reinforcement.

Undocumented Immigrants

Unauthorized immigrants are the other unwilling participants in the recent reconstruction of a horizontal dimension of insiders and outsiders. A flood of analyses shows not only that most Americans deeply oppose illegal immigration but also that some assume that most newcomers are poorly educated, non-White, criminal, and here illegally. At the worst,

> In one critical way, . . . Mexicans are much worse off than black Americans. . . . [O]ne-fifth of all Mexican Americans lack any legal claim on American society because they are present without authorization. . . . Not only will its [the resulting underclass's] members be exploited and excluded, but they will be outside the law itself, deportable at a moment's notice and perhaps even at serious risk of incarceration for the felonious crime of living and working in the United States without permission.

This grim analysis finds that "undocumented migrants are not perceived as fully human . . . , thus opening a door to the harshest, most exploitive, and cruelest treatment that human beings are capable of inflicting on one another."[56]

This claim is overdrawn. Hitler, Stalin, Pol Pot, and Idi Amin engaged in the cruelest treatment humans can inflict on one another; not even Sheriff Arpaio matches them. Nonetheless, unauthorized immigrants are subject to more and broader governmental prohibitions based on group status than any other set of Americans (as the phrase "illegal aliens" implies). They are ineligible in many states for social services such as food stamps, welfare, Medicaid, and in-state college tuition rates. Restricted access to savings and checking accounts, drivers' licenses, and credit, as well as other forms of "social exclusion," may harm not only their own economic and psychological well-being but also their children's development. They can take most jobs only under false credentials, with all of the insecurity that implies. As one young woman put it, "if you don't have papers and you do own something, the day that something happens it just all goes away. . . . I think maybe I'm gonna work hard for it, and have it, and then like, all of a sudden you know my dream just shattered, and I think [about what] if I had papers, and I got ahead, and I know it would be mine and nobody could take it away."[57]

Restrictions have themselves created a new form of heterogeneity, since many families are comprised of a complicated mix of unauthorized immigrants, legal noncitizen immigrants, naturalized immigrants, and native-born Americans. Some family members can vote, hold office, pay in-state tuition rates to a public university, or receive publicly funded social services, while others cannot. Instability deepens when, as is common, the children but not the parents are American citizens, thus reversing a family's usual pattern of authority and status. As of 2009, four million U.S.-born children had at least one undocumented parent; put another way, almost two-fifths of adult unauthorized immigrants have children who are American citizens. Not surprisingly, such circumstances can generate anxiety and conflict. A teenaged Guatemalan undocumented immigrant has no medical insurance—but for his younger native-born brother, "whenever he's sick they always take him to the hospital, and stuff like that, because the government pays for him. . . . My mom takes him to the dentist yearly, to the doctor, you know, but if I feel really sick, like I have to be dying to go to the hospital."[58]

Even greater problems lie in the restrictive social relations that unauthorized immigrants face outside their community, and in their difficulties in pursuing economic success. Americans' opposition to illegal immigration is much stronger than opposition to generic immigration. In one 2006 survey that typifies others in the late 2000s, three-quarters of a sample of registered voters were concerned that illegal immigration would "lead to an increase in crime"; two-thirds thought it might "lead to an increase in terrorism" or "take jobs away from U.S. citizens"; and over half were concerned that it would "change the culture of the country." Even in a survey of immigrants, three-tenths agreed that "illegal immigrants cost the taxpayers too much by using government services like public education and medical services."[59]

Mobility under these circumstances is, not surprisingly, difficult to attain. Very few surveys identify immigration status, but even the very rough stand-in of Mexican nationality shows the blockage. For example, the mean occupation scores for Mexican-born children brought to the

United States at very young ages are slightly lower than those of native-born citizens while the scores of young immigrant Koreans and Vietnamese are much higher. Controlling for a variety of characteristics, young Mexican American men who entered the labor force in the mid-1990s had significantly lower earnings than did otherwise comparable Whites.[60] If these analysts could distinguish the undocumented from Mexicans or from immigrants more generally, they would presumably find more upward mobility for most immigrants and even less for those without legal standing in the United States. This pattern ominously resembles that of Blacks, in which those with some resources are increasingly able to participate in creating a new racial order in which they can advance while the poor or incarcerated risk being left behind—politically, cognitively, normatively, and emotionally.

Even though most native-born Americans endorse a path toward citizenship or at least a stable guest worker program, the politics of immigration status are hardening. In 2010, Arizona passed a law that, as described by CNN, "orders immigrants to carry their alien registration documents at all times and requires police to question people if there's reason to suspect they're in the United States illegally. It also targets those who hire illegal immigrant laborers or knowingly transport them." As written, the law permits police to request proof of legal status after a stop for offenses as trivial as traffic violations or noncompliance with local housing ordinances. Close on the heels of a traffic stop is the possibility of deportation.

When signing the bill, the governor asserted the need to "enforce the law evenly"; President Obama, in contrast, described it as "threaten[ing] to undermine basic notions of fairness that we cherish as Americans." The Department of Justice filed suit to prevent implementation and as of this writing a federal court has issued an injunction against most of the law's provisions. Other public officials also opposed it: "Police were deeply divided on the matter, with police unions backing it but the state police chief's association opposing the bill, contending it could erode trust with immigrants who could be potential witnesses."[61] Los Angeles County supervisors voted to boycott Arizona; two academic associations issued statements condemning it, as did the American School Boards Association. Los Angeles Cardinal Roger Mahoney likened the law to "German Nazi and Russian Communist techniques" and called it "the country's most retrogressive, mean-spirited, and useless anti-immigrant law." San Francisco's police chief said the law "will have a catastrophic effect on policing." Protesters used both a light touch and a heavy hand (see figures 6.4 and 6.5).

Nevertheless, legislators in roughly half of the states indicated that they would propose a similar bill; by mid-2011, Georgia and Alabama had

Figure 6.4. "Los Suns."
Source: Photo by Christian Petersen, Getty Images Sport/Getty Images.

passed similar laws and Utah had passed one with some similar provisions. The attorney general of Virginia ruled that state police already have the authority granted by SB 1070 to Arizona's police.[62]

Not surprisingly, political calculations play a role in public actors' support or opposition. In a flurry of polls soon after its passage, anywhere from a plurality to a solid majority of Americans endorsed the new law (although when asked, many agreed that they did not really understand it or know what it contained).[63] Protests against the "illegal alien invasion" (as shown in figure 6.6) arguably bolstered wavering legislators. Crucially, Latinos comprise barely 12 percent of Arizona's voters although they are almost a third of the population; the unauthorized population grew very rapidly during the 2000s as did the Hispanic share of children and newborns. Even apart from its tradition of conservative or libertarian politics, the state presents a textbook case of William Frey's cultural generation gap.

Generational politics may determine whether Americans continue on the path of pushing undocumented immigrants into the status of permanent poor outsiders or whether they find a route to legalization and the chance for upward mobility. On the one hand, six states have very large racial and ethnic generation gaps, in which the White percentage of the child (nonvoting) population is much smaller than the White percentage

Figure 6.5. "Arizzona."
Source: grayson-green.blogspot.com/2010/05/for-mothers-day-10-reasons-to-op
pose.html.

of the elderly (heavily voting) population. Arizona leads the list with a
gap of 40 percentage points, but Nevada, California, Texas, New Mexico,
and Florida are close behind with differences of 30 points or more.[64] In
the short run, this invites exclusion: non-White children cannot vote,
non-White young men may seem threatening, many of their parents are
unauthorized or recent legal immigrants who also cannot vote, and children require a relatively high proportion of public expenditures through
schooling and perhaps social welfare services.

Figure 6.6. "Stop illegal alien invasion," October 15, 2007.
Source: http://www.stoptheNorthamericanunion.com/Subversion.html.

However, children grow up and the elderly eventually disappear from
the political scene. Even some conservative elected officials are treading
warily due to their perception of Hispanics' or immigrants' new or potential electoral impact: "in states with larger and more established Hispanic
populations, politicians considering anti-immigrant messages have to
think seriously about blowback. . . . Behind the scenes, GOP strategists
are said to be urging their candidates not to go there." Reaction against
California's analogous Proposition 187 in 1994 led many new voters—
White as well as Hispanic and Asian—to become Democrats. At least in
California, Republicans do not want to relearn that bitter lesson. As a
nonpartisan elections analyst puts it, "The reason Republicans [in Cali-
fornia] aren't taking on illegal immigration like they used to is there's no
benefit in it. The smart Republicans have figured out that Latinos are
moving into the middle class very rapidly and are fundamentally conservative on economic issues. There is a lot of growing wealth in Latino and
Asian communities. So there's caution that this is a major voting bloc and
one that Republicans want to get a piece of."[65]
The cultural generation gap may narrow even before young Latinos
become voters since, as we have shown earlier, young Whites are considerably more liberal on the issue of immigration than are their elders.
"Many older Americans feel threatened by the change that immigration
presents," says one college senior. "Young people today have simply been
exposed to a more accepting worldview." Even with a long series of controls, young adults in three western counties were significantly more favorable than were their elders to the 2006 immigrant rights demonstrations.[66] Our analysis of seven polls from 2007 to mid-2010 found no
question on which young adults were less sympathetic than older adults

to immigrants or less supportive of immigration. On six of the eight relevant items, they were noticeably more so.[67] In 2010, "California voters aged 18 to 29 represented the majority of those who opposed the denial of [public] services [to undocumented immigrants] across all ethnic groups by a margin of nearly 30 points." This result was not due to the fact that a disproportionate share of young California voters are themselves immigrants or their children; young adult Whites held essentially the same views as young adult non-Whites. More than half of California voters under, but not over, age forty-five agreed that unauthorized immigrants are "a net benefit to the state" and strongly supported a path to legalization.[68] Another poll six weeks later found a clear age gradient in views about Arizona's new law. About three-fifths of Whites aged eighteen to twenty-nine opposed it; opposition declined and support rose with each subsequent age group until only a third of Whites aged sixty-five and over opposed it. By 2011, the age gap had generalized; twice as many young as old registered voters in California agreed that "recent immigration has improved the quality of life" both in the state and in their own community, while half as many agreed that immigration had worsened Californians' quality of life.[69]

If SB 1070 and its kin are implemented, undocumented immigrants and their families and communities will be even more economically and politically constrained. If young Black men continue to be incarcerated at very high rates, they and their families and communities will also face perhaps insuperable constraints. If wealth disparities are not reduced, the chance to change relative group positions will be severely undermined. If Muslims (or Arabs) are treated as synonymous with terrorists, the barrier from exclusion to inclusion will not be breached. If non-Whites feel that they must cling to group identity to fend off persistent and debilitating discrimination, rather than simply because they cherish their heritage and identity, they will not engage in creating a new racial order. The mixed evidence of this chapter shows that alternative pathways are feasible; the next few decades will make the difference.

PART III

POSSIBILITIES

society's structural failure to provide decent jobs and adequate education, "the transformation of . . . our limited welfare state into a neoliberal project with an emphasis on privatization and personal responsibility; [and] the move to incarceration in place of employment." But the sociologist Orlando Patterson concludes that "the United States has worked harder and gone farther than any other advanced majority-white nation in confronting and righting the wrongs of its racist past."[1]

How do we make sense of this tricky evidence that seems to point uncompromisingly in several directions at once? Holmes, of course, found no difficulty in sorting out what truly mattered from what only appeared to matter and then drawing the right conclusion—but that is why he is fictional. In the world outside 221B Baker Street, this book has grappled with at least five distinct types of complexity: any racial order has by our definition five components; four forces are promoting the creation of a new American racial order; structural barriers and laws impede this creation; groups and people in them engage with the American racial order in distinct ways; and the evidence for any argument is mixed. Obeying Holmes's injunction to "shift your own point of view a little," in this chapter we combine these multiple forms of complexity in a new way in the hopes of showing clearly the political and personal choices facing Americans. We conclude with some urgent pleas for policies that will promote the right kind of transformation and retard the wrong kind, dissolve the worst blockages, and bring Americans closer to Madison's vision of a republic with no dominant faction.

Components of the American Racial Order, Redux

Chapters 2 through 5 each focused on one transformative force—immigration, multiracialism, genomics, or cohort change—analyzed through the five components of a racial order. We now reverse the logic, focusing on how each component of the racial order is affected by the combination of the four transformative forces.

What Is a Race?

Immigration has disrupted Americans' twentieth-century assumptions of what constitutes a race.[2] Most consequential is the question of whether Hispanicity is best understood in racial terms, as in "Black, White, Asian, and Hispanic," or as an ethnicity, as in "Hispanics may be of any race." Politicians' campaign strategies, judges' decisions, advocacy groups' choices for organizing, and individuals' identities and behaviors all will vary depending on whether they understand Latinos to be a single group, a disparate set of nationalities, immigrants, or mostly White ethnics.

Also as a consequence of immigration, it is becoming less clear what it means to be Black in the United States. Early in his presidential campaign, Obama was described as not Black enough or not authentically Black in part because he did not have deep roots in African American history; as a child and young man, he engaged with that concern himself. By 2010, he classified himself simply as Black. In 2011, however, the prominent intellectual Cornel West once more raised the issue of how to understand Blackness in the context of immigration: Obama "has a certain fear of free black men. It's understandable. As a young brother who grows up in a white context, brilliant African father, he's always had to fear being a white man with black skin." Immigrants from Africa and other parts of the world wrestle with sorting out the relationships among race, nationality, immigration status, appearance, and identity. As West's comments imply, this issue is politically fraught as well as empirically messy: "The Black community in the United States . . . stands at a point in the collective struggle against racial subordination that may threaten its racial and ethnic solidarity forever. . . . Blacks are compelled to think about whether they should look at their Black brothers and sisters from the Mother Country, West Indies, or other parts of the world with different eyes and hearts than their brothers and sisters who come from families with many generations in the United States."[3] As with Latinos, how Blackness is defined and bounded will affect politicians' strategies, judges' decisions, advocacy groups' choices, and individuals' lives.

The same point holds for Whites and for multiracials. Whiteness, often understood as the unmoved mover, can be porous. On the one hand, the Supreme Court has declared that (putatively White) Iraqis could sue their (White) employer for racial discrimination and that Whites charged with defacing synagogues could be prosecuted for a crime of racial hatred; those decisions are evidence of splitting. On the other hand, "it seems likely that an increasing number of Latinos—those who have fair features, material wealth, and high social status, aided also by Anglo surnames—will both claim and be accorded a position in U.S. society as fully white."[4] That is evidence of joining. If multiracials become another race— so that the canonical list becomes Black, White, Asian, Latino, multiracial—politicians' strategies, judges' decisions, and so forth will be affected in roughly the same ways as if Hispanics become a race. That is complication enough. But if multiracials represent a fluid, indeterminate group that defines a race only in context or with inclination, that will deeply disrupt the first component of the American racial order.

Within a few decades, genomic science will not simply add another race, make groups more heterogeneous, or blur group boundaries; it may transform the very meaning of race. In what direction is not yet clear. Individualized medicine may undermine the need for racial (or any other group) identification, and recognition of the arbitrariness of categorical lines dividing the continuum of human variation will undermine fixed boundaries. Alternatively or at the same time, claims of finding medically or behaviorally meaningful genomic clusters that correspond to intelligible population groups may reintroduce an element of biology into our understanding of race. Whatever direction genomics takes us, Americans' current understanding and practice of race will eventually seem as quaint as nineteenth-century phrenology and "fractions of blood" do now. Science can never be innocent of politics, and as genomic science evolves so will conceptions of race.

Immigration and multiracialism are mutually reinforcing. Recent immigrants' descendants are a disproportionate share of those marrying across group lines, and immigrants, like multiracials, are especially likely to define races fluidly or inconsistently. Once DNA tests become as common as blood tests are now, many will reveal a varied ancestry; that fact may affect young adults' racial self-definition. Cohort change will magnify all of these disruptions of the old racial order. Immigrants are disproportionately young adults, an increasing proportion of young adults marry across group lines, and young adults will be the first generation profoundly affected by genomic science. Young adults by definition have collective racial memories different from those of the cohort raised in the civil rights struggle and first years of the new immigration. Young adults will not be color-blind or post-racial, whatever those terms mean—but for many, what counts as a race in their eyes will be complex and nuanced, and their choices about how to practice race may be more voluntary and less imposed. If the postmodernists are right, that the categories with which we make sense of our world shape our collective and individual actions in it, the question of what is a race implies the possibility of creating a new racial order in the United States.

How Are Individuals Classified?

The same four forces are changing how people understand themselves and others. Immigrants' identity shifts from nationality or region to ethnicity to pan-ethnicity to hyphenated American to American, and back again, depending on context and motivation. Immigrant parents, children, and grandchildren define themselves differently from one another. People with mixed parentage or ancestry may identify as racially mixed, as a member of one group, or as a member of whichever group seems right at that moment. Genetic ancestry searches will confirm some people's racial identity and challenge that of others.

As with the first component of the racial order, these forces operate both independently and interactively. Young adults can be imaginative, even playful in their self-definitions, calling themselves "nomadic mixed" or "latino in some situations." They find models for self-invention in former secretary of state Condoleezza Rice or President Obama, in musical or film stars and sports figures, and in each other. They are learning about genomics in high school and taking ancestry or genetic medical tests in college. Although not ignoring race, a generation that sees their own and their friends' racial labels as an object of play has moved a long way from one-drop-of-blood rules, blood quanta, or the policing of group authenticity. After all, "what does a sense of solidarity mean when half of the black population thinks that blacks should get away from thinking of themselves as part of a racial group?"[5]

Relative Group Positions

There are two questions here. First, are groups shifting their location or losing a distinct location in a relatively fixed vertical hierarchy or along a horizontal axis of inclusion and exclusion? Second, are the endpoints on either the vertical or the horizontal axis moving further apart or coming closer together, such that hierarchy and exclusion are themselves changing shape?

The answer to the first question is a qualified "yes." To some degree, groups are changing positions and they are certainly becoming more internally heterogeneous. White Americans still hold a disproportionate share of political and economic resources, and they are still the quintessential insiders. However, the median Asian American is better off than the median Anglo American in education, income, occupational status, and likelihood of living in an integrated community—though not in political power or attainment of positions of economic and social leadership. Conversely, Blacks still occupy a disproportionate share of the least desirable social and economic positions in the United States. But the median Black immigrant is better educated than the median native-born White, and there is now a robust native-born Black middle class with political and some economic or social clout. Blacks, at least those whose families have been in the United States for generations, are insiders; as Jorge Klor de Alva put it, "Blacks are Americans. They're Anglos. . . . They're Anglos of a different color, but they're Anglos."[6]

Hispanic descendants of legal immigrants are moving into the middle class and sometimes attaining insider status. A Texan dismisses fears of nonincorporation: "the power of America is undeniable. People may check 'Hispanic' on the census, but in San Antonio they are Tejanos, Texans of Mexican ancestry. . . . Kids . . . consider themselves American. We are already your neighbors and fellow workers, and are or soon will be your in-laws." Some Muslims are similarly moving up and in. "Detroit's Unlikely Saviors" are opening stores and schools ("if McDonald's can have restaurants all over the Arab world, then why can't I have kebab shops all over America?"), while "Muslim populations across the United States . . . [are developing] more assertive, tactically adaptive expressions of American identity."[7]

One must not overstate the changes in groups' relative positions. Non-White groups are making gains in educational attainment and achievement but slowly and fitfully—and schooling gains are only slightly reflected in higher incomes. Wealth holdings remain rigidly fixed by race and class. So long as that remains the case, so long as young Black men in poor communities are likely to be incarcerated and to have little chance of success once released, and so long as unauthorized immigrants lack a pathway to citizenship and upward mobility, the hierarchy of relative group positions and the distinction between insider and outsider are being only partly altered. Political choices—some of which we outline below—can lower if not eliminate these structural blockages, but such choices require commitments that most Americans at present seem unwilling to make.

Relative group positions are changing more rapidly in the political arena, however, and that could be key to making different economic and social policy choices over the next few decades. Electoral and protest politics are not being deracialized—far from it, as an army of social scientists is eager to show.[8] Instead, something more interesting is happening: Blacks, and more slowly Hispanics, are gaining office through some combination of geographic concentration, demographic change, young White adults' willingness to support non-White candidates, non-White candidates' and officeholders' increasing ability to speak across group and ideological lines, and Blacks' overwhelming support for many candidates of their own race. Barack Obama won the presidency through all of these means, and he is not unique. If growing political and administrative power translates into changes in policy choices and policy implementation, the public sector may eventually do more than it currently does to promote transformation in relative group positions.

Groups, then, are slowly becoming more internally heterogeneous both economically and in terms of inclusion in the American mainstream; these changes could promote more such change. Nothing in our analysis, however, suggests a transformation of the structure of the status hierarchy itself. Economic inequality is growing, and even recent policies to promote some downward redistribution of wealth such as health care reform are doing little to reverse that trend.[9] So the answer to the second question about relative group positions is "no." Further discussion of change in the whole American economic system remains outside our scope.

What Is Permitted, Required, or Forbidden?

The United States now has only a few official state policies to pro-hibit, promote, or require actions by members of a specified group. How much and what kind of impact they have, and whether unofficial state-sponsored actions that disproportionately affect particular groups have stepped in to fill the discriminatory void, are deeply contentious issues.

The evidence cuts in several directions. Whites no longer have first claims on jobs, schools, and neighborhoods, but the benefits of affirmative action for whites in earlier state policies persist in huge wealth disparities.[10] The Department of Homeland Security stripped Sheriff Arpaio of his power to use federal law to arrest suspected illegal immigrants, but he continues to arrest them and officials in other communities retain that power. Arizona's immigration law, if implemented, will have the effect if not the intent of harassing Latino residents, but governmental actions have blocked it so far. NSEERS specified disparate treatment for nationals of several predominantly Muslim states, but NSEERS is being shut down and public officials have defended American Muslims' right to construct mosques. President Obama, citing his young daughters, endorses the use of forensic biobanks, while federal task forces warn of discriminatory use of genetic material for law enforcement purposes. Airlines and police eschew racial profiling, but anecdotes about flying while Arab or driving while Black proliferate.

So the extent and trajectory of state-sponsored prohibitions remains an open question. Two conclusions nonetheless seem warranted. First, there is much more political contestation around these policies and practices—and many more victories for advocacy groups—than around the deeper structural impediments of unequal wealth, disproportionate incarceration, and barriers to legal status for unauthorized immigrants. Individuals challenge discrimination in court with help from MALDEF, the Legal Defense Fund, or the ACLU. Sports teams pressure states to change their laws; as Phoenix Suns guard Steve Nash explained the "Los Suns" uniforms (shown in chapter 6), "the law [SB 1070] is . . . to the detriment of our society and our civil liberties. I think it's very important for us to stand up for things we believe in. As a team and as an organization, we have a lot of love and support for all of our fans. The league is very multicultural. We have players from all over the world, and our

Latino community here is very strong and important to us."[11] Genomic scientists and museums warn against research purporting to find genes for violence or intelligence. The harms of state-sponsored prohibitions are real and recurrent, but the American state itself as well as societal forces provide tools and resources with which people can fight them, and sometimes win.

Second, transformation in the other components of the racial order has the capacity to keep this component from halting further transformation. As more immigrants come to the United States and become naturalized and voting citizens, the less incentive most elected officials will have to pass immigrant-bashing laws. Already immigration reform "'is becoming the third rail of politics, for Republicans in particular. . . . It's almost impossible to talk about immigration reform without sounding anti-immigrant.'"[12] Scientists' prestige and their revulsion against the past two centuries' racial science will contend against claims that particular groups have a genetic tendency toward specific behaviors or traits. The more that young adults jettison norms, stereotypes, activities, and living patterns that isolate them from one another, the harder it will be for state actors to justify treating Muslims, immigrants near the Mexican border, or young Black men differently from everyone else. As we have said so often, none of this is certain; it depends on Americans' choices in both public and private arenas. But group-based permissions have disappeared, and the conditions are in place for using protest, litigation, and electoral pressure against remaining or new, implicit or explicit, group-based prohibitions.

Social Relations

Immigrants' social relations range from complete isolation to easy incorporation into American society. The unauthorized are constrained by economic and legal barriers, while native-born children are moving to Frey's melting pot metros[13] and adopting American cultural norms altogether too quickly from their parents' vantage point. Mixed-race families and multiracial individuals almost by definition embody transformation of social relations. Even Blacks and Whites, the most maritally segregated groups, are finding that their families are heterogeneous in novel ways, ranging from blended families to surprising results in DNA ancestry testing. As genomic science shows more and more clearly how genes interact with environment even after a person reaches adulthood, pressures for more attractive and healthy living conditions for all could strengthen.

Above all, cohort change is driving Americans' creation of new social relations. Young adults are especially likely to be immigrants or multiracials or to interact with them. Their generation will develop the consequences of understanding interactions among genes and environment, as well as myriad other discoveries in genomics, For many young adults, group membership is more contextual, controllable, idiosyncratic, and normatively relaxed than it has been for their parents. Surprising juxtapositions are becoming common: "U.S. Catholic Universities Seeing Influx of Muslim Students," according to one headline.[14] Incorporation can take unexpected forms: asked why he chose a building for a Muslim community center so close to the former World Trade Center, thereby triggering strong protest, the owner answered, "Listen, do you have any clue how the Manhattan real-estate market works, what is involved? . . . This is New York. . . . Do you know how many places I looked at?"[15]

Most generally, young Whites tend to be more racially liberal than their parents are, young Blacks and Latinos are sometimes more conservative than their parents are, and the views of young adults sometimes converge on issues around which their parents continue to fight. Young adults are moving into the political realm with shared memories, from Hurricane Katrina to a Black president, that differ dramatically from their elders' memories of civil rights marches and exile from a homeland.

The definition of a race, classification of individuals, and social relations—that is, concepts, attitudes, and behaviors—have changed more over the past decade than have relative group positions and governmental prohibitions—that is, structures and institutions. The Jim Crow racial order was transformed into that of the late twentieth century in exactly the opposite way: structures and institutions of segregation and discrimination were abolished before the composition of the population or attitudes and behaviors had changed much (and concepts of race never did change between those two orders). The analysis in this book presents the question of whether changed understandings and behaviors, in conjunction with new citizens and newly heterogeneous groups, will be solidified into new institutions and diminished hierarchies. Only if all components of the American racial order are transformed will a new racial order be stably created.

Race, Class, and Policy Choices

Evidence of a new racial order is more fragmentary and subject to contradiction than we wish analytically or ideologically. And in any case, a new order will have both good and bad features. But complexity is not just an occupational hazard of social scientists who enter such a contentious arena as American racial and ethnic dynamics; it is itself our central point. That is, the conditions for creating a new racial order are in place—but so are old and new barriers to its accomplishment. There are no certainties here, and lacking Sherlock Holmes's genius we make no confident predictions.

To put the point more analytically, the outcome of the contest between transformative and entrenched forces will be decided through political actions not yet taken. This is not a new circumstance: Gunnar Myrdal wrote during World War II that "if America wants to make the . . . choice, she cannot wait and see. She has to do something big and do it soon. . . . America can demonstrate that justice, equality, and cooperation are possible between white and colored people."[16] America did eventually choose to jettison the Jim Crow racial order that Myrdal investigated so thoroughly and to substitute a racial order that retained the old groups but struggled with partial success to change relative group positions, abolish governmental prohibitions, and improve social relations. New institutions emerged, and heterogeneity within and across groups grew.

As a result, knowing the race or ethnicity of a person who begins life with some resources gives us less and less leverage in predicting that person's eventual beliefs and behaviors. But knowing a poor person's race, ethnicity, or immigration status still enables a good forecast of his or her life chances. As Debra Dickerson puts it, "class is the new black. . . . All the traditional coalitions and alliances are offline. . . . Let's talk class, not race—problem areas, not the pigment of those living within them."[17]

This is not the place for detailed policy proposals on how to promote the best features of transformation, offset the worst, and eliminate the blockages to further change. However, our analysis suggests general directions for accomplishing those goals: taking political advantage of demographic change and growing heterogeneity is the driving mechanism, and changing structures of wealth holding and exclusion is the essential task.

Over the next quarter century, the cohort of workers born in the two decades after World War II will retire. As the sociologist Richard Alba points out, their retirement "will open up a huge swath of positions, running from the bottom to the top of the workforce. Because of the disproportionate concentration of white baby boomers in the middle and upper ranges of the occupational structure, the potential for racial and ethnic shifts will be especially large there. . . . There will be much more ethnoracial diversity at the middle and higher levels of the United States within the next few decades." Table 7.1 shows the beginning of this transformation. Even before baby boomers have begun retiring in large numbers, one can see a decline in the proportion of top jobs held by Anglos and a rise in the proportion of top jobs held by people of color.

Alba is cautious about projecting from these results, since the differences shown in table 7.1 are subject to two very different, though not mutually exclusive, interpretations—cohort change and aging. "In one,

Table 7.1
Share of High-Level Jobs Held by Various Groups, 2005–6

Age in 2006	U.S.-born non-Hispanic Whites	U.S.-born non-Hispanic Blacks	U.S.-born Hispanics	Foreign-born Hispanics	U.S.-born Asians	Foreign-born Asians
			Top decile			
26-31	64.9	5.0	4.5	2.5	4.2	12.6
62-71	81.7	2.2	1.1	1.9	0.8	5.5
			Rest of top quartile			
26-31	69.4	7.3	6.1	3.3	2.6	6.2
62-71	82.0	4.4	1.7	1.7	0.5	3.1
			Second quartile			
26-31	69.9	8.0	8.0	5.5	1.8	2.8
62-71	79.9	5.4	2.5	3.2	0.7	2.8

Source: Alba 2009, table 4.3. Data are from ACS 2005, 2006.
Note: The rows do not sum to 100 percent because foreign-born non-Hispanic Whites and foreign-born non-Hispanic Blacks are not included.

they express historical changes in life chances, which are reflected in the attainments of different birth cohorts because they reach maturity under varying conditions; in the other, they express variations across the life cycle, which each cohort experiences as its members age." He also worries that African Americans, American Indians, and second-generation Hispanics will not be positioned to move into the newly vacated high-status jobs if the United States does not reduce racial and ethnic gaps in schooling quality and attainment. Nevertheless, "the blurring of major ethno-racial boundaries is a plausible prospect for the near future."[18]

Another demographer also envisioned disruption in relative group statuses by "imagin[ing] who would help fill the void behind our aging adults and how the boomers and immigrants might share a rendezvous with destiny."[19] He focuses less on the labor market and more on two other essential societal interactions—paying taxes and buying houses. In states such as California and Arizona where the elderly are mostly White and the young are increasingly non-Anglo, incorporation of newcomers is not merely ideologically desirable (to liberals, in any case) but in the direct interests of current homeowners and taxpayers—that is to say, voters. They will suffer unless the United States ensures that Hispanics "play a vital role in shouldering the burden of a graying society."[20] After all, when aging baby boomers seek to sell their homes and move to condominiums near the grandchildren, they need buyers with resources; those will increasingly not be other Whites. Figure 7.1 provides the projections.

An aging population also needs a lot of publicly funded services, especially but not only Medicare and Social Security. To meet that need, either taxes must be raised or more younger adults must pay taxes. For this reason too, in states with an ethnic generation gap, voters' self-interest implies a need to ensure steady if not high wages for the expanding population of immigrants and their descendants.

Young native-born Blacks and Whites are also essential, of course, if the arithmetic of the dependency ratio is to work out, that is, if today's children and young adults are to be able to sustain the economy and society of the future. Myers spells out the overall logic: "Growing the new base of middle-class taxpayers is closely related to building a skilled workforce. Both hinge on the crucial matter of educational attainment. . . . The added feature in the case of taxpayers is the relationship between education level and earnings. Higher-income taxpayers obviously can contribute more to the social support of seniors and others than can those who are not paid as well."[21]

Unlike most demographers, Myers considers what political configuration is needed to upgrade jobs and, most urgently, schooling so that there will be a population able to move into Alba's top-tier positions, buy

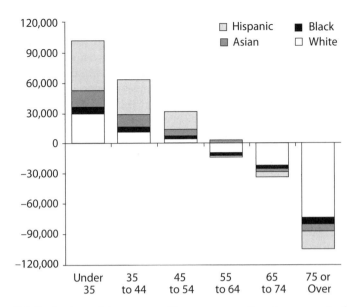

Figure 7.1. Projection of the excess of buyers over sellers, by age and ethnicity, California in 2020.
Source: Myers 2007, 237.

houses, and pay taxes.[22] While many have warned of the "intensifying confrontation between the gray and the brown,"[23] Myers outlines a more optimistic intergenerational social contract in what he calls the cycle of roles. Children and young adults receive publicly funded and high-quality education. That positions them as adults to become workers, home buyers, and taxpayers. As these contributing members of society mature, they are able to make financial and political contributions to their communities and perhaps to the nation as a whole. Finally, as mature adults age into being seniors, they are rewarded with health care, pensions, and the ability to sell their home.

None of these outcomes is easy to attain and no policy proposal will be free of conflict, of course. Myers's point is that it is in everyone's interest for this virtuous cycle to dominate the vicious cycle of pushing immigrants (and poor Blacks) out and down. The crucial question is whether some combination of demographic change, voters' and leaders' public spiritedness, and self-interest (and, we would add, a decline in barriers among racial groups) will generate the political will to keep trying until Americans fulfill the new intergenerational social contract.

The need for sustained political will points us to a final concern: an ominous proportion of residents in some communities are not eligible to vote. About a quarter of Los Angelenos are noncitizens, as are a third of the residents of Miami and a fifth in Houston. The proportion of noncitizen residents of the United States is greater now than at any time since the early twentieth century. In 1970, fewer than 2 percent of adult American residents were ineligible to vote.[24] By 2000, about 43 percent of adult immigrants were naturalized citizens, which meant that about 6 percent of adult Americans were ineligible to vote (setting aside disenfranchised felons). Furthermore, in the years around 2000, second- and third-generation Hispanics (that is, native-born citizens) voted at lower rates than did the immigrant generation of Hispanics. In fact, proportionally fewer third-generation Latinos voted than in any other immigrant group or generation.[25]

Whether Americans create a new racial order will depend to a considerable degree on whether voting and other forms of political participation change. Young voters, or new voters in a given racial or ethnic group, cannot be assumed to share policy preferences; that is part of what we mean by saying that groups are becoming more heterogeneous and that race and ethnicity no longer permit solid predictions of views and activities. But one can assume that young or new voters will be as capable of looking out for their interests as older or established ones are—which means that they will take the main responsibility for managing the new racial order. Political action by new participants, in short, is both an effect and a cause of further transformation of the American racial order.

Managing demographic change is largely a matter of immigrants and their children. But most Blacks and badly off native-born Whites will benefit from the same policies that help immigrants, most crucially improvements in education and jobs. Further policy changes are needed to overcome the blockages of alienation and despair in the inner city, as well as the individual and collective harms resulting from excessive incarceration. We see some momentum on the issue of imprisonment and its consequences: the number of people in city and state jails is leveling off, disenfranchisement of ex-felons is being beaten back, and some new preventive or rehabilitative programs seem to be effective: "New York cut its incarceration rate by 15% between 1997 and 2007, while reducing violent crime by 40%."[26] This is a start, and we hope *The Economist* is right in predicting that politicians who tackle the injustices and inefficiencies of the U.S. criminal justice system will "get some credit" and therefore keep working at it.[27]

Isolated and despairing neighborhoods are not unique to Blacks, but desperately poor inner cities are perhaps the blockages to transformation of which Americans should be most ashamed. William Julius Wilson used to promote universalistic policies roughly on the theory that a rising tide lifts all boats; he now argues that "in framing public policy, we should not shy away from an explicit discussion of the specific issues of race and poverty; on the contrary, we should highlight them in our attempt to convince the nation that these problems should be seriously confronted and that there is an urgent need to address them."[28] Behind this careful wording is a moral passion that we share: as Americans move through the twenty-first century, we owe it to our children to ensure that their most important collective racial memory is Chicago's Grant Park on election night 2008, not the planes crashing into the World Trade Center or the New Orleans Superdome in the days after Hurricane Katrina.

Notes

Introduction

1. We have been influenced in our understanding of changing racial orders by, among many others, Berlin 1998; Klinkner and Smith 2002; Morgan 1975; Hollinger 2006; Woodward 1971; Marx 1998; Wilson 1980; Fredrickson 2002; Montejano 1987; King and Smith 2005, 2008; and Kim 2000.

Chapter 1. Destabilizing the American Racial Order

The sources for the epigraphs are as follows: Lucas 2000, 467; Hitt 2005, 47; "Census, Welfare, California, New York City" 2004.

1. Coon 1939. Coon anticipates the supposedly recent view that race is socially constructed. The first paragraph of the introduction to his book states, "If there is one consistent theme in this book, it is that physical anthropology cannot be divorced from cultural and historical associations and that there is no such thing as 'pure' biology, at least in reference to human beings" (vii).

2. Darwin 2010 [1871], 170.

3. Criminal race: Hughes 1988, 167, quoting *Edinburgh Review*; ethnicity: Sollors 1989 and Hattam 2004; Yale: Smith 2009.

4. "Self-definition" means that an individual chooses his or her own racial label. By "identity," we mean that the person sees his or her racial self-definition to be an important constitutive part of who he or she really is, with political, emotional, behavioral, or cultural implications. By "identification," we mean that an external actor or agency (e.g., employer, census bureau, another person) is giving a racial or ethnic label to a person; that label may or may not correspond with the person's self-definition. Rockquemore, Brunsma, and Delgado (2009) provide a similar, though not identical, set of definitions and their implications.

5. Kim 1999 elegantly lays out this two-dimensional model.

6. Mexican middle class: Vallejo 2009, 1; Black segregation: "Black Segregation in US Drops to Lowest in Century," 2010, using data from Frey 2010a; live in suburbs: Frey 2010a, 51.

7. California teens: New American Media 2007a; California voters: Field Poll 2010; Minnesota: Carew 2010; Gallup Poll: Witters 2010.

8. Deputizing local police: Government Accountability Office 2009; Democracy Now 2009; "not even past": Sugrue 2010.

9. The first prominent use of this idea that we have found was a story on National Public Radio in early 2008:

> Welcome to the latest buzz word in the political lexicon, post-racial. It is what Senator Barack Obama signals in his victory speech in South Carolina. . . .
> The post-racial era, as embodied by Obama, is the era where civil rights

veterans of the past century are consigned to history and Americans begin to make race-free judgments on who should lead them. . . . The *New Yorker* wrote of a post-racial generation and indeed, the battle-scarred veterans of the civil rights conflict of 40 years ago seemed less enchanted with Obama than those who were not yet alive then (Schorr 2008).

Since 2008, a variety of commentators have approvingly used the phrase and a plethora of academics have denied its validity. We do not share the views of all of those scholars, but this book concurs that post-racial is not an appropriate description of the current American racial order.

10. Powell 2010; see also Hochschild and Powell 2008.

11. See Prewitt forthcoming on the Blumenbachian typology of American racial definitions.

12. With the curious exception of American Indians, for whom government policy promoted incorporation during much of the first half of the twentieth century.

13. King and Smith 2005, 75; Kim 1999; Fredrickson 2002, 6; Omi and Winant 1994, 35.

14. Segregation: Massey and Denton 1993, Drake and Cayton 1993 [1945]; labor: Wacquant 2002; miscegenation: Myrdal 1944, Fortner 2010, Kennedy 2003; middle class: Pattillo-McCoy 1999; power: Horton 1995, Stepick et al. 2003; Browning, Marshall, and Tabb 1984, Sonenshein 1993, Mollenkopf and Sonenshein 2009.

15. Influence: authors' analysis of Sapiro et al. 2007 and American National Election Studies (ANES) 2009; "much in common": authors' analyses of Pew Research Center 2009b; friends: New American Media 2007a.

16. Another deep structural problem is the persistence of deeply poor and dysfunctional American Indian communities on reservations. We do not address this issue in any detail in this book.

Chapter 2. Immigration

The sources for the epigraphs are as follows: Klor de Alva, Shorris, and West 1998, 184; e-mail message of Linda Dwyer, quoting a student, to h-ethnic@h-net. msu.edu, March 20, 2005; Yoplac 2010.

1. The Hart-Celler act allotted 170,000 immigrant slots per year to the eastern hemisphere, with a limit of 20,000 from any one country, and 120,000 annually to the western hemisphere. The quotas included preference for highly skilled workers in the arts and sciences, made provisions for admitting refugees, and eliminated discriminatory policies against Asians. Crucially, immediate family members of American citizens were exempt from the allotments. The new law eliminated the old provision that granted 70 percent of immigration slots to Great Britain, Ireland, and Germany. Often almost half had gone unused, while other countries generated long waiting lists since, in some cases, they had been limited to about 100 people per year.

Hochschild and Burch 2007 analyze the politics behind the 1965 immigration law, as well as providing full citations for all quotations in this chapter from 1964 and 1965.

2. There was also no passionate group activism or partisan politics; immigration reform was driven by elites' foreign policy considerations. President Truman linked immigration reform to "the conduct of our foreign relations and to our responsibilities of moral leadership in the struggle for world peace." Presidents Eisenhower and Kennedy concurred. Kennedy's assassination, Johnson's and his allies' legislative skill, mounting cold war geopolitical pressures, and concern for refugees fleeing communism or political persecution lay behind the passage of the 1965 law (Tichenor 2002; Zolberg 2006).

3. The UN estimates that the United States had received 42.8 million people of "migrant stock" by 2009, compared with the Russian Federation with 12.3 million, Germany with 10.8 million, and Saudi Arabia, Canada, France, the United Kingdom, and Spain with 6 to 7 million each. Data on the 1960s are in United Nations Dept. of Economic and Social Affairs 2003. For 2009, see United Nations 2009.

The UN predicts that migration will continue to rise, to at least 4 percent of the world's population by 2020. The Gallup Organization found in 2009 that about 16 percent of the world's adults, 700 million people, would like to migrate permanently if they had a chance. The United States is the preferred destination of a quarter, or 165 million (Esipova and Ray 2009).

4. Department of Homeland Security 2008, table 1.

5. Bullet points are from, respectively, Frey 2007b, 16; Frey 2010b, 2009; Camarota 2010; Frey 2006; Su 2011, Dougherty 2011.

6. Mountain states: Frey 2007a; proportion of White children: Frey 2007b; intermarriage: Frey 2009. See Metropolitan Policy Program 2010 for changes in the one hundred largest metropolitan areas.

7. Data are from Hoefer, Rytina, and Baker 2011; Passel and Cohn 2009; and McCabe and Meissner 2010.

8. Passell and Cohn 2009. Passel reminds readers that "*the data do not necessarily support the idea that the share of Mexican migration that is unauthorized has been increasing in recent years.* The earlier cohorts (i.e. pre-1990) had also been largely unauthorized when they had been in the country for shorter durations. That is, *the Mexican-born population in the United States for less than 5 years was found to be at least 75% unauthorized in estimates made for 1995, 1990, 1986, and 1980.* These earlier entry cohorts are now almost all legal as result of three processes: 1) a 'normal' transition from unauthorized to legal through sponsorship and 245(i); 2) the legalization programs of the late 1980s; and 3) selective return migration to Mexico by unauthorized migrants" (Passel 2005, 16, emphases in original).

9. Handlin 2002, 3; Cato Institute 1995, 146.

10. In federal parlance, NHOPI is Native Hawaiian and Other Pacific Islander; AIAN is American Indian and Alaska Native; A.O.I.C. is "alone or in combination (with one or more other races)."

11. McBride 1996.

12. Again from the OMB report, "the racial and ethnic categories set forth in the standards should not be interpreted as being primarily biological or genetic in

reference. Race and ethnicity may be thought of in terms of social and cultural characteristics as well as ancestry." Unless otherwise noted, all quotations in this and the next paragraph are from Office of Management and Budget 1997. NAS comment is from Edmonston, Goldstein, and Lott 1996, 35; see also Passel and Taylor 2009.

13. A 1976 law required "Hispanic" in order to "assist state and federal governments, and private organizations in the accurate determination of the urgent and special needs of Americans of Spanish origin or descent" (Public Law 94-311). In 2004, Congress required Some Other Race in the census. The census bureau had sought to eliminate what it perceived to be an imprecise catchall category. But Representative José Serrano (D-NY) described that move as "a bit strange and out of touch with reality" since "many Hispanics have a complicated relationship with their racial identities. . . . [W]e don't fit neatly into the Census' tidy little boxes." Retaining "other," he argued, avoids "tainted demographic data" (Serrano 2004).

14. The American Indian category also uniquely includes a political criterion. The person must "maintain . . . tribal affiliation or community attachment," and the census form instructs respondents to "Print name of enrolled or principal tribe."

15. Mulatto: Gratton and Gutman 2000, Schor 2005. Distinct race: in 1930, the census bureau added "Mexican" to the "Color or race" inquiry, instructing enumerators that "practically all Mexican laborers are of a racial mixture difficult to classify, though usually well recognized in the localities where they are found. In order to obtain separate figures for this racial group, it has been decided that all persons born in Mexico, or having parents born in Mexico, who are definitely not white, Negro, Indian, Chinese, or Japanese, should be returned as Mexican." After much protest on both sides of the border, the bureau retreated, the director noting wryly that "the classification by race or color of . . . populations is not only very difficult, but is a very delicate matter to the United States Government." He decreed that henceforth "Mexicans are Whites and must be classified as 'White'. This order does not admit of any further discussion, and must be followed to the letter." See Hochschild and Powell 2008 for more details and citations to internal quotes; for histories of contestation over Mexican Americans' Whiteness, see Rosales 1985, 81; Rodriguez 2000; and Gross 2007.

16. Patterson 2001; see also Cobas, Duany, and Feagin 2009.

17. Endorsement of Hispanic race: Haney López 1997, 1148; see also Broh and Minicucci 2008 and Gómez 2009. Fear of Hispanic race: http://www.you tube.com/watch?v=ZSTdGC4z6io.

18. LNS results for 2006: Fraga et al. 2010; 2010 census results: Bureau of the Census 2011; characterizations quoted in El Nasser 2011 (ellipses in quotation are in original).

19. Corey 1998; Mr. Frank's answer was not reported. "*Our* people": Diaz 2004, 8; Haitians: Kretsedemas 2008, 832.

20. Bureau of the Census 2002, 37.

21. Shiao and Tuan 2008, 1023. Junn and Masuoka 2008 similarly point to "a surprising degree of malleability in Asian American racial group attachment" (729).

22. Survey researcher: Porter 2001; health care officials: Buescher, Gizlice, and Jones-Vessey 2005. More generally, mothers of the almost 118,000 North Carolina newborns gave dozens of different responses to the race question on birth certificates. (At that time, the agency's rules held that the father's race was irrelevant to the child's race.)

23. Brazilians: Martes 2008, 237; see also McDonnell and de Lourenço 2009. Dominicans: letter to the editor, quoted in San Martin 2007; Somalis: Gilbert 2009, 374, 380–81; see also Williamson 2008.

24. Census analysis: Bennett 2003; recontact survey: Groeneman 2001.

25. Census 2000: Marrow 2008b, McDonnell and de Lourenço 2009; conceptual explanation: Rumbaut 2009, 29.

26. Marrow 2004; see also Marrow 2003.

27. Dominicans: Itzigsohn 2004; census and CPS: del Pinal and Schmidley 2005. They also found differences in Hispanic identification between the census and the CPS for immigrants from Spain, Brazil, and other Central and South American countries.

28. CILS: Rumbaut 2009; rates of Mexican identification: Duncan and Trejo 2008, 26; see also Bean, Brown, and Bachmeier 2010; Brown et al. 2011.

29. Racial or ethnic identities: Waters 1995, 1999 and Rogers 2006; fraught allegiances: Wamba 1999, 47; external identification: quoted in Escobar 1999; context matters: Oropesa, Landale, and Greif 2008.

30. College student: Bush 2002, 32; Albanian: Winerip 2005; Middle Eastern: Abdulrahim 2009.

31. Tafoya, Johnson, and Hill 2004, 4.

32. All evidence in this and the following few paragraphs are from the authors' analysis of August 2009 CPS, unless otherwise noted.

33. See also Logan and Deane 2003; Logan 2003.

34. After twenty years: Vigdor 2009, 64; 1994 to 2004: White and Glick 2009, 119.

35. Schooling attainment and earnings: Haskins 2007, quotation on p. 2; White and Glick 2009. Occupation scores: Vigdor 2009.

36. Concerns: Fraga 2009, 177, 178 (internal numbering not included). Politics of demonization: Massey 2007, 132, 146, 150, 157. Ismaili 2010 similarly depicts a governmental "war on immigrants" in the 2000s.

37. Massey and Sánchez 2010, 121. In 1999, over 90 percent of Latinos agreed that "the opportunity to get ahead is better in the United States" than in their home country. By 2010, that proportion had declined, but over 80 percent still concurred (Pew Hispanic Center 2010).

38. *Plyler v. Doe*, (1982); *Lau v. Nichols* (1974). In addition, the main federal education law, No Child Left Behind (NCLB), requires schools to evaluate English-language learners through math and reading exams starting in the third grade. At least in the letter of the law, schools face penalties if the students' test scores do not improve. NCLB also mandates annual tests on and evidence of improvement in English proficiency and promotes the involvement of parents through information and direct engagement.

39. *United States v. Brignoni-Ponce* (1975).

40. Immigration and Customs Enforcement 2008. For contrasting views on

the use of Section 287(g), see Center for Immigration Studies 2009; Chishti 2009; Democracy Now 2009; Rodríguez et al. 2010; and Department of Homeland Security 2010. Quote is from Government Accountability Office 2009, preface.

41. Pew Hispanic Center 2010.

42. Public Agenda and Carnegie Corporation of the United States 2009.

43. The federal Justice Department filed suit against Sheriff Arpaio in 2010 on the grounds that he would not cooperate with an investigation into violation of immigrants' rights under Title VI of the Civil Rights Act. At the same time, a federal grand jury was determining whether he had abused his authority and intimidated county workers. The Maricopa County Board of Supervisors, although controlled by Republicans, is seeking to bring Arpaio under closer budgetary and administrative control, and numerous lawsuits have been filed against him and his department. As of this writing, he remains sheriff. For a recent analysis, see Waslin 2010.

44. Office of Inspector General 2003; Sheridan 2004; Cole 2002.

45. On Enhanced Border, see Bureau of Consular Affairs 2010b and Gorman 2009; on NSEERS, see Immigration and Customs Enforcement 2010 and Bureau of Consular Affairs 2010a.

46. Department of Justice 2003b; blogger: Davis 2009 (capitalization in original).

47. Department of Transportation: Gardner and Hsu 2009; Department of Homeland Security: Office for Civil Rights and Civil Liberties 2008.

48. Reich and Barth (2010) provide a good analysis of why states make different choices on this issue.

49. Quotation and bill analysis are in Bada et al. 2010, 19, following the Migration Policy Institute's Data Hub. Bada et al. offer further examples of new state and local actions with regard to immigrants; see also Chavez and Provine 2009; Schuck 2009; and Varsanyi 2010.

50. Headline: Favro 2007; local ordinances: Ramakrishnan and Wong 2010; jurisdictional patchwork: Varsanyi et al. 2010, 3; see also Lewis and Ramakrishnan 2007 and Hopkins 2010.

51. Benjamin Franklin famously worried about too many Germans; a century later, people with English ancestry castigated Irish newcomers and rioted against Catholics, while western European Jews scorned the recently arrived eastern European Jews. Most Whites, including recent immigrants, hated Asians. During World War II, most Americans opposed unrestricted movement between the United States and Canada, Australia, and other countries in the British Empire; up to three-quarters opposed opening the borders to "selected" or "political" European refugees (Roper/*Fortune* Survey, 1938, 1939, 1942, 1947).

Throughout the book, unless otherwise noted, references to individual survey items are available at Roper Center for Public Opinion Research 2010 and often at PollingReport.com.

52. On Sotomayor's name: Krikorian 2009; increase or decrease levels of immigration: PollingReport.com 2010; thermometer scale: Greenberg Quinlan Rosner, various polls.

53. A good thing: Gallup Poll, various; do more to help the country: ABC News, various; contribute to this country: CBS News/*New York Times*, various.

54. Join society: Fox News/Opinion Dynamics Poll, July 11–12, 2006; mainly positive impact: *Los Angeles Times*/Bloomberg Poll, November 30–December 3, 2007; food, music, art: Gallup Poll, various.

55. Loyal Americans: Public Agenda 1998; Constitution: Public Agenda, July 20–24, 2002. Welcome all immigrants: 2007: CBS/*New York Times*, May 18–23, 2007; 2010: CBS/*New York Times*, April 28–May 2, 2010.

56. Economic benefit or threat: NBC News/*Wall Street Journal* Poll, March 31–April 3, 2005; Associated Press/Ipsos-Public Affairs Poll, May 15–17, 2006. In a 2005 survey with very similar results, Republicans were a few points more likely than Democrats to agree that "today's immigrants work harder than people born here" (CBS News, October 3–5, 2005). All data in this paragraph are from *Polling Report*.

57. Prejudice: ABC News Poll, September 27–30, 2007.

58. Chinese immigrants: Committee of 100, 2007; Asian Americans good for America, succeed, take jobs: Committee of 100, 2009; nationality improve the United States: Knight Ridder, 1997.

59. Gallup Poll: June 1–3, 1984, August 23–24, 1990, February 6–9, 1992, July 9–11, 1993, June 3–9, 2002, June 8–25, 2006.

60. Good for America: Committee of 100, 2009; Pew Hispanic Center Immigration Poll, February 8–March 7, 2006; 1993 and 1997: Gallup/CNN/*USA Today*, July 1993; Pew News Interest Index Poll, April 1997.

61. Princeton Survey Research Associates International/*Newsweek* Poll, January 14–15, 2009.

62. All results are in Ha 2010.

63. Gallup Poll: June 11–17, 2001, June 3–9, 2002, June 12–18, 2003, June 6–25, 2005, June 8–25, 2006, June 4–24, 2007, June 5–July 6, 2008, July 10–12, 2009, July 8–11, 2010.

64. A version of this question has been asked since 1984, and in each iteration, at least two-thirds agree with "mostly take low-paying jobs Americans don't want."

65. Make contribution: Associated Press/Ipsos, March 28–30, 2006. Government services: Gallup Poll, June 8–25, 2006, June 5–July 6, 2008, June 11–13, 2010.

66. For example, Fox News/Opinion Dynamics Poll, May 4–5, 2010; NBC News/MSNBC/Telemundo Poll, May 20–30, 2010.

67. Apply for legal status: CBS/*New York Times*, May 18–23, 2007; pay a fine: ABC/*Washington Post*, April 21–24, 2009. Become U.S. citizens: *Los Angeles Times*/Bloomberg Poll, April 7–9, 2006, CNN Poll, May 5–7, 2006, *Los Angeles Times*/Bloomberg Poll, June 8–25, 2006, Gallup/*USA Today* Poll, March 2–4, 2007, Public Religion Research Institute, September 1–14, 2010; Pew Research Center, February 22–March 14, 2011.

68. Rasmussen Reports 2010.

69. A systematic review of American public opinion on immigrants and immigration since 1997 comes to the same conclusion: "The current review reveals mixed attitudes, dualities in Americans' thinking, and splits on immigration issues. . . . Public opinion is at times ambivalent, espousing certain attitudes that challenge others" (Segovia and DeFever 2010, 375).

70. Increasing public attention: Pew Hispanic Center 2008. The remaining results in this paragraph are in Public Agenda and Carnegie Corporation of the United States 2009, quote on p. 14.

71. Fraga et al. 2007.

72. Those proportions have declined slightly since 2002. The sampling procedures for the two surveys were somewhat different, however, so comparisons should be made cautiously (Public Agenda and Carnegie Corporation of the United States 2003).

73. Public Agenda and Carnegie Corporation of the United States 2009.

74. 1990s: Fasenfast, Booza, and Metzger 2006, 102. 2000s: Iceland 2009, 4, 6, 134.

75. Immigrants fanned out: Tavernise and Gebeloff 2010; see also Metropolitan Policy Program 2010. Fifty metropolitan areas: Frey 2010a; one hundred largest metro areas: Frey 2010d, 2, 3.

76. Los Angeles mayor: Sonenshein 1993; University of Texas: Guinier and Torres 2002; Los Angeles schools: Kim and Lee 2002.

77. Mahoney 2006; Heredia 2009; United States Conference of Catholic Bishops 2003; Milkman 2006; Ethnic Media Network 2010. See also Ramakrishnan and Bloemraad 2008 and Wong 2006.

78. Quoted in Dionne 1999. See also Williamson 2011.

79. Interlopers: Kim 2000; McClain 2006; Rogers 2004; Marrow 2008a. Government treats immigrants better: Cohen 2009; see also Gay 2006. Compton: Simmons and Sewell 2010; see also McClain et al. 2008. Immigrant rights march: Bada et al. 2010.

80. Modan 2007, 120, emphasis in original; see also Florida 2002, but see Putnam 2007.

81. O'Connor 2011.

82. Quoted in Pluviose 2006; see, similarly, Gonzalez 2010.

Chapter 3. Multiracialism

The sources for the epigraphs are as follows: Hardy Drew and the Nancy Boys, "There's No One as Irish as Barack O'Bama," http://www.youtube.com/watch?v=EADUQWKoVek; Brown 2001, 47; Barack Obama quoted in Gardner 2008.

1. Many states never had anti-miscegenation laws; beginning in the 1950s, others began to repeal them. *Loving v. Virginia* (1967) eliminated the remaining laws in the southern and border states.

2. Bureau of the Census 2001.

3. Vasconcelos 1979 [1925].

4. We use "mixed race," "multiracial(ism)," "biracial," and "racial mixture" interchangeably. We specify where relevant whether Hispanics or Latinos are a "race" for purposes of this analysis; except as noted, we do not treat people of mixed nationalities (Japanese Korean or Swedish Armenian) as multiracial. Quotation is from Omi and Winant 1994, vii.

5. A sample of the recent outpouring of writing on this topic includes Haney López 1996; Sollors 2000; Nobles 2000; Moran 2001; Johnson 2003; Hollinger

2003; Kennedy 2003; Romano 2003; Ingersoll 2005; Lubin 2005; Hattam 2007; Hochschild and Powell 2008; Novkov 2008; Gross 2008; and Pascoe 2009.

6. For the history of multiracial advocacy, see Jones 2000; DaCosta 2004; and Williams 2006. NAS reports included Edmonston and Schultze 1995 and Edmonston, Goldstein, and Lott 1996. Experts included authors in Smith and Edmonston 1997; Hirschman, Kasinitz, and DeWind 1999; and Goldstein and Morning 2000. Wallman 1998 gives the government analysis, and Williams 2006 analyzes state activity.

7. Some advocates were disappointed that the OMB gave the option of choosing one or more races rather than establishing a stand-alone category of "multiracial." In their eyes, "multiracial" would have signaled a distinct group identity, whereas "mark one or more" permits analysts to reallocate mixed-race individuals back into their component races.

As figure 1.1 shows, the 2010 census similarly asks, "What is Person 1's race? Mark one or more boxes."

8. Prewitt 2001, 40. Prewitt implemented the decision but did not hold the position of census director when the OMB issued the 1997 *Revisions*.

9. Department of Justice 2001.

10. Equal Employment Opportunity Commission 2005, 71295; Department of Education 2007, 59267.

11. Communication with authors, January 2008.

12. Broh and Minicucci 2008.

13. The number of major corporations permitting multiracial self-definition is rising rapidly; in 2008, only thirty-five permitted the choice of two or more races. (Eighteen permitted only one response, and the rest did not ask for race or we could not obtain the information.) For Chamber of Commerce, see Equal Employment Opportunity Commission 2005, 71296.

14. Nevins 1958. School superintendent quoted in Chandler and Glod 2009.

15. Pew Research Center 2010b.

16. 2007: Frey 2009, quotes from p. 6. Before 2007: Farley 2007; Qian and Lichter 2007; Lee and Edmonston 2005, 2006; Yen 2010; Qian and Lichter 2007; Lee and Edmonston 2005, 2006; Yen 2010. 2008: Pew Research Center 2010b. Generally, see Lee and Bean 2010.

17. See citations in previous note.

18. Intermarriage patterns were broadly similar for men. These estimates are conservative, since the data do not take into account the third-generation "loss" of Hispanics into White-only identity or the higher intermarriage rate of Some Other Race identifiers, who are disproportionately Hispanic (Stevens, McKillip, and Ishizawa 2006). See also Fraga et al. c. 2007. Nonmarital partnerships: Fryer 2005.

19. The decline in intermarriage does not hold for native-born Asians; see Fryer 2005, figure 1. See also Pew Research Center 2010b and Stevens, McKillip, and Ishizawa 2006 on intermarriage among children and grandchildren of immigrants. These data exclude Hispanics; adding them would make the trajectories steeper.

20. Quotation from Perlmann 2002, 15–16. Another projection: Edmonston and Passel 1999, 389.

21. Children below eighteen: Farley 2007; mixed-race children outside marriage: Bureau of the Census 2003; households with children under eighteen: Pew Research Center 2010b.

22. Fraction of Whites: Goldstein, communication with the authors, January 29, 2009; immediate family member: Pew Research Center 2010b.

23. Stone 1908, 401. Although his view was unusual, Stone's contemporaries energetically debated the biological differences between what they called pure and hybrid races. A letter to the *New York Times*, for example, reported the "pretty well-established fact that the hybrids produced by such fusion ["between the Indo-European and Ethiopian races in this country"] cease to bear children, in fact, become sterile, at the third or fourth generation" (Shufeldt 1907).

24. Quotes are from, respectively, Steinberg n.d.; DaCosta 2007, 56–57; and Rockquemore and Brunsma 2002, 42.

25. Quotes are from, respectively, Moore 2001, 3; U.S. House of Representatives 1997, 383–84; MAVIN Foundation 2006; and Association of MultiEthnic Americans 2001.

26. Anthony Appiah, quoted in Wright 1994, 46.

27. Census 1870: Census Office 1872, xiii. "Then, what is white?": *Ex parte Shahid* (1913); transformative logic: Rockquemore, Brunsma, and Delgado 2009, 19.

28. Direct comparisons between census 2000 and later ACSs are difficult because the census bureau's imputation rules for allocating respondents into racial categories differ across years. In addition, the sampling frame and procedures for the ACS have only recently been stabilized, and some demographers doubt the comparability to the census of even recent data. The census bureau's Annual Population Estimates differ from the ACS because of different imputation rules as well as different strategies for calculating groups' sizes. The official estimates take into account births, deaths, and net migration but not self-reports in the years after the census; they therefore do not incorporate changes in people's propensity to identify with multiple races, as the ACS can do. Finally, the NHIS differs from both census bureau measures, presumably because of sampling strategies, question wording and placement, and other house effects.

For the 2000 census itself, it may be appropriate to drop respondents who chose Some Other Race (SOR) + one of the standard races from the category of multiracial, on the grounds that many chose White and wrote in Hispanic or an equivalent term—that is, they are White Hispanics rather than being of mixed race as that term is commonly used. Deleting SORs from the 2000 census leaves a self-identified multiracial population for that year of 1.4 percent.

29. Data in Bureau of the Census 2011; quote from Saulny 2011a. The proportion of multiracials choosing Some Other Race + a named race declined dramatically, from 17.1 in the 2000 census to 8.1 percent in the 2009 ACS, suggesting that multiracialism is less frequently a stand-in for White Hispanics than when first introduced.

30. Population under eighteen: http://factfinder.census.gov/, table B01001G; immigrants: Tafoya, Johnson, and Hill 2004, 5.

31. Increase in states: Ferguson 2001; profitable: Whitaker 2002; liberating: quoted in Nagel 1995, 959.

32. 2001 survey: Massey et al. 2003; CILS: authors' analysis of Portes and Rumbaut 1991–2006. Californians: Lee 2004, 15; law students: Panter et al. 2009; thirty-one colleges and universities: Broh and Minicucci 2008. More generally, unlike several decades ago, the better-educated among Blacks, Whites, and Asians are more likely to intermarry (Fryer 2007). This analysis did not examine Hispanics.

33. Analysis for the authors by UCLA staff (Cooperative Institutional Research Program, various years). Data include only full-time students at four-year institutions and institutions with at least a 60 percent participation rate. Sample sizes range from 142,000 to 286,000 annually, across hundreds of institutions chosen by a complex stratification system. The analysis weighted the results to be representative of all first-year students.

34. Saulny 2011b, quoting Matthew Snipp.

35. Root 1993.

36. Add Health Blacks: Harris and Sim 2002, 619; Add Health Hispanics: Brown, Hitlin, and Elder 2006. Try to fit in: Jiménez 2004, 91, emphasis in original; see also Miville et al. 2005. Depends on what day it is: Rockquemore and Brunsma 2002, 48.

37. Just to add to the confusion, half of those who had said earlier in the survey that they considered themselves of mixed race agreed that they "always identify . . . [themselves] as a particular race." Only 28 percent of the same group "always identify [themselves] as mixed race" (Kaiser Family Foundation/Harvard University/*Washington Post* 2001).

38. Hitlin, Brown, and Elder 2006, 1305–6. See also Doyle and Kao 2007 and Panter et al. 2009.

39. Authors' analysis of Portes and Rumbaut 1991–2006; quote in Miville et al. 2005, 512, brackets and first two ellipses in original.

40. Malay food: Tariq 2010, 73; "passing as black": Khanna and Johnson 2010, 387, 394. Panter et al. 2009 suggest the same strategic action among law school applicants, but we have no direct evidence of why the law students who switched from monoracial minority to multiracial, when given the chance after admission, did so.

41. Beal et al. 2006; Beal to Jennifer Hochschild, e-mail communication, August 1, 2005.

42. Farley 2004; see also Roth 2005.

43. Metaphor for America: Kalb 2006; "I have the blues": Gates 2006.

44. Kaiser Family Foundation/Harvard University/*Washington Post* 2001; Pew Research Center and National Public Radio 2009. For a detailed analysis of the *Washington Post* survey, see Masuoka 2011.

45. Further analyses show that the proportions holding professional or managerial jobs, proportions with less than high school education, and proportions unemployed follow the same patterns.

46. Relative group positions are also destabilized when one looks at the reverse of the usual phenomenon—that is, when one pays closer attention to people who identify monoracially even if they have ancestors from different groups. "Medical forms that ask patients to identify a single race can alter patterns of racial health disparities because some multiracial adults identify with single-race

groups whose health experience is different from their own. . . . [In particular], multiracial adults who say 'white' best describes themselves are 38 percent more likely than single-race whites to report their health as fair or poor" (Rice University 2011, paraphrasing Bratter and Gorman 2011).

47. Office of Management and Budget 2000.

48. NAACP LDF: Holmes 2000; MAVIN: Matt Kelley, quoted in Moore 2001; policy analysts: Goldstein and Morning 2002.

49. Chapter 6 addresses whether this expansion simultaneously and inadvertently harms people who remain in disadvantaged groups.

50. Large public university: Levin 2007; young Californians: New American Media 2007a; New York City: Kasinitz et al. 2008.

51. New American Media 2007a; the survey excluded Whites. See also Kaiser Family Foundation/Harvard University/*Washington Post* 2001.

52. *New York Times* quoted in Hochschild, Weaver, and Powell 2008; Gallup Organization 2007.

53. Pew Research Center 1999; Gallup/CNN/*USA Today*, 2001. 2007 results: Gallup Organization 2007; 2009 results: Pew Research Center 2010b.

54. Louis Harris and Associates, February 1971; Nixon: Savage 2009; Kaiser Family Foundation/Harvard University/*Washington Post* 2001.

55. Survey of biracial couples: Kaiser Family Foundation/Harvard University/*Washington Post* 2001. Difficult relationships: Bratter and Eschbach 2006; Hohmann-Marriott and Amato 2008; Bratter and King 2008; Zhang and Van Hook 2009. Hostility: Sanchez and Bonam 2009; Miville et al. 2005.

56. 1995 survey: authors' analysis of *Newsweek* 1995; 2001 survey of multiracials: Kaiser Family Foundation/Harvard University/*Washington Post* 2001.

57. It is hard to know what to make of the results in the survey of interracial marriages; among other things, it is not reported whether spouses or children were present during the survey. Law school students: Panter et al. 2009; college students: Levin 2007.

58. Quillian and Redd 2009, 279. Doyle and Kao 2006 find similar patterns.

59. *Newsweek* 1995; Kaiser Family Foundation/Harvard University/*Washington Post* 2001; see also Masuoka 2008. Freshmen survey: authors' analysis of Massey and Charles 2006; IAT: Heiphetz et al. 2009.

Robert Putnam and David Campbell make a parallel argument about religious faith in the United States: although most Americans are deeply committed to their faith, religion provides a "civic glue, uniting rather than dividing"—unlike in, for example, Ireland, the Middle East, or India. Part of the reason is the high level of interfaith marriage over the past half century; approximately half of Americans are married to someone who grew up practicing a different religion, and that fact makes people highly tolerant of differences in religious belief (Putnam and Campbell 2010, 517).

60. Analysis for authors by staff at UCLA's Cooperative Institutional Research Program, various years.

61. DaCosta 2006, 199.

62. Models: Wallace 2008; see also Stevenson 2004 and Texiera 2005. Betty Crocker: Stanfield 1999.

63. Edwards, Caballero, and Puthussery 2010, 955, quoting the father of a multiracial child.

64. DaCosta 2006; Waterston 2004.

65. Lab experiments: Ho et al. 2011; for similar results, see Herman 2010. Views of Obama's race: Pew Research Center and National Public Radio 2009. See Peery and Bodenhausen 2008 for experimental evidence showing the same result.

On Obama's race: "The first black president! I'm proud to be able to say that. That's unless you screw up. And then it's going to be, 'What's up with that half-white guy?'" (Wanda Sykes, at 2009 White House Correspondents' Association dinner).

66. First quote in McClain 2004, 43; second is from Harris-Perry 2010. See also Edwards, Caballero, and Puthussery 2010, for example, p. 959.

67. *Philadelphia Tribune* quoted in Thornton 2009, 117; see also Squires 2007. Stalking horse: Gallagher 2006, 103; whitespace: Horton 2006, 117; choose blackness: Ibrahim 2009, 30. For a more analytic version of this argument, see Bean and Lee 2009.

Chapter 4. Genomics

The sources for the epigraphs are as follows: "Biology's Big Bang" 2007; J. Craig Venter, in Buerkle 2000, 1; Cohn 2006, 553. Barkley's response to Snoop Dog: "I'll just call you Whitey from now on." http://www.youtube.com/watch?v=Exz0yNdvksg.

1. Genome definition at http://www.genome.gov/11006943; genomics definition at WordNet® 3.0 n.d.

2. All quotations in this paragraph are from Zwart 2007. The internal quote is from International Human Genome Sequencing Consortium (IHGSC) 2004, 860.

3. For helpful timelines, see http://www.genomenewsnetwork.org/resources/timeline/timeline_overview.php and http://www.ornl.gov/sci/techresources/Human_Genome/project/timeline.shtml. Human Genome Project: Venter et al. 2001; International Human Genome Sequencing Consortium 2001.

4. Singularity Hub: Kleiner 2008; asymptoting to free: Altman 2008; Illumina: Henderson 2009.

5. *New York Times*: Wade 2009; see also Goldstein 2009, and Kraft and Hunter 2009. Rare diseases: Maugh 2009. Wailoo and Pemberton 2006 provide the recent history of a few such diseases. PricewaterhouseCoopers: Ray 2009.

6. Smith 2010.

7. "'My goal is to get the residents involved and tell them that together, we can make our environment clean,' Tika Bar-On, the city's chief veterinarian, told Reuters news agency," quoted in "DNA to Be Used in Dog Mess Fight" 2008. On sushi: Chinnici 2008.

8. "This kit analyzes your dog's DNA and identifies the breeds in its ancestry. It provides scientific confirmation of the physical characteristics, behavioral ten-

dencies, personality traits, and potential health risks your mixed-breed dog has inherited." http://www.skymall.com/shopping/detail.htm?pid=102908967&c.

9. "I like the mtDNA to be the same on both female lines of a horse. It just makes me happy." http://forums.about.com/n/pfx/forum.aspx?tsn=6&nav=mess ages&webtag=ab-horseracing&tid=17088.

10. DNA cruise ship: http://www.genepartner.com/. Poster: http://www.dna11 .com/gallery_portraits.asp; smartphone: http://www.dna11.com.

11. Lewontin 1972; Rosenberg et al. 2002. Quotes from Cavalli-Sforza, Menozzi, and Piazza 1994, 19.

12. National Human Genome Research Institute 2010b; American Anthropological Association 1998.

13. Social Science Research Council: Social Science Research Council c. 2005. Howard University: National Human Genome Center 2004; hunter-gatherers: Schuster et al. 2010, 943. Francis Collins: Collins and Mansoura 2001.

14. Jacobs 2008.

15. A cline is "a gradual change in an inherited characteristic across the geographic range of a species, usually correlated with an environmental transition such as altitude, temperature, or moisture. . . . In species in which the gene flow between adjacent populations is high, the cline is typically smooth, whereas in populations with restricted gene flow the cline usually occurs as a series of relatively abrupt changes from one group to the next" (*The American Heritage® Science Dictionary*).

16. Jacobs 2008; see also Price et al. 2008.

17. For a similar study of genetic diversity across Mexico, with a similar graph showing mixtures of four conventionally defined racial groups, see Silva-Zolezzi et al. 2009.

18. Quotes from Brewer 2006, 513, 514 (latter quote is attributed to Duster 2003).

19. MacArthur 2009.

20. Cavalli-Sforza, Menozzi, and Piazza 1994, 136; Fullwiley 2007, 4.

21. Quoted in Bliss 2012.

22. Li et al. 2009; "Racial Clues in Bowel Cancer Find" 2008; Bryc et al. 2010.

23. One medical anthropologist usefully distinguishes geneticists' use of "statistical race" from the earlier understanding of "typological race." The latter was the view of nineteenth- and early twentieth-century race scientists: "humans are divided into natural, discrete groups that are easily distinguished by their intrinsic properties revealed in appearance, temperament, morality, and intelligence." That view has been almost entirely discredited. Statistical race, in contrast, relies "on numerical data to represent population differences. The differences it identifies and represents as racial derive from the fact that people of common ancestry are more likely to share certain genes or alleles (versions of genes) than those who do not share ancestry. This is because to some extent both ancestry and genetic variation are geographically distributed" (Sankar 2008, 275, 276).

24. Justification for BiDil quoted in Duster 2005, 1050. Significant step: Kahn 2007; Asian patients: Payne 2008, 586, quoting from FDA Alert.

25. Iressa has been licensed for sale in some non-Asian countries, albeit in many cases with restrictions.

ostak et al. 2009, 79. Disadvantaged see genetics as more impor-
ent items: Shostak et al. 2009, quote on p. 88. See also Schnitt-
owell 2000.

overage: National Science Foundation 2010, table 7.2; newspa-
child and Sen 2011.

Closing the Net on Common Disease Genes" 2007, 821; Mary-
er Lectures on Human Values, Harvard University, November
g was the lead researcher in determining the role of BRCA1 and
ertain forms of breast cancer.

revolution: Kleiner 2008; *Genome Technology*, June 2010, 3;
rt 2007.

t Change

r the epigraphs are as follows: Powell and Roberts 2009, A14;
; de Tocqueville 1966 [1848], 441; Robinson 2010, 4.
93; Harris 2006.

nises underlie the idea of a collective memory. "Memory is elic-
nized in social contexts . . . remembering is as much social as
tive memories perform "culture work for those in the pres-
] is thought to advance and validate identities, fuel grievances
nemies), and give meaning and narrative coherence to individu-
ies" (Griffin 2004, 544). See also Griffin and Hargis 2008 and
dgers 2004 for citations to the extensive literature.

e and young adulthood: Griffin 2004, 545; William Ayres:
10.

Black respondents showed "evidence of a critical period effect,
having been mentioned primarily by those in their adolescent or
during the height of the civil rights movement in the 1950s and
arp decrease in mentions by those ages in later years" (Schuman
4, 246). Griffin 2004 shows a similar critical period effect.

nalysis of Schuman and Rodgers 2006.

ks to Howard Schuman for finding and providing to us the civil
pen-ended responses to the 1985 survey. They are deeply mov-
to Schuman and Amy Corning for sharing their results from the

munity is so diverse: Pew Research Center 2007c; no general
: Harris and Langer 2008.

r, those in the middle age groups held views between the oldest
ews in 2003 lay between those of 1987 and 2009 (authors' anal-
7, Pew Research Center 2003, 2009b; see also Pew Research
he central issue in analyzing changing attitudes over time is sort-
fects from period or age effects. Caren, Ghoshal, and Ribas 2011
d Dixon 2010 provide elegant demonstrations of how to do so.
2005, 158–59.
007.

26. FDA defends: Temple and Stockbridge 2007; passion against this paradigm: Yancy 2007.

27. Cohn 2006, 552, 553. See also Cooper, Kaufman, and Ward 2003 and
reply in Burchard et al. 2003; Tang et al. 2005; Ferdinand 2008.

28. Both quotes on opponents of race-specific medications are in Brody and
Hunt 2006, 557. Asian race: Payne 2008, 586.

29. Kahn 2005; Krieger 2005; "Symposium on Race, Pharmaceuticals, and
Medical Technology" 2008; Braun et al. 2007.

30. Jones and Goodman 2005.

31. Focus of future research: O'Malley 2005, 292; see also Tutton et al. 2008.
Pharmacogeneticist quoted in Tutton et al. 2008, 467–68.

32. Smith 2009.

33. All quotations from DNA Print Genomics n.d.

34. Newsome 2007.

35. Slaten 2009; Lamason et al. 2005; Sulem et al. 2007; Christine 2010.

36. Ossario and Duster 2005, 121.

37. Fullwiley 2008; see also Tallbear 2008.

38. Stump quoted in Willing 2006; Simpson quoted in Gibson 2007. Another
example: a woman with some European ancestry nevertheless became strongly
attached to the African heritage she found through genealogical genetics: "[I] am
also from the Temne Tribe of Sierra Leone. I am also in touch with a fellow
Tribesman. . . . It is so wonderful to talk to your fellow Tribesman. . . . We clicked
real quick. [I] can't explain it. He told me he's been waiting" (Nelson 2004).

39. Hitt: Hitt 2005; Villarreal: Lomax 2005; enthusiast quoted in Wright and
Roth 2011.

40. Quotes from Gates 2009, 10. Lexis-Nexis search: Hochschild and Sen
2010. This is far from a complete population, of course. There are five layers of
selection in this group of persons: who chose to take a DNA ancestry test; which
test(s) they took; whether they were profiled by a journalist; what they told the
journalist; and what the journalist reported and editor accepted. Nevertheless, it
is the broadest evidence we know of on who takes DNA ancestry tests and how
they respond to the results.

41. Nash 2004; Abu El-Haj 2004. Hirschman and Panther-Yates 2008 describe the yearning search for Celtic and Viking ancestry, and Wright and Roth
2011 show the same for Aboriginal or Native American ancestry.

42. Lei 2007.

43. Bryc et al. 2010; see also Tishkoff et al. 2009 and Zakharia 2009. For
ancestral mixture in groups other than Blacks, see Bonnen 2010; Eaaswarkhanth
et al. 2010; Kayser 2010; O'Rourke and Raff 2010; Majumder 2010; and Soares
2010.

44. Gillette quoted in Willing 2006; Lee quoted in Harmon 2006, 18; Kunte
Kinte: quoted in Kilgannon 2007.

45. All quotations in Daly 2005.

46. Hirschman and Panther-Yates 2008, 63; see also Tutton 2004. Royal et al.
2010 canvass the commercial genetic ancestry firms in the United States as of
2010 and give an excellent overview of the science and sociology of the
enterprise.

47. "Potential negative consequences": Shriver and Kittles 2008, 208, 209. For additional warnings, see Nordgren and Juengst 2009 and Skinner 2006. "Genetic essentialism": Nelson 2008; Nordgren and Juengst 2009, 157.

48. Rick Kittles quoted in Koerner 2005. Kittles continues, "there will be people who say they have 100 percent African blood. I can show them that they have significant European ancestry, too."

49. American Museum of Natural History: Mary Jeanne Kreek, in DeSalle and Yudell 2005, vii; Institute of Medicine: Hernandez and Blazer 2006, 1.

50. Early meta-analysis: Miles and Carey 1997, 207; delinquency: Guo, Roettger, and Cai 2008, 543. Scholars have also reported genetic bases for political orientations and levels of political participation (Alford, Funk, and Hibbing 2005; Fowler, Baker, and Dawes 2008).

51. Jews' genetic diseases: Cochran, Hardy, and Harpending 2006. Both quotes are in Wade 2005. *Science*: Mekel-Bobrov et al. 2005; Evans et al. 2005. Collins quoted in Regalado 2006. For reactions, see Hsu 2006.

52. Quotations from Duster 2005, 1051 and Kohn 2006. See also Kahn 2005 and "Symposium on Race, Pharmaceuticals, and Medical Technology" 2008. For an interesting discussion of the concern about racial attributions for criminal propensities, and possible solutions, see Koops and Schellekens 2006.

53. About twenty states and the federal government also maintain an Arrestee Index, which can include detained immigrants (Berson 2009; Gorman 2009).

54. "A DNA profile distills a person's complex genomic information down to a set of 26 numerical values, each characterizing the length of a certain repeated sequence of 'junk' DNA that differs from person to person. . . . Tabulating the number of repeats creates a unique identifier, a DNA 'fingerprint.'. . . These records include none of the health and biological data present in one's genome as a whole" (Seringhaus 2010).

55. CODIS is growing by the number of people convicted of a felony in the United States each year, minus those whose samples are already in the DNA database. Cass 2010a provides an excellent brief overview.

56. DNA can be used to verify family ties for immigration based on family reunification. In 2007, France mandated the use of DNA testing on immigrants with family already in France, but the law was scrapped in 2009 before its scheduled implementation (Carvajal 2007; "France Stops Controversial DNA Testing Law" 2009). The United States continues to use these tests through voluntary participation, although what "voluntary" means in some cases has been questioned (Aizenman 2006). Canada also enables the use of DNA blood tests to overcome delays related to immigration processing for certain family members (Citizenship and Immigration Canada 2010).

57. For a good, albeit hostile, explanation of familial searching, see Grimm 2007. On state law, see the three postings at http://www.scienceprogress.org/author/nram. On Grim Sleeper: Steinhauer 2010. Farahany 2009 provides an array of expert views, and Kaye 2009 argues for using offender databases for research.

58. Privacy concerns in Offender Index: Joh 2006; Lazer 2004; Henning 2009. Wilson 2008 provides a sensible middle-of-the-road strategy for negotiating the twin claims of privacy rights and pursuit of criminal justice, especially with re-

gard to surreptitious sampling 2008; Garrett and Neufeld 20

59. Henning 2009. At this with regard to the constitutio from arrestees (Cass 2010b).

60. Potential value: Lazer 2 Etzioni 2004.

61. On non-Anglo populati Racial disparity in partial mat

62. False positives: Scientifi Hoc Committee on Partial Ma cate is more succinct: expansio arrests is "building Jim Crow's 2004 and Duster 2004.

63. Grimm 2007, 1165–66.

64. Both quotes from Greely

65. National Research Coun

66. Gross et al. 2005, 547, 2008b.

67. Spokesperson: Zero Antl

68. Dawn Riggs, posting on 2006.

69. New genetic tests, and w ous; interested in human genom Egg and sperm: National Scienc 2006, 2008.

70. Papaioannou 2009; Dive

71. Deny coverage or job: Mi search Institute 2010c; Rothstei

72. "Defective genes," etc.: Di the employer conducted genetic case was quickly settled in favor Research Institute 2010a).

73. Hjörleifsson and his colle mation and neglect of uncertaint ise" (Hjörleifsson, árnason, and versely, is overestimation of risk either to benefits or to people's a

74. Trust scientists: National ing: Virginia Commonwealth Un

75. One 2001 question asked discrimination from genetic testi (46 percent) and no (43 percent whether respondents were thinkir crimination based on medical cor

76. Singer, Antonucci, and van

77. Whites accept genetic expl

and quoted in Sl tant, and subseq ker, Freese, and

78. Network per stories: Hoc

79. *Science*: " Claire King: Tar 15, 2006. Dr. Ki BRCA2 genes in

80. Midst of philosopher: Zv

Chapter 5. Coh

The sources Cooper 2009, 1

1. Kammen 1

2. Several pr ited by and org personal." Coll ent. . . . [Memo (and thus define als and collecti Schuman and R

3. Adolescer Magliocca 200

4. Both time [with civil right early adult year 1960s, with a s and Rodgers 2

5. Authors' a

6. Many tha rights–oriented ing. And thank 2009 survey.

7. Black cor Black experien

8. In each y and youngest; yses of Pew 1 Center 2007b). ing out cohort and Fullerton a

9. Rumbaut

10. Hattam

11. As Eugene Robinson puts it, "Just as it's wrong to ignore the overlapping pathologies of poverty, hopelessness, unemployment, crime, incarceration, and family disintegration that plague black Americans disproportionately, it's also wrong to deny that the rise of the black Mainstream is truly a great American success story—arguably, the greatest of all" (2010, 85).

12. Hacker and Pierson 2010; Bartels 2008; McCarty, Poole, and Rosenthal 2008.

13. Asian/Pacific Islanders' and Hispanics' share of the total number of bachelor's degrees conferred also rose during those three decades. But so did their share of the overall young adult population, so their relative gains are more ambiguous (National Center for Education Statistics 2010, table 285).

Another way to indicate the rise of non-Whites in higher education: in 1988 only 9 percent of undergraduates (both full- and part-time) were Black; by 2008 14 percent were, which is higher than Blacks' share of the population ("Undergraduate Diversity" 2010).

14. One young author describes education as "the great divide splitting black communities today. . . . The money and opportunities hitched to the education star have rocketed beyond some people's wildest dreams. This new prospect of opportunity is pulling the rug out from under conventions" (Womack 2010, 145–46). Fryer 2011 shows the power of high-quality schooling in reducing racial and ethnic income gaps.

15. National Assessment of Educational Progress 2010.

16. As we noted in chapter 1, one cannot say without a much more detailed analysis how much of this change is actual loss of income rather than changing self-definitions as Native American.

17. The figures in this paragraph are derived from the authors' analysis of the 1980 census and the 2009 ACS.

18. But note that poverty among young Asians also rose.

19. Among native-born young adults, Whites' median incomes rose by about $2,000 from $48,000, while Asians gained an astonishing $12,000 above their 1980 median income of $50,000. Latinos' median income began and ended the period at about $37,000. Native American and African American median incomes declined among young adults, from $36,000 to $33,000 for the former and from $35,000 to $31,000 for the latter.

20. Among native-born fifty-five- to sixty-four-year-olds with incomes at the 90th percentile of their group, Whites' and Indians' incomes both rose from 1980 to 2000 then held steady over the next decade (from very different bases, of course). Older native-born Blacks' and Asians' incomes at the 90th percentile rose until 2000, then declined slightly (again from very different bases). Unlike the other groups, older native-born Latinos' incomes at the 90th percentile continued to rise over the 2000s.

21. Acs and Zimmerman 2008. These analysts also show that being White was associated with a slight but statistically significant decrease in the likelihood of slipping into the bottom quintile in the later period, though not in the earlier one.

22. Isaacs 2007, 6–7.

23. Gillespie 2010 and Harris 2009a, 2009b provide several ways to rethink the old and increasingly unhelpful dichotomy between racial and deracialized

campaigns. Ford 2009b provides a way to sort out urgent racially inflected politics and policies from frivolous or inappropriate ones.

24. A new day: Pinckney 2009, 10; San Francisco: Anderson 2009; Boston City Council: Cooper 2009, 19.

25. Bakari Sellers: Ifill 2008; conservative candidate: Seelye 2010; Philadelphia, MI: Dawidoff 2010, 32.

26. The overall number of state legislators declined slightly over these two decades, so the proportion of state legislators who were Black rose from 5.8 to 8.5 percent.

27. Our thanks to Richard Hart of the Joint Center for Political and Economic Studies for providing these and other data on Black elected officials. These data are incomplete for mayors of small places in recent years, so the number of Black mayors is probably greater than reported here.

28. Many districts represented by Black elected officials have a majority of non-Anglos. When we examine districts with a majority of Latinos and Blacks in combination, we also see a decline in the proportion of Black elected officials representing majority Anglo districts.

29. Brady and Karlan 2009, 22; for comparisons of voters by age, period, and cohort, see Luks and Elms 2005 and Levine, Flanagan, and Gallay 2009.

30. Dawidoff 2010, 35. As we have noted several times, in our view the judge is mistaken; race is different for young people but not a non-issue.

31. Harris/ABC poll, 2008. In the ANES surveys of 1976, 2000, and 2008, more young than older White adults agreed that Blacks had too little and Whites too much influence. The proportions endorsing greater Black influence and the proportions preferring less White influence rose, especially among the youngest adults, from 1976 to 2000 (but fell a little by 2008).

32. Majority-white constituency: Ansolabehere, Persily, and Stewart 2010, 1409; percentage of White support: Clayton 2010; suburbanites, etc.: "Election Results" 2008; Kenski, Hardy, and Jamieson 2010.

33. Thirteen-percentage-point gap and young Black, Hispanic, and White voters: Pew Research Center 2008b; age was significantly related: Lewis-Beck 2009, 481. For more detail, see Fisher 2010; Ramakrishnan et al. 2009; and Tesler and Sears 2010. Racial resentment: Tesler and Sears 2010.

34. Obama's margin of victory: Lewis-Beck and Tien 2009; Campbell 2008; Hopkins 2009; Jacobson 2009. Early political experiences: Alwin and Krosnick 1991; Plutzner 2002; Abramowitz 2009; Stoker and Kent 2008.

35. Ansolabehere and Stewart 2009, emphasis added. See also Ansolabehere, Persily, and Stewart 2010 and Jackman and Vavreck 2010.

36. "Younger Voters" 2011.

37. Thanks to Mingus Mapps and Kim Williams for data on the race of mayors and urban populations over the past few decades. Bills passed: Griffin and Newman 2008 and Volden and Wiseman 2009; alienation: Cohen 2009.

38. Vote for incumbents: Hajnal 2007; Howell and Perry 2004. Al Sharpton quoted in Bai 2010.

39. Department of Justice 2003b. Fit the description: Powell 2006; Black teens: Crutchfield et al. 2009. Chicago: Skogan 2006; New York City police

stops: Fagan et al. 2010. See also Gabbidon and Higgins 2009 and Gelman et al. 2007.

A 2006 survey found, in contrast, that young adult Whites and Blacks had been arrested at the same rate, whereas older Blacks were more likely than older Whites to have been arrested (authors' analysis of Kaiser Family Foundation/ *Washington Post*/Harvard University 2006). We lack the evidence to explain the differences between the results in this survey and in others.

40. Pew Hispanic Center 2009a.

41. Treat Latinos fairly: Fraga et al. 2010; enforcing the law: Pew Hispanic Center 2009a; victims of crime: Bureau of Justice Statistics 2010c, 2010d.

42. The GSS asked about appropriate levels of government spending for "halting the rising crime rate" twenty-six times between 1973 and 2008; responses followed the same pattern. Two-thirds of White and three-fourths of Black respondents aged eighteen to twenty-nine consistently agreed that the United States spends too little; in only one year did more young White than Black adults perceive underspending. (The pattern and percentages are similar for Blacks and Whites aged forty-five and over.) This question, however, did not ask respondents how they would prefer to have funds devoted to crime control spent; one can imagine wide variation in their answers.

43. Overpolicing: Hagan, Shedd, and Payne 2005 and Hurwitz and Peffley 2005. Bad personal treatment: Skogan 2005; Rosenbaum et al. 2005; Weitzer and Tuch 2006; Peffley and Hurwitz 2010.

44. See also Danigelis, Hardy, and Cutler 2007.

45. There is no significant age difference in the use of "discrimination" or "lack of education" to explain Blacks' relative poverty.

46. For similar findings, including for young Hispanics, with a more sophisticated statistical treatment, see Hunt 2007.

47. Hollinger 2006.

48. Quote in Cornish 2007. Data on historically Black colleges and universities: National Center for Education Statistics 2004, 2010, tables 227 and 240, respectively.

Just over two-fifths of Latinos attended a Hispanic-serving institution in 2007, and Latino students are increasingly likely to attend such schools. But most have a much smaller proportion of Hispanic students compared with the traditional proportion of Black students at historically Black colleges and universities, and Hispanic-serving institutions lack the deep historical resonance of the Black institutions (National Center for Education Statistics 2004, table 238).

49. Morgan State University 2009. Spelling has been left as in the original notes.

Their elders can get frustrated when young adults don't place their own understanding of race at the center of identity. A middle-aged African American leading a community discussion on intergroup relations insisted to an observer that, despite the recent arrival of immigrants from several countries, "we're not trying to be all things to all people. . . . I want us to address race. Diversity is fine. All of those other things are fine, but what ails us is what we feel about the issue of race. We're going to set race right in the middle of the table and I don't care how you come in, that's what we're focused on." To his dismay, the fact that "I don't let the program go off in a thousand different directions . . . has made some people upset" (Walsh 2007, 91–92).

50. Kelderman 2010. In 2004, more than one-fourth of the grandchildren of Mexican immigrants in metropolitan Los Angeles saw their ethnic identity as "not too important" (Bean, Brown, and Bachmeier 2010, 263). In a survey three years later of late adolescent Californians (of whom barely a third were Anglos), 27 percent chose "music or fashion preference" as "the most important characteristic that defines [their] identity." Only 15 percent chose religion, ethnicity, or race (New American Media 2007a). There are no comparisons over time for these results, so we cannot be sure that they represent cohort change rather than the possibility that teens have not yet focused on their racial or ethnic identity.

51. Quote is in Sullivan 2010; it is from one of the authors of the study, which can be found at Wimmer and Lewis 2010.

52. Weaver 2008.

53. We found a similar pattern of results in 2008 (authors' analysis of data in Pew Research Center 2008a). There was no pattern by age for preferences to live in a heterogeneous religious or political community, or in a community with members of the same social and economic class, which suggests that the results are not only a function of social desirability. These questions were not asked earlier so we cannot compare results over time.

54. 2007 survey: Pew Research Center 2007c; 2008 survey: CBS Poll, November 2008.

55. Loc Dao, age sixteen, quoted in Howe and Strauss 2000, 221.

56. Cross-sectional data sometimes reinforce this evidence of change over time. In 2004 younger Blacks perceived less personal discrimination than did older ones, and in 2005 younger Blacks were more likely to describe interactions with Whites as "excellent" (2004: Jackson et al. 2004; 2005: Dawson, Harris-Lacewell, and Cohen n.d.). Results were similar in 2008 (Harris and Langer 2008). In 2007 young adult Mexicans and Puerto Ricans perceived less discrimination against Hispanics in schools than did older ones. In 2009 young adults at all educational levels were less likely to see widespread societal discrimination than were older ones (2007: Pew Hispanic Center 2007; 2009: Pew Research Center and National Public Radio 2010).

57. In 2004, for example, older Hispanics perceived less discrimination than did younger ones (Jackson et al. 2004), and in 2006 younger Hispanics (especially Puerto Ricans) were less optimistic about the gains from hard work (Fraga et al. 2010). Even though they saw less discrimination in schools and no differences in the workplace, young Latinos in 2007 were more likely than older ones to see discriminatory impediments to Latinos' ability to succeed in American society (Pew Hispanic Center 2007).

In 2005, younger Blacks and Whites were more likely than older ones to see severe economic inequality by race (Dawson, Harris-Lacewell, and Cohen n.d.). In 2008, young Black adults were more likely than older ones to agree that Blacks have achieved racial equality—but immediately thereafter they were more likely to report that Blacks in their community often experience racial discrimination (Harris and Langer 2008).

Cathy Cohen's survey of urban youth (2010) provides the most extensive grounds for disagreement with our thesis about the transformation of social relations among young adults. Her evidence points to one of the main blockages to creating a new racial order: class disparities among African Americans. We address that issue in chapter 6.

58. Non-Whites in different age groups: Frey 2010a; New York public school students: Stiefel, Schwartz, and Conger 2003. Montgomery County students: Gartner 2011; Brooklyn: Davidson 2010, 54. An official of New York's planning department explains how so much heterogeneity is manageable: "There's a gentleman's agreement. We don't have to love each other, but we tolerate each other" (Fessenden and Roberts 2011).

59. Frey 2010a, 2010d.

60. Cultural generation gap: Frey 2010b; Implicit Association Test: Nosek et al. 2007. These results hold even with controls for gender, ethnicity, and political orientation. "Press the button": Cave 2010. For more complete analyses, see Kasinitz et al. 2008; Kasinitz, Mollenkopf, and Waters 2004.

61. McBride 2009, 71–72; Robinson 2010, 188.

Chapter 6. Blockages to Racial Transformation

The sources for the epigraphs are as follows: Joseph 2009; "Hallowed Ground" 2010; Lamont, age seventeen, quoted in Brown-Dean c. 2010, 32. The last epigraph is reprinted by the kind permission of Yale University Press.

1. Kallen 1997 [1924], 116; Walzer 1992, 77; Sandel 1994, 1768.

2. Roediger 2008, B8; Joseph 2009.

3. Shelby 2005, 202.

4. Cohen 2010, 117–32. Young adults' overall agreement with both negative and positive assertions about American racial dynamics may indicate "diffuse support . . . [in which,] while young black Americans are disgusted with the current running of the nation's political system and are willing to withhold their specific support, they are conflicted about whether there is any hope, short of revolution, that can right the country's democracy" (132). An alternative explanation is response set, in which people tend to agree with a difficult or abstract survey item that is framed to offer only one viewpoint.

5. Mississippi Chinese: Loewen 1971; honorary Whites: Hacker 1992, 12, 13, 22.

6. First quote: Bratter 2007, 824; second quote: Gaines 2010, 204–5. Gaines provides no citations to such exponents. For other explorations of the question of whether immigrant assimilation is tantamount to becoming White, see Gerstle 1993; Hollinger 1993; Brodkin 1998; Jacobson 1998; Roediger 2005; and Ignatiev 1996, among others. A good review is Kolchin 2002.

7. Pawnee chief: quoted in Nabokov 1999, 38; Irish S.O.B.: Waters 1990, 54.

8. The Abandoned: Robinson 2010, 197; Lamont: Brown-Dean c. 2010, 32.

9. Discrimination and poverty: Tate 2010; "Who you gonna sock?": Terkel 1974, 2–3. Or as Peter Schmidt (pseudonym) told one of us, he wanted a college education "but there wasn't too much money around, and somehow or other,

when I really needed the big money behind me, it wasn't there" (Hochschild 1981, 143). His children are in the same situation. For a fuller discussion of the difficulties in seeing racial discrimination when it appears to be diminishing, see Hochschild 1995, part 4.

10. We focus on incarceration and its effects rather than severe disadvantage in arenas such as education or jobs for several reasons. First, we have already pointed to the impact of inequalities of schooling and income, and will address unemployment below. In addition, schooling for the worst off may be slowly improving while the trends in incarceration remain huge and unequivocal. On the necessity of school reform for the worst off (of all groups), see Hochschild and Scovronick 2003.

11. U.S. jails: Bureau of Justice Statistics, 2008, table 6.13.2008. United Kingdom jails: International Centre for Prison Studies 2010; some time during their life: Department of Justice 2003a.

12. Percent of different groups imprisoned: authors' calculations from Bureau of Justice Statistics 2010b, table 18. Most disadvantaged: Western and Pettit 2010.

13. Uggen, Manza, and Thompson 2006, 287, 290. Slightly older data permit comparisons with Hispanics also: as of 2001, the lifetime risk of incarceration was 6 percent for White men, 32 percent for Black men, and 17 percent for Latinos (Bureau of Justice Statistics 2003).

14. Nellis and King 2009. See also Doerner and Demuth 2010.

15. Job prospects for ex-felons: Western 2006 and Pager 2003; Black male dropouts: Western and Pettit 2010.

16. Marriage and divorce: Western 2006 and Western et al. 2004; health: Massoglia 2008, 290; behavior problems: Wildeman 2008; children with a parent in prison or jail: Western and Pettit 2010. Wildeman 2009 provides higher estimates of the number of children with an imprisoned parent, with the same racial disparity.

17. New York City: Fagan, West, and Holland 2003. Detroit and other cities: Urban Institute c. 2006; Braga, Papachristos, and Hureau 2009; Chicago: Sampson and Loeffler 2010, 23–24.

18. Families and neighborhoods: Burch 2008 and Clear 2007; reinforcing social process: Sampson and Loeffler 2010, 27. Feedback loop: Fagan, West, and Holland 2003; "imprisoned communities": Sampson and Loeffler 2010, 25.

19. Black men and 2008 election: Sentencing Project 2010b. In at least six states, 20 percent of Blacks could not cast a vote. Latinos: MALDEF 2003.

20. Michelle Alexander (2010) points out that more Black men have lost the franchise today than in 1870, the year the Fifteenth Amendment enfranchised Black citizens. This is mainly a rhetorical point, of course, since the Black male population has grown dramatically over the past 150 years—but it does suggest the extent of felon disenfranchisement.

21. Most states in the MALDEF study of Latino felon disenfranchisement have liberalized their laws; Arizona and California, however, are crucial exceptions. Bar felons from voting for life: Sentencing Project 2010a.

22. Although this point is disputed, we find the evidence compelling that links

higher Black crime rates to isolated neighborhoods with concentrated poverty, poor schools, and high levels of joblessness. Those conditions act as a "social multiplier" on crime. Among others, see Chiricos 1987 and Glaeser, Sacerdote, and Scheinkman 2003. Careful analyses of the relation between commission of crime and incarceration find the links to be weak, complex, and less strong than they used to be (Tonry and Melewski 2008; Sampson and Loeffler 2010; Western and Pettit 2010).

23. Drug arrests: Beckett, Nyrop, and Pfingst 2006; drug and weapons offenses: Mauer 2006.

24. Gelman, Fagan, and Kiss 2007, 815. As the authors point out, the data were from 1999; since then the New York City Police Department has established an "extensive" system for accurate reporting of stops and continuous monitoring of racial proportionality. Recent reports come to opposite conclusions on its effect (Ridgeway 2007; Fagan 2010). See also Ayres and Borowsky 2008.

25. Demuth and Steffensmeier 2004; McDougall et al. 2003; Engen et al. 2003.

26. Quotations from Hout 1984, 308 and Hogan and Featherman 1978, 101. Unless otherwise noted, throughout this discussion of wealth, "White" refers to non-Hispanic Whites, and "non-Whites" refers to everyone else combined. A few of the studies do separate Blacks from other non-Whites.

27. Median: Masterson, Zacharias, and Wolff 2009; mean: Masterson, Wolff, and Zacharias 2009. The census bureau's measure of extended income shows similar results. The mean values of non-White to White household income rose from 0.60 in 1959 to 0.76 in 2004. The median values were, respectively, 0.57 and 0.74 (Masterson, Wolff, and Zacharias 2009).

The LIMEW includes not only median or mean income but also income from wealth (including imputed rent on owner-occupied housing), cash and noncash transfers, public consumption such as the cost of schooling, and household production.

28. Authors' calculations from Survey of Consumer Finances 2009.

29. For different measures of income and wealth and different analytic logics but the same basic findings, see Scholz and Levine 2004 and Elmelech 2008.

Being an immigrant is not strongly associated with wealth holding. Overall, when race and years of schooling are controlled, immigration status has no statistically significant relationship with net worth or the probability of having a positive net worth. A more fine-grained analysis shows that immigrant Hispanics have significantly lower net worth than native-born Hispanics—hardly a surprise—and that immigrant Asians perhaps have lower net worth than native-born Asians ($p < .10$) (Hao 2007).

30. High-risk assets: Terrell 1971; Straight 2002; Hanna and Wang 2007. Buying first house: Dowell Myers, communication with authors, October 31, 2010.

31. Black or Latino neighborhoods: Squires 2009; Been, Ellen, and Madar 2009; Rugh and Massey 2010; Lee, Rosentraub, and Kobie 2010. Unfavorable mortgage terms: Pew Hispanic Center 2009b.

32. Sen 2010. When she relaxed the assumption that borrowers went to the same lenders, Sen found much greater disparities between Black and White bor-

rowers and somewhat greater disparities between Hispanic and White borrowers. She again found that Asians were offered fewer subprime mortgages than were Whites. Thus overall, Blacks and Hispanics were disadvantaged, and Asians advantaged, compared with White mortgage seekers.

33. Federal Reserve report: Haughwout, Mayer, and Tracy 2009, quote on p. 53. Pattern of foreclosures: Immergluck 2010.

34. Bureau of Labor Statistics 2010.

35. Joint Economic Committee 2010, table 1.

36. Note, nonetheless, that although much smaller proportions of Blacks and Latinos received wealth transfers between 1989 and 2007 and the absolute value of the transfers was lower, the mean and median present values of those transfers rose much more over the period for Blacks than for Whites (for Hispanics, the change over time differed depending on whether one considers mean or median). In other words, there are fewer well-off Blacks than Whites and they have less wealth, but the growth in disparity between the best-off Blacks and all others was greater in the early 2000s than was the comparable growth among Whites (Wolff and Gittleman 2011).

37. "There is at once a pervasive invisibility that is a shared experience among Asian Americans at all levels of organizations, and leadership invisibility at the senior levels of organizations. . . . [T]his invisibility . . . exists across local and federal governments, private sector, and educational institutions" (Thatchenkery and Sugiyama 2011, 1).

38. CBS News, September 13, 2001, September 20, 2001, January 5, 2002, September 2, 2002; National Conference for Community and Justice, January 13, 2005; CBS News, August 17, 2006, August 11, 2006.

About a fifth of Muslims in the United States are African American (Pew Research Center 2007a). However, as this wording suggests, almost all survey questions implicitly equate Muslims with immigrants from the Middle East. We found no questions later than 1996 in the Roper Center's iPOLL database that include both the term "Islam" (or "Muslim") and the term "Black" (or "Afro-American" or "African American"). Unless otherwise noted, our discussion of Muslims or Islam refers to recent immigrants or to descendants of immigrants from the Middle East.

39. Same legal rights: National Public Radio/Kaiser Foundation/Harvard University, August 9, 2002; closely monitoring the whereabouts: *Newsweek* Poll, September 20, 2001; scrutinizing more closely: *Los Angeles Times,* November 10, 2001; mass detentions: *Newsweek* Poll, July 11, 2007.

40. In a 2002 Fox News poll, a slight majority supported "sealing borders and stopping all immigration of young Arab men while the search for terrorists is conducted." This response may, however, reflect general dismissal of civil liberties rather than a specific issue of Arabs, since only a slightly smaller proportion of respondents supported stopping all (unspecified) immigration to search for terrorists (Fox News/Opinion Dynamics, May 14, 2002). Given how unusual these results are, furthermore, one must be attentive to house effects of the survey sponsor or organization.

A more focused question generated more enthusiasm for security over civil liberties. In 2010, seven in ten Americans favored "special, more intensive security checks before boarding U.S. flights" for "airline passengers who fit the profile of terrorists based on their age, ethnicity, or gender" (Gallup Organization 2010). Using a 2004 survey, Schildkraut 2009 provides a nuanced analysis of support for ethnic profiling. Davis 2007 provides the broadest analysis.

41. Loyal to the United States: National Public Radio/Harvard University/Kaiser Family Foundation, October 31, 2001; support American traditions: Fox News/Opinion Dynamics Poll, September 12, 2006. More agreed with the same question about unspecified "immigrants."

42. Headscarves in class: Princeton Survey Research Associates International/*Newsweek* Poll, October 31, 2001. More peaceable: *Newsweek* Poll, July 11, 2007; face discrimination: Pew Research Center 2009a.

43. Schafer and Shaw 2009.

44. CNN/Opinion Research Corporation Poll, June 22–24, 2007. This was perhaps an unusually bloodthirsty sample: 6 percent agreed that (and another 4 percent couldn't decide whether) they themselves would be "willing to kill another person in order to uphold a religious belief or advance a religious cause."

The proportion who concur that Islam encourages violence more than do other religions has varied unsystematically between 35 and 45 percent since 2002 (Pew Forum on Religion and Public Life 2010).

45. Pew Forum, August 1, 2007. In the same exercise with regard to Mormons, 27 percent chose negative and 23 percent chose positive terms—hardly a strong endorsement but not quite as much hostility.

Knowledge about Islam is low but growing. In a series of polls since 2002, the proportion of Americans answering two factual questions correctly rose from a third to two-fifths (Pew Research Center 2009a). See also ABC News/*Washington Post* Poll, 2006.

46. Pew Forum on Religion and Public Life 2010. In 2007, almost the same proportions were unfavorable toward Mormons as toward American Muslims, and many more—about half of the respondents—disapproved of atheists (Pew, August 2007).

47. ABC News/*Washington Post* Poll, August 2010; see also Schafer and Shaw 2009.

48. Some hostile feelings: ABC News/*Washington Post* Poll, 2006; know a Muslim personally: Pew Research Center 2009a. Three-quarters of non-Hispanic Whites supported profiling in air travel, compared with just over three-fifths of non-Whites (Gallup Organization 2010).

49. Pew Weekly News Interest Index Poll, October 12–15, 2010; news coverage: Pew Research Center 2010a; holds up with controls: Wike and Grim 2010. ANES and Pew surveys: Kalkan, Layman, and Uslaner 2009.

50. Willingness to vote: Pew Forum on Religion & Public Life/Pew Research Center Survey, June 24–July 8, 2003; *Los Angeles Times*/Bloomberg Poll, June 24–26, 2007. Overclaim support for women and Blacks: Hopkins 2009.

51. Pew Research Center 2007a; Baker et al. 2009.

52. Need thick skins: Vitello 2010: first quote from author, second from executive director of Muslim American Society. Perceive discrimination: Public Agenda and Carnegie Corporation of the United States 2009, 34.

53. Scared for our safety: Cainkar 2009, 29; EEOC: Greenhouse 2010; young adults: Pew Research Center 2007a.

54. George W. Bush: "Bush" 2007; House of Representatives: "Ramadan Resolution" 2007; Obama's administration: Elliott 2010, A1. Los Angeles police: Goodstein 2011.

55. Quoted in Gardner 2010.

56. Massey 2007, 157, 150.

57. Children's development: Yoshikawa et al. 2008; Yoshikawa 2011. Quotation is in Gonzales 2009, 419.

58. U.S.-born children: Passel and Taylor 2010. For the long-term impact of these complex family structures, see Brown et al. 2011 and Bean et al. 2011. Teenaged Guatemalan: Menjivar and Abrego 2009, 178–79.

59. 2006 survey: Fox News/Opinion Dynamics Poll, April 4–5, 2006; survey of immigrants: Public Agenda and Carnegie Corporation of the United States 2009.

60. Vigdor 2009; White and Glick 2009.

61. Riccardi 2010.

62. Commonwealth of Virginia, Office of the Attorney General 2010.

63. See, for example, Associated Press/Univision/GfK Poll, May 7–11, 2010; Field Poll, July 16, 2010; *The Economist*/YouGov poll, May 1–4, 2010; CNN Poll, May 21–23, 2010, and July 16–21, 2010; *Los Angeles Times*, May 12, 2010; *New York Times*, May 29, 2010; and NBC News Survey, May 20–23, 2010. Bishop (2010) issues useful cautions about whether these views are substantively meaningful.

64. Frey 2010c.

65. Treading warily: Kilgore 2010; reaction against Proposition 187: Bowler, Nicholson, and Segura 2006; Republicans in California: Watanabe et al. 2010.

Economic costs—from legal defense of SB 1070, boycotts, and loss of low-paid workers—also generate resistance to similar laws in other states and to further penalties against unauthorized immigrants in Arizona. As newspaper headlines put it, "Arizona, Bowing to Business, Softens Stand on Immigration" (Oppel 2011) and "More States Toss Costly Immigration Legislation in Final Days of Session" (Hoy 2011).

66. College senior: Cave 2010; 2006 immigrant marches: Cohen-Marks, Sanchez, and Nuño 2009.

67. The polls were conducted by Pew Research Center 2007b, 2007c; *Newsweek,* January 2009; Pew Research Center 2009c; CBS/*New York Times*, April 2009; ABC News/*Washington Post*, April 2009; Gallup Poll, July 2009; NBC News/*Wall Street Journal*, May 2010; and NBC News/MSNBC/Telemundo, May 2010.

An analysis of six pooled surveys from the Public Policy Institute of California found that even with a long string of controls, age was positively related to agreement that immigration is a burden to California (Newman, Hartman, and Taber forthcoming).

68. Hoy 2010; see Cave 2010 for the same pattern in a *New York Times* poll.

69. SB 1070: Hispanics of all ages opposed the law. Results were not reported

for Blacks and Asians by age (Greenberg Quinlan Rosner and American Viewpoint 2010). On quality of life: Field Poll, 2011.

Chapter 7. The Future of the American Racial Order

The sources for the epigraphs are as follows: Robinson 2010, 159; Chafets 2010, 41; Cohen 2010, 113; Doyle 2005 [1891], 107–8.

1. Quotations and paraphrases are from, respectively, Massey 2007, 150; Alba 2009, 16; Joseph 2009; Cohen 2009; Cohen 2010, 1, 2; Patterson 2009.

2. The same is true for Europeans: see Alba 2005.

3. Obama's race: Obama 2007; Cornel West: Hedges 2011, 2; Black community: Brown 2009, 298.

4. Haney López 2006, B8.

5. See further examples of imaginative self-definition in the survey of 45,000 college students described in chapter 1. Sense of solidarity: Harris 2009b, 43.

6. Klor de Alva, Shorris, and West 1998, 184.

7. Tejanos: Chafets 2010, 42; Detroit's saviors: Ghosh 2010; American identity: Shyrock 2008, 200; see also other chapters in the same volume.

8. Tesler and Sears 2010; King and Smith 2011; Sugrue 2010.

9. Bartels 2008; Hacker and Pierson 2010; McCarty, Poole, and Rosenthal 2008.

10. Katznelson 2005.

11. Bare Left 2010.

12. Hotline OnCall 2010, quoting a Republican pollster.

13. Tavernise and Grebeloff 2010.

14. A student explains, "because it is an overtly religious place, it's not strange or weird to care about your religion here, to pray and make God a priority. They have the same values we do." Some Catholic universities are "unsure how to adapt," while others are "creating prayer rooms . . . and hiring Islamic chaplains" (Wan 2010).

15. Quoted in Jacobson 2010, 26.

16. Myrdal 1944, 1022.

17. Dickerson 2009, 46, 47. A young filmmaker similarly "used to be obsessed with race. I'm more obsessed with class now" (Lim 2009). See Hollinger 2008 and Ford 2009a for excellent discussions of intersections between race and class in the Obama era.

18. All quotations from Alba 2009, 92, 19, 119, 225.

19. Myers 2007, xiii.

20. Tienda and Mitchell 2006, 14, quoted in Myers 2007.

21. Myers 2007, 214.

22. By Roland Fryer's calculations, as of the mid-2000s, "black men earn 39.4% less than white men; black women earn 13.1% less than white women. Accounting for educational achievement drastically reduces these inequalities—39.4% to 10.9% for black men and 13.1% *lower* than whites to 12.7% *higher* for black women. . . . Hispanic men earn 14.8% less than whites in the

raw data ... which reduces to 3.9% more than whites when we account for AFQT [a standard measure of educational achievement]. ... Hispanic women earn six percent less than white women ... without accounting for achievement. Adding controls for AFQT, Hispanic women earn sixteen percent *more* than comparable white women" (Fryer 2011, 859). In short, schooling is crucial, as are policies to reduce the racial achievement gap. In the same chapter, Fryer canvasses programs that have shown success in that endeavor.

23. Brownstein 2010.

24. Census of Population 1970, http://www.census.gov/.

25. Logan, Oh, and Darrah 2009. The opposite pattern held for immigrant Asians and Blacks and their descendants; there was no clear pattern for foreign-born Whites and descendants of White immigrants.

26. Leveling off: Bureau of Justice Statistics 2010a; Pew Center on the States 2010. Rehabilitative programs: Abramsky 2010; Kleiman 2010; Weisberg and Petersillia 2010; Braga, Piehl, and Hureau 2009. New York: "Rough Justice" 2010.

27. "Rough Justice" 2010.

28. Wilson 2009, 141.

References

Abdulrahim, Raja. 2009. "Students Push UC to Expand Terms of Ethnic Identification." *Los Angeles Times*, March 31.

Abramowitz, Alan. 2009. "Barack Obama and the Transformation of the American Electorate." http://papers.ssrn.com.

Abramsky, Sasha. 2010. "Is This the End of the War on Crime?" *The Nation*, July 5, pp. 11–17.

Abu El-Haj, Nadia. 2004. *"A Tool to Recover Past Histories": Genealogy and Identity after the Genome.* Princeton, NJ: Institute for Advanced Study.

Acs, Gregory, and Seth Zimmerman. 2008. *U.S. Intergenerational Economic Mobility from 1984 to 2004: Trends and Implications.* Washington, DC: Pew Charitable Trust.

Aizenman, N. C. 2006. "DNA Testing a Mixed Bag for Immigrants." *Washington Post*, October 25.

Alba, Richard. 2005. "Bright vs. Blurred Boundaries: Second-Generation Assimilation and Exclusion in France, Germany, and the United States." *Ethnic and Racial Studies* 28 (1): 20–49.

———. 2009. *Blurring the Color Line: The New Chance for a More Integrated America.* Cambridge, MA: Harvard University Press.

Alexander, Michelle. 2010. *The New Jim Crow: Mass Incarceration in the Age of Colorblindness.* New York: The New Press.

Alford, John, Carolyn Funk, and John Hibbing. 2005. "Are Political Orientations Genetically Transmitted?" *American Political Science Review* 99 (2): 153–67.

Altman, Russ. 2008. "Genotyping Cost Is Asymptoting to Free." *Building Confidence*, October 8. http://rbaltman.wordpress.com/2008/10/08/genotyping-cost -is-asymptoting-to-free/.

Alwin, Duane, and Jon Krosnick. 1991. "Aging, Cohorts, and the Stability of Sociopolitical Orientations over the Life Span." *American Journal of Sociology* 97 (1): 169–95.

American Anthropological Association. 1998. "Statement on 'Race.'" *American Anthropologist* 100: 712–13.

Anderson, Tomika. 2009. "Leaders of the New School." *Essence* 39 (10): 106.

Ansolabehere, Stephen, and Charles Stewart III. 2009. "Amazing Race: How Post-Racial Was Obama's Victory?" *Boston Review*, January/February. http:// www.bostonreview.net/BR34.1/ansolabehere_steward.php.

Ansolabehere, Stephen, Nathaniel Persily, and Charles Stewart III. 2010. "Race, Region, and Vote Choice in the 2008 Election: Implications for the Future of the Voting Rights Act." *Harvard Law Review* 123 (6): 1386–1436.

Aronson, Jay, and Simon Cole. 2009. "Science and the Death Penalty: DNA, Innocence, and the Debate over Capital Punishment in the United States." *Law & Social Inquiry* 34 (3): 603–33.

Association of MultiEthnic Americans. 2001. "AMEA Responds to Multiracial

Census Data." March 12. http://www.ameasite.org/census/031201censusdata
.asp.

Ayres, Ian, and Jonathan Borowsky. 2008. *A Study of Racially Disparate Outcomes in the Los Angeles Police Department.* Prepared for ACLU of Southern
California. http://islandia.law.yale.edu/ayres/Ayres%20LAPD%20Report.pdf.

Bada, Xóchitl, et al. 2010. *Context Matters: Latino Immigrant Civic Engagement
in Nine U.S. Cities.* Washington, DC: Woodrow Wilson International Center
for Scholars.

Bai, Matt. 2010. "Still Too Hot to Touch." *New York Times,* July 25, pp. Wk1, 4.

Baker, Wayne, et al. 2009. *Citizenship and Crisis: Arab Detroit after 9/11.* New
York: Russell Sage Foundation.

Bare Left. 2010. "Phoenix Suns Stand Up for Civil Liberties." *Daily Kos,* May 5.
http://www.dailykos.com/story/2010/05/05/863738/-Phoenix-Suns-stand
-up-for-civil-liberties.

Bartels, Larry. 2008. *Unequal Democracy: The Political Economy of the New
Gilded Age.* Princeton, NJ: Princeton University Press.

Beal, Anne, et al. 2006. "The Changing Face of Race: Risk Factors for Neonatal
Hyperbilirubinemia." *Pediatrics* 117 (5): 1618–25.

Bean, Frank, and Jennifer Lee. 2009. "Plus ça Change. . .? Multiraciality and the
Dynamics of Race Relations in the United States." *Journal of Social Issues* 65
(1): 205–19.

Bean, Frank, Susan Brown, and James Bachmeier. 2010. "Comparative Integration Contexts and Mexican Immigrant-Group Incorporation in the United
States." In *Managing Ethnic Diversity after 9/11: Integration, Security, and
Civil Liberties in Transatlantic Perspective,* ed. Ariane Chebel d'Appollonia
and Simon Reich. New Brunswick, NJ: Rutgers University Press. 253–75.

Bean, Frank, et al. 2011. "The Educational Legacy of Unauthorized Migration:
Comparisons across U.S.-Immigrant Groups in How Parents' Status Affects
Their Offspring." *International Migration Review* 45(2): 348–385.

Beckett, Katherine, Kris Nyrop, and Lori Pfingst. 2006. "Race, Drugs, and Policing: Understanding Disparities in Drug Delivery Arrests." *Criminology* 44 (1):
105–37.

Been, Vicki, Ingrid Ellen, and Josiah Madar. 2009. "The High Cost of Segregation: Exploring Racial Disparities in High Cost Lending." *Fordham Urban
Law Journal* 36 (1): 361–94.

Bennett, Claudette. 2003. "Exploring the Consistency of Race Reporting in Census 2000 and the Census Quality Survey." Paper presented at the annual meeting of the American Statistical Association, San Francisco, August 3–7.

Berlin, Ira. 1998. *Many Thousands Gone: The First Two Centuries of Slavery in
North America.* Cambridge, MA: Harvard University Press.

Berson, Sarah. 2009. "Debating DNA Collection." *National Institute of Justice
Journal* 264. http://www.nij.gov/journals/264/debating-DNA.htm.

"Biology's Big Bang." 2007. *The Economist,* June 14, p. 13.

Bishop, George. 2010. "How Immigration Poll Majorities Are Born in the USA."
PollSkeptics Report, May 28. http://www.stinkyjournalism.org/latest-journal
ism-news-updates-184.php.

"Black Segregation in US Drops to Lowest in Century." 2010. *Huffington Post,*

December 14. http://www.huffingtonpost.com/2010/12/14/black-segregation -in-us-d_n_796357.html.

Bliss, Catherine. 2012. *Race Decoded: The Genomic Fight for Social Justice.* Palo Alto, CA: Stanford University Press.

Bonnen, Penelope, et al. 2010. "European Admixture on the Micronesian Island of Kosrae: Lessons from Complete Genetic Information." *European Journal of Human Genetics* 18: 309–16.

Bowler, Shaun, Stephen Nicholson, and Gary Segura. 2006. "Earthquakes and Aftershocks: Race, Direct Democracy, and Partisan Change." *American Journal of Political Science* 50 (1): 146–59.

Brady, David, and Pamela Karlan. 2009. "Reflection on the Election and Its Consequences." *Bulletin of American Academy of Arts and Sciences* (spring): 15–22.

Braga, Anthony, Andrew Papachristos, and David Hureau. 2009. "The Concentration and Stability of Gun Violence at Micro Places in Boston, 1980–2008." *Journal of Quantitative Criminology* 26 (1): 33–53.

Braga, Anthony, Anne Piehl, and David Hureau. 2009. "Controlling Violent Offenders Released to the Community: An Evaluation of the Boston Reentry Initiative." *Journal of Research in Crime and Delinquency* 46 (4): 411–36.

Bratter, Jenifer. 2007. "Will 'Multiracial' Survive to the Next Generation?: The Racial Classification of Children of Multiracial Parents." *Social Forces* 86 (2): 821–49.

Bratter, Jenifer, and Karl Eschbach. 2006. "'What about the Couple?' Interracial Marriage and Psychological Distress." *Social Science Research* 35 (4): 1025–47.

Bratter, Jenifer, and Bridget Gorman. 2011. "Does Multiracial Matter? A Study of Racial Disparities in Self-Rated Health." *Demography* 48 (1) : 127–52.

Bratter, Jenifer, and Rosalind King. 2008. "'But Will It Last?': Marital Instability among Interracial and Same-Race Couples." *Family Relations* 57 (2): 160–71.

Braun, Lundy, et al. 2007. "Racial Categories in Medical Practice: How Useful Are They?" *PLoS Medicine* 4 (9): 1423–28.

Brewer, Rose. 2006. "Thinking Critically about Race and Genetics." *Journal of Law, Medicine, and Ethics* 34 (3): 513–19.

Brodkin, Karen. 1998. *How Jews Became White Folk: And What That Says about Race in America.* New Brunswick, NJ: Rutgers University Press.

Brody, Howard, and Linda Hunt. 2006. "BiDil: Assessing a Race-Based Pharmaceutical." *Annals of Family Medicine* 4 (6): 556–60.

Broh, C. Anthony, and Stephen Minicucci. 2008. "Racial Identity and Government Classification: A Better Solution." Paper presented at the annual meeting of the Association for Institutional Research, Seattle, May 28.

Brown, J. Scott, Steven Hitlin, and Glen Elder Jr. 2006. "The Greater Complexity of Lived Race: An Extension of Harris and Sim." *Social Science Quarterly* 87 (2): 411–31.

Brown, Kevin. 2009. "Now Is the Appropriate Time for Selective Higher Education Programs to Collect Racial and Ethnic Data on Its Black Applicants and Students." *Thurgood Marshall Law Review* 34: 287–321.

Brown, Susan, et al. 2011. "Legalization and Naturalization Trajectories among Mexican Immigrants and Their Implications for the Second Generation." In *The Next Generation: Immigrant Youth in a Comparative Perspective*, ed. Richard Alba and Mary Waters. New York: New York University Press. 31–45.

Brown, Ursula. 2001. *The Interracial Experience: Growing up Black/White Racially Mixed in the United States*. Westport, CT: Praeger.

Brown-Dean, Khalilah. Forthcoming. *Once Convicted, Forever Doomed: Punishment, Citizenship, and Civil Death*. New Haven, CT: Yale University Press.

Browning, Rufus, Dale Rogers Marshall, and David Tabb. 1984. *Protest Is Not Enough: The Struggle of Blacks and Hispanics for Equality in Urban Politics*. Berkeley, CA: University of California Press.

Brownstein, Ronald. 2010. "The Gray and the Brown: The Generational Mismatch." *National Journal*, July 24. http://www.nationaljournal.com/magazine/the-gray-and-the-brown-the-generational-mismatch-20100724.

Bryc, Katarzyna, et al. 2010. "Genome-Wide Patterns of Population Structure and Admixture in West Africans and African Americans." *PNAS* 107 (2): 786–91.

Buerkle, Tom. 2000. "The 'Wondrous Map' of Gene Data: Historic Moment for Humanity's Blueprint." *New York Times*, June 27, p. 1.

Buescher, Paul, Ziya Gizlice, and Kathleen Jones-Vessey. 2005. "Discrepancies between Published Data on Racial Classification and Self-Reported Race: Evidence from the 2002 North Carolina Live Birth Records." *Public Health Reports* 120 (4): 393–98.

Burch, Traci. 2008. "Trading Democracy for Justice? The Spillover Effects of Imprisonment on Neighborhood Voter Participation." Unpublished paper, Northwestern University, Department of Political Science.

Burchard, Esteban, et al. 2003. "The Importance of Race and Ethnic Background in Biomedical Research and Clinical Practice." *New England Journal of Medicine* 348 (12): 1170–75.

Bureau of Consular Affairs. 2010a. *Frequently Asked Questions—Visa Applicants from State Sponsors of Terrorism Countries*. Washington, DC: Department of State.

———. 2010b. *Safety & Security of U.S. Borders/Biometrics*. Washington, DC: Department of State.

Bureau of Justice Statistics. 2003. *Prevalence of Imprisonment in the U.S. Population, 1974–2001*. Washington, DC: Department of Justice.

———. 2010a. *Correctional Populations in the United States, 2009*. Washington, DC: Department of Justice.

———. 2010b. *Prison Inmates at Midyear 2009—Statistical Tables*. Washington, DC: Department of Justice.

———. 2010c. *Sourcebook of Criminal Justice Statistics*. Washington, DC: Department of Justice.

———. 2010d. "Victims: Key Facts at a Glance." http://bjs.ojp.usdoj.gov/content/glance/race.cfm.

Bureau of Labor Statistics. 2010. *Labor Force Statistics from the Current Population Survey*. Washington, DC: Department of Labor.

Bureau of the Census. 2001. *The Two or More Races Population: 2000.* Washington, DC: Department of Commerce.

———. 2002. *Measuring America: The Decennial Censuses from 1790 to 2000.* Washington, DC: Department of Commerce.

———. 2003. *Married-Couple and Unmarried-Partner Households: 2000.* Washington, DC: Department of Commerce.

———. 2009. *Annual Estimates of the Resident Population by Sex, Race, and Hispanic Origin for the United States: April 1, 2000 to July 1, 2008.* http://www.census.gov/popest/national/asrh/NC-EST2008-srh.html.

———. 2011. *Overview of Race and Hispanic Origin, 2010.* Washington, DC: Department of Commerce.

"Bush: All Religions Pray to 'Same God.'" 2007. *World Net Daily,* October 7. http://www.wnd.com/?pageId=43906.

Bush, Melanie. 2002. "Breaking the Code of Good Intentions: Everyday Forms of Whiteness." *Souls* 4 (4): 25–44.

Cainkar, Louise. 2009. *Homeland Insecurity: The Arab American and Muslim American Experience after 9/11.* New York: Russell Sage Foundation.

Camarota, Steven. 2010. "Census: Population up 27 Million in Just 10 Years." *Center for Immigration Studies News.* http://cis.org/2010CensusPopulation.

Campbell, James. 2008. "An Exceptional Election: Performance, Values, and Crisis in the 2008 Presidential Election." *The Forum* 6 (4): article 7. http://www.bepress.com/forum/vol6/iss4/art7.

Caren, Neal, Raj Ghoshal, and Vanesa Ribas. 2011. "A Social Movement Generation: Cohort and Period Trends in Protest Attendance and Petition Signing." *American Sociological Review* 76 (1): 125–51.

Carew, Emma. 2010. "Minnesota Colleges Find Diverse Ways to Say 'Welcome.'" *Chronicle of Higher Education,* January 17, pp. A1, A26.

Carvajal, Doreen. 2007. "French Council Approves DNA Testing for Immigrants." *New York Times,* November 15.

Cass, James. 2010a. "The Cost of Making Crime Not Pay: Obama, CODIS and Forensic DNA." *Genomics Law Report,* March 23. http://www.genomicslawreport.com/index.php/2010/03/23/the-cost-of-making-crime-not-pay-obama-codis-and-forensic-dna.

———. 2010b. "Keeping up with CODIS and Katie's Law." *Genomics Law Report,* June 7. http://www.genomicslawreport.com/index.php/2010/06/07/keeping-up-with-codis/.

Cato Institute. 1995. *The Cato Handbook for Congress: Policy Recommendations for the 104th Congress.* Washington, DC: Cato Institute.

Cavalli-Sforza, L. Luca, Paolo Menozzi, and Alberto Piazza. 1994. *The History and Geography of Human Genes.* Princeton, NJ: Princeton University Press.

Cave, Damien. 2010. "Baby Boomers Are Backing Arizona's Tough New Law While Young People Are Rejecting It." *New York Times,* May 18, pp. A13, A17.

"Census, Welfare, California, New York City." 2004. *Migration News* 11 (2). http://migration.ucdavis.edu/mn/more.php?id=2994_0_2_0.

Census Office. 1872. *The Statistics of the Population of the United States.* Washington, DC: Government Printing Office.

Center for Immigration Studies. 2009. *The 287(g) Program: Protecting Home Towns and Homeland*. Washington, DC: Center for Immigration Studies.

Chafets, Zev. 2010. "The Post-Hispanic Hispanic Politician." *New York Times Magazine*, May 9, pp. 38–43.

Chandler, Michael, and Maria Glod. 2009. "Multiracial Pupils to Be Counted in a New Way." *Washington Post*, March 23, p. A1.

Chavez, Jorge, and Doris Provine. 2009. "Race and the Response of State Legislatures to Unauthorized Immigrants." *Annals of the American Academy of Political and Social Science* 623 (1): 78–92.

Chinnici, Christina. 2008. "DNA Testing Uncovers Suspect Sushi." CNN, August 22. http://articles.cnn.com/2008-08-22/tech/sushi.dna_1_mark-stoeckle -bar-coding-dna-bar?_s=PM:TECH.

Chiricos, Theodore. 1987. "Rates of Crime and Unemployment." *Social Problems* 34 (2): 187–212.

Chishti, Muzaffar. 2009. *Testimony: Hearing on Examining 287(g): The Role of State and Local Law Enforcement in Immigration Law*. Washington, DC: U.S. House of Representatives, Committee on Homeland Security.

Citizenship and Immigration Canada. 2010. "Sponsorship of a Spouse, Common-Law Partner, Conjugal Partner, or Dependent Child Living Outside Canada." http://www.cic.gc.ca/english/pdf/kits/guides/3912e.pdf.

Clayton, Dewey. 2010. *The Presidential Campaign of Barack Obama: A Critical Analysis of a Racially Transcendent Strategy*. New York: Routledge.

Clear, Todd. 2007. *Imprisoning Communities: How Mass Incarceration Makes Disadvantaged Neighborhoods Worse*. New York: Oxford University Press.

"Closing the Net on Common Disease Genes." 2007. *Science*, May 11, pp. 820–22.

Cobas, José, Jorge Duany, and Joe Feagin, eds. 2009. *How the United States Racializes Latinos: White Hegemony and Its Consequences*. Boulder, CO: Paradigm Publishers.

Cochran, Gregory, Jason Hardy, and Henry Harpending. 2006. "Natural History of Ashkenazi Intelligence." *Journal of Biosocial Science* 38 (5): 659–93.

Cohen, Cathy. 2009. "From Kanye West to Barack Obama: Black Youth, the State, and Political Alienation." In *The Unsustainable American State*, ed. Lawrence Jacobs and Desmond King. New York: Oxford University Press. 255–95.

———. 2010. *Democracy Remixed: Black Youth and the Future of American Politics*. New York: Oxford University Press.

Cohen, Steve. 2009. "Letter to the Editor." *New York Times*, September 18.

Cohen-Marks, Mara, Gabriel Sanchez, and Stephen Nuño. 2009. "Look Back in Anger? Voter Opinions of Mexican Immigrants in the Aftermath of the 2006 Immigration Demonstrations." *Urban Affairs Review* 44 (5): 695–717.

Cohn, Jay. 2006. "The Use of Race and Ethnicity in Medicine: Lessons from the African-American Heart Failure Trial." *Journal of Law, Medicine, and Ethics* 34 (3): 552–54.

Cole, David. 2002. "Enemy Aliens." *Stanford Law Review* 54 (5): 953–1004.

Cole, Simon, and Michael Lynch. 2006. "The Social and Legal Construction of Suspects." *Annual Review of Law and Social Science* 2: 39–60.

Collins, Francis, and Monique Mansoura. 2001. "The Human Genome Project: Revealing the Shared Inheritance of All Humankind." *Cancer* 91 (1 Suppl.): 221–25.

Commonwealth of Virginia, Office of the Attorney General. 2010. *Letter to the Honorable Robert G. Marshall, Member, Virginia House of Delegates.* July 30. http://www.oag.state.va.us/OPINIONS/2010opns/10-047-Marshall.pdf.

Coon, Carleton. 1939. *The Races of Europe.* New York: MacMillan.

Cooper, Kenneth. 2009. "Young, Black, and in the Running." *Boston Globe Magazine,* July 19, pp. 17–22.

Cooper, Richard, Jay Kaufman, and Ryk Ward. 2003. " Race and Genomics." *New England Journal of Medicine* 348 (12): 1166–70.

Cooperative Institutional Research Program. Various years. *Freshman Survey.* Los Angeles: UCLA, Graduate School of Education and Information Services, Higher Education Research Institute.

Corey, William. 1998. "More Work to Be Done." *Standard-Times,* April 10.

Cornish, Audie. 2007. "Students Uncertain about Historically Black Schools." *NPR: All Things Considered,* February 23.

Crutchfield, Robert, et al. 2009. "Racial Disparities in Early Criminal Justice Involvement." *Race and Social Problems* 1 (4): 218–30.

DaCosta, Kimberly. 2004. "All in the Family: The Familial Roots of Racial Division." In *The Politics of Multiracialism,* ed. Heather Dalmadge. Albany, NY: State University of New York Press. 19–41.

———. 2006. "Selling Mixedness: Marketing with Multiracial Identities." In *Mixed Messages: Multiracial Identities in the "Color-Blind" Era,* ed. David Brunsma. Boulder, CO: Lynne Rienner Publishers. 183–99.

———. 2007. *Making Multiracials: State, Family, and Market in the Redrawing of the Color Line.* Palo Alto, CA: Stanford University Press.

Daly, Emma. 2005. "DNA Tells Students They Aren't Who They Thought." *New York Times,* April 13, p. A18.

Danigelis, Nicholas, Melissa Hardy, and Stephen Cutler. 2007. "Population Aging, Intracohort Aging, and Sociopolitical Attitudes." *American Sociological Review* 72 (5): 812–30.

Darwin, Charles. 2010 [1871]. *The Descent of Man, and Selection in Relation to Sex (Part 1).* Vol. 21 of *The Works of Charles Darwin.* New York: New York University Press.

Davidson, Justin. 2010. "19: Because Brooklyn and Queens Are Competing to Be the Most Diverse Counties in America (and Maybe the World)." *New York Magazine,* December 20–27, pp. 52–54.

Davis, Darren. 2007. *Negative Liberty: Public Opinion and the Terrorist Attacks on America.* New York: Russell Sage Foundation.

Davis, Yvonne. 2009. "'Flying While Arab' Continues to Soar." *Huffington Post,* March 16. http://www.huffingtonpost.com/yvonne-r-davis/flying-while-arab -continu_b_174367.html.

Dawidoff, Nicholas. 2010. "The Visible Man." *New York Times Magazine,* February 28, pp. 31–37, 44.

Dawson, Michael, Melissa Harris-Lacewell, and Cathy Cohen. n.d. *The 2005*

Katrina, Race, and Politics Study. Chicago, IL: University of Chicago. http://www.michaeldawson.net/data/.

del Pinal, Jorge, and Dianne Schmidley. 2005. *Matched Race and Hispanic Origin Responses from Census 2000 and Current Population Survey February to May 2000.* Washington, DC: U.S. Bureau of the Census, Population Division.

Democracy Now. 2009. *Department of Homeland Security Expands Controversial 287(g) Program Empowering Local Police to Enforce Immigration Laws.* http://www.democracynow.org/2009/10/19/department_of_homeland_security_expands_controversial.

Demuth, Stephen, and Darrell Steffensmeier. 2004. "Ethnicity Effects on Sentence Outcomes in Large Urban Courts: Comparisons among White, Black and Hispanic Defendants." *Social Science Quarterly* 85 (4): 994–1011.

Department of Education. 2007. "Final Guidance on Maintaining, Collecting, and Reporting Racial and Ethnic Data to the U.S. Department of Education." *Federal Register* 72 (202): 59266–79.

Department of Homeland Security. 2008. *Yearbook of Immigration Statistics: 2008.* Washington, DC: Department of Homeland Security.

———. 2010. *The Performance of 287(g) Agreements.* Washington, DC: Department of Homeland Security.

Department of Justice. 2001. "Guidance Concerning Redistricting and Retrogression under Section 5 of the Voting Rights Act, 42 U.S.C. 1973c." *Federal Register* 66 (12): 5412–14.

———. 2003a. *Prevalence of Imprisonment in the U.S. Population, 1974–2001.* Washington, DC: Department of Justice, Bureau of Justice Statistics.

———. 2003b. *Guidance Regarding the Use of Race by Federal Law Enforcement Agencies.* Washington, DC: Department of Justice, Civil Rights Division.

DeSalle, Rob, and Michael Yudell. 2005. *Welcome to the Genome: A User's Guide to the Genetic Past, Present, and Future.* New York: Wiley-Liss.

Diaz, Johnny. 2004. "A Little Respect." *Boston Globe*, February 15, pp. 1, 8.

Dickerson, Debra. 2009. "Class Is the New Black." *Mother Jones* (January/February): 46–47.

Dionne, E. J. 1999. "Construction Boon: It's No Accident That the GOP Is Being Rebuilt by Its Governors." *Washington Post*, March 14, p. B01.

Diver, Colin, and Jane Maslow Cohen. 2001. "Genophobia: What Is Wrong with Genetic Discrimination?" *University of Pennsylvania Law Review* 149 (5): 1439–82.

DNA Print Genomics. n.d. "Forensics." http://www.dnaprint.com/welcome/productsandservices/forensics/.

"DNA to Be Used in Dog Mess Fight." 2008. BBC News. http://news.bbc.co.uk/2/hi/middle_east/7619179.stm.

Doerner, Jill, and Stephen Demuth. 2010. "The Independent and Joint Effects of Race/Ethnicity, Gender, and Age on Sentencing Outcomes in U.S. Federal Courts." *Justice Quarterly* 27 (1): 1–27.

Dougherty, Conor. 2011. "New Faces of Childhood: Census Shows Hispanic and Asian Children Surging as Whites, Blacks Shrink." *Wall Street Journal*, April 6.

Doyle, Arthur Conan. 2005 [1891]. *The New Annotated Sherlock Holmes*. Vol. 1. Ed. Leslie Klinger. New York: Norton.

Doyle, Jamie, and Grace Kao. 2006. "Friendship Choices of Multiracial Adolescents: Racial Homophily, Blending, or Amalgamation?" *Social Science Research* 36 (2): 633–53.

———. 2007. "Are Racial Identities of Multiracials Stable? Changing Self-Identification among Single and Multiple Race Individuals." *Social Psychology Quarterly* 70 (4): 405–23.

Drake, St. Clair, and Horace Cayton. 1993 [1945]. *Black Metropolis: A Study of Negro Life in a Northern City*. Chicago, IL: University of Chicago Press.

Duncan, Brian, and Stephen Trejo. 2008. *Intermarriage and the Intergenerational Transmission of Ethnic Identity and Human Capital for Mexican Americans*. Bonn, Germany: Institute for the Study of Labor.

Duster, Troy. 2003. *Backdoor to Eugenics*. 2nd ed. New York: Routledge.

———. 2004. "Selective Arrests, an Ever-Expanding DNA Forensic Database, and the Specter of an Early-Twenty-First-Century Equivalent of Phrenology." In *DNA and the Criminal Justice System: The Technology of Justice*, ed. David Lazer. Cambridge, MA: MIT Press. 315–34.

———. 2005. "Race and Reification in Science." *Science* 307 (5712): 1050–51.

Eaaswarkhanth, Muthukrishnan, et al. 2010. "Traces of Sub-Saharan and Middle Eastern Lineages in Indian Muslim Populations." *European Journal of Human Genetics* 18: 354–63.

Edmonston, Barry, and Jeffrey Passel. 1999. "How Immigration and Intermarriage Affect the Racial and Ethnic Composition of the U.S. Population." In *Immigration and Opportunity: Race, Ethnicity, and Employment in the United States*, ed. Frank Bean and Stephanie Bell-Rose. New York: Russell Sage Foundation. 373–414.

Edmonston, Barry, and Charles Schultze. 1995. *Modernizing the U.S. Census*. Washington, DC: National Academy Press.

Edmonston, Barry, Joshua Goldstein, and Juanita Lott, eds. 1996. *Spotlight on Heterogeneity: The Federal Standards for Racial and Ethnic Classification*. Washington, DC: National Academy Press.

Edwards, Rosalind, Chamion Caballero, and Shuby Puthussery. 2010. "Parenting Children from 'Mixed' Racial, Ethnic, and Faith Backgrounds: Typifications of Difference and Belonging." *Ethnic and Racial Studies* 33 (6): 949–67.

El Nasser, Haya. 2011. "Hispanic Responses on Race Give More Exact Breakdown." *USA Today*, March 9.

"Election Results 2008." 2008. *New York Times*, November 5.

Elliott, Andrea. 2010. "White House Quietly Courts Muslims in U.S." *New York Times*, April 19, pp. A1, A16.

Elmelech, Yuval. 2008. *Transmitting Inequality: Wealth and the American Family*. New York: Rowman and Littlefield.

Engen, Rodney, et al. 2003. "Discretion and Disparity under Sentencing Guidelines: The Role of Departures and Structured Sentencing Alternatives." *Criminology* 41 (1): 99–130.

Equal Employment Opportunity Commission. 2005. "Agency Information Collection Activities: Notice of Submission for OMB Review, Final Comment Request." *Federal Register* 70 (227): 71294–71303.

Escobar, Gabriel. 1999. "Dominicans Face Assimilation in Black and White." *Washington Post*, May 14, p. A3.

Esipova, Neli, and Julie Ray. 2009. "700 Million Worldwide Desire to Migrate Permanently." Princeton, NJ: Gallup Organization.

Ethnic Media Network. 2010. "Conservatives Back Immigration Reform." http://newamericamedia.org/2010/04/conservatives-back-immigration-reform.php.

Etzioni, Amitai. 2004. "DNA Tests and Databases in Criminal Justice: Individual Rights and the Common Good." In *DNA and the Criminal Justice System: The Technology of Justice*, ed. David Lazer. Cambridge, MA: MIT Press. 197–223.

Evans, Patrick, et al. 2005. "Microcephalin, a Gene Regulating Brain Size, Continues to Evolve Adaptively in Humans." *Science* 309 (5741): 1717–20.

Ex parte Shahid. 1913. 205 F. 812 (E.D.S.C. 1913).

Fagan, Jeffrey. 2010. *Report, in Floyd et al. v. City of New York.* New York: United States District Court, Southern District of New York.

Fagan, Jeffrey, Valerie West, and Jan Holland. 2003. "Reciprocal Effects of Crime and Incarceration in New York City Neighborhoods." *Fordham Urban Law Journal* 30 (5): 1551–1602.

Fagan, Jeffrey, et al. 2010. "Street Stops and Broken Windows Revisited: The Demography and Logic of Proactive Policing in a Safe and Changing City." In *Race, Ethnicity, and Policing: New and Essential Readings,* ed. Stephen Rice and Michael White. New York: New York University Press. 309–48.

Farahany, Nita, ed. 2009. *The Impact of Behavioral Sciences on Criminal Law.* New York: Oxford University Press.

Farley, Reynolds. 2004. "Identifying with Multiple Races: A Social Movement That Succeeded But Failed?" In *The Changing Terrain of Race and Ethnicity,* ed. Maria Krysan and Amanda Lewis. New York: Russell Sage Foundation. 123–48.

———. 2007. "The Declining Multiple Race Population of the United States: The American Community Survey, 2000 to 2005." Paper presented at the annual meeting of the Population Association of America, New York City, March 29–31.

Fasenfast, David, Jason Booza, and Kurt Metzger. 2006. "Living Together: A New Look at Racial and Ethnic Integration in Metropolitan Neighborhoods, 1990–2000." In *Redefining Urban and Suburban America: Evidence from Census 2000.* Vol. 3. Ed. Alan Berube, Bruce Katz, and Robert Lang. Washington, DC: Brookings Institution Press. 93–117.

Favro, Tony 2007. "US Cities Offer Very Different Ways of Dealing with Illegal Immigration." http://www.citymayors.com/society/us-illegals.html.

Federal Bureau of Investigation. 2010. *Uniform Crime Reports.* Washington, DC: Department of Justice.

Ferdinand, Keith. 2008. "Fixed-Dose Isosorbide Dinitrate-Hydralazine: Race-Based Cardiovascular Medicine Benefit or Mirage?" *Journal of Law, Medicine, and Ethics* 36 (3): 458–63.

Ferguson, Ellyn. 2001. "Indian Ancestry Makes Mark on Census." *Salt Lake Tribune*, March 11.

Fessenden, Ford, and Sam Roberts. 2011. "Then as Now: New York's Shifting Ethnic Mosaic." *New York Times*, January 23, p. 26.

Field Poll. 2010. *The Growing Importance of California's Ethnic Voter Population*. San Francisco: Field Research Corporation.

———. 2011. *Plurality Says Immigration Not Affecting the State's Quality of Life*. San Francisco: Field Research Corporation.

Fisher, Patrick. 2010. "The Age Gap in the 2008 Presidential Election." *Society* 47 (4): 295–300.

Florida, Richard. 2002. *The Rise of the Creative Class: And How It's Transforming Work, Leisure, and Everyday Life*. New York: Basic Books.

Ford, Richard. 2009a. "Barack Is the New Black: Obama and the Promise/Threat of the Post–Civil Rights Era." *Du Bois Review* 6 (1): 37–48.

———. 2009b. *The Race Card: How Bluffing about Bias Makes Race Relations Worse*. New York: Picador.

Fortner, Michael. 2010. "The Color of Intimacy: Local Social Orders and National Equilibria in American Race Politics." Unpublished paper, Drexel University, Department of Political Science.

Fowler, James, Laura Baker, and Christopher Dawes. 2008. "Genetic Variation in Political Participation." *American Political Science Review* 102 (2): 233–48.

Fraga, Luis. 2009. "Building through Exclusion: Anti-Immigrant Politics in the United States." In *Bringing Outsiders In: Transatlantic Perspectives on Immigrant Political Incorporation*, ed. Jennifer Hochschild and John Mollenkopf. Ithaca, NY: Cornell University Press. 176–92.

Fraga, Luis, et al. 2007. *Redefining America: Key Findings from the 2006 Latino National Survey: Presentation for the Woodrow Wilson International Center for Scholars*. Seattle: University of Washington, Institute for the Study of Ethnicity, Race, and Sexuality.

Fraga, Luis, et al. c. 2007. "Redefining America: Findings from the 2006 Latino National Survey: House of Representatives Presentation." http://depts.washington.edu/uwiser/LNS.shtml.

Fraga, Luis, et al. 2010. *Latino National Survey (LNS), 2006*. Ann Arbor, MI: Inter-university Consortium for Political and Social Research.

"France Stops Controversial DNA Testing Law." 2009. UPI.com. September 15.

Fredrickson, George. 2002. *Racism: A Short History*. Princeton, NJ: Princeton University Press.

Frey, William. 2006. "Immigrants Are Everywhere." *Milken Institute Review*, second quarter, pp. 6–7.

———. 2007a. "Boomer Seniors." *Milken Institute Review*, second quarter, pp. 6–7.

———. 2007b. "The Racial Generation Gap." *Milken Institute Review*, third quarter, pp. 16–17.

———. 2009. "Mixed Race Marriages." *Milken Institute Review*, second quarter, pp. 5–7.

———. 2010a. "New Racial Segregation Measures for States and Large Metropolitan Areas: Analysis of the 2005–2009 American Community Survey." http://www.psc.isr.umich.edu/dis/census/segregation.html.

———. 2010b. "Race and Ethnicity." In *The State of Metropolitan America: On the Front Lines of Demographic Transformation*, ed. Brookings Metropolitan Policy Program. Washington, DC: Brookings Institution Press. 50–63.

———. 2010c. "Will Arizona Be America's Future?" Up Front Blog. http://www .brookings.edu/opinions/2010/0428_arizona_frey.aspx.

———. 2010d. "Census Data: Blacks and Hispanics Take Different Segregation Paths." *State of Metropolitan America* 21. Washington, DC: Brookings Institution. http://www.brookings.edu/opinions/2010/1216_census_frey.aspx.

Fryer, Roland Jr. 2005. http://www.economics.harvard.edu/faculty/fryer/files/in terracial_marriage_onlineappendix_figs.pdf.

———. 2007. "Guess Who's Been Coming to Dinner? Trends in Interracial Marriage over the 20th Century." *Journal of Economic Perspectives* 21 (2): 71–90.

———. 2011. "Racial Inequality in the 21st Century: The Declining Significance of Discrimination." In *Handbook of Labor Economics*. Vol. 4B. Ed. Orley Ashenfelter and David Card. San Diego, CA: North Holland. 855–972.

Fullerton, Andrew, and Jeffrey Dixon. 2010. "Generational Conflict or Methodological Artifact? Reconsidering the Relationship between Age and Policy Attitudes in the U.S., 1984–2008." *Public Opinion Quarterly* 74 (4): 643–73.

Fullwiley, Duana. 2007. "The Molecularization of Race: Institutionalizing Human Difference in Pharmacogenetics Practice." *Science as Culture* 16 (1): 1–30.

———. 2008. "Can DNA 'Witness' Race?: Forensic Uses of an Imperfect Ancestry Testing Technology." *Gene-Watch* 21 (3–4): 12–14.

Gabbidon, Shaun, and George Higgins. 2009. "The Role of Race/Ethnicity and Race Relations on Public Opinion Related to the Treatment of Blacks by the Police." *Police Quarterly* 12 (1): 102–15.

Gaines, Kevin. 2010. "Of Teachable Moments and the Specters of Race." *American Quarterly* 62 (2): 195–213.

Gallagher, Charles. 2006. "Color Blindness: An Obstacle to Racial Justice?" In *Mixed Messages: Multiracial Identities in the "Color-Blind" Era*, ed. David Brunsma. Boulder, CO: Lynne Rienner Publishers. 103–16.

Gallup Organization. 2007. "Most Americans Approve of Interracial Marriages." http://www.gallup.com/poll/28417/Most-Americans-Approve-Interracial -Marriages.aspx.

———. 2010. "Americans Back Profiling Air Travelers to Combat Terrorism." http://www.gallup.com/poll/125078/americans-back-profiling-air-travelers -combat-terrorism.aspx.

Gardner, Amy. 2010. "Tea Party's Judson Phillips Defends Essay Attacking Congressman for Being Muslim." *Washington Post*, October 28.

Gardner, Amy, and Spencer Hsu. 2009. "Airline Apologizes for Booting 9 Muslims." *Washington Post*, January 3.

Gardner, David. 2008. "'Most Shelter Dogs Are Mutts Like Me': Obama Defies Political Correctness at First Press Conference." *London Daily Mail*, November 8.

Garrett, Brandon. 2008a. "Claiming Innocence." *Minnesota Law Review* 92 (6): 1629–1724.

———. 2008b. "Judging Innocence." *Columbia Law Review* 108: 55–142.

Garrett, Brandon, and Peter Neufeld. 2009. "Invalid Forensic Science Testimony and Wrongful Convictions." *Virginia Law Review* 95 (1): 1–97.

Gartner, Lisa. 2011. "More Children of Immigrants Enrolling in Earliest Grades." *Washington Examiner*, February 7.

Gates, Henry Louis Jr. 2006. "My Yiddishe Mama." *Wall Street Journal*, February 1, p. A14.

———. 2009. *In Search of Our Roots: How 19 Extraordinary African Americans Reclaimed Their Past.* New York: Crown.

Gay, Claudine. 2006. "Seeing Difference: The Effect of Economic Disparity on Black Attitudes toward Latinos." *American Journal of Political Science* 50 (4): 982–87.

Gelman, Andrew, Jeffrey Fagan, and Alex Kiss. 2007. "An Analysis of the New York City Police Department's 'Stop-and-Frisk' Policy in the Context of Claims of Racial Bias." *Journal of the American Statistical Association* 102 (479): 813–23.

Gerstein, Josh. 2010. "President Obama Backs DNA Test in Arrests." March 9. http://www.politico.com/news/stories/0310/34097.html.

Gerstle, Gary. 1993. "The Working Class Goes to War." *Mid-America* 75 (3): 303–22.

Ghosh, Bobby. 2010. "Arab Americans: Detroit's Unlikely Saviors." *Time Magazine*, November 8, pp. 50–53.

Gibson, Lydialyle. 2007. "Long Way Home." *University of Chicago Magazine* 100 (3). http://magazine.uchicago.edu/0812/features/kittles.shtml.

Gilbert, Lauren. 2009. "Citizenship, Civic Virtue, and Immigrant Integration: The Enduring Power of Community-Based Norms." *Yale Law and Policy Review* 27: 335–97.

Gillespie, Andra, ed. 2010. *Whose Black Politics? Cases in Post-Racial Black Leadership.* New York: Routledge.

Glaeser, Edward, Bruce Sacerdote, and Jose Scheinkman. 2003. "The Social Multiplier." *Journal of the European Economic Association* 1 (2): 345–53.

Goldstein, David. 2009. "Common Genetic Variation and Human Traits." *New England Journal of Medicine* 360 (17): 1696–98.

Goldstein, Joshua. 1999. "Kinship Networks That Cross Racial Lines: The Exception or the Rule?" *Demography* 36 (3): 399–407.

Goldstein, Joshua, and Ann Morning. 2000. "The Multiple-Race Population of the United States: Issues and Estimates." *Proceedings of the National Academy of Sciences* 97 (11): 6230–35.

———. 2002. "Back in the Box: The Dilemma of Using Multiple-Race Data for Single-Race Laws." In *The New Race Question: How the Census Counts Multiracial Individuals*, ed. Joel Perlmann and Mary Waters. New York: Russell Sage Foundation. 119–36.

Gómez, Laura. 2009. "Opposite One-Drop Rules: Mexican Americans, African Americans, and the Need to Reconceive Turn-of-the-Twentieth-Century Race

Relations." In *How the United States Racializes Latinos: White Hegemony and Its Consequences*, ed. José Cobas, Jorge Duany, and Joe Feagin. Boulder, CO: Paradigm Publishers. 87–100.

Gonzales, Roberto. 2009. "On the Rights of Undocumented Children." *Society* 46 (5): 419–22.

Gonzalez, Jennifer. 2010. "Community Colleges Build Programs That Fit Immigrants' Needs." *Chronicle of Higher Education*, February 28.

Goodstein, Laurie. 2011. "Police in Los Angeles Step Up Efforts to Gain Muslims' Trust." *New York Times,* March 10, p. A17.

Gorman, Anna. 2009. "U.S. to Collect DNA Samples of Arrested Immigrants." *Los Angeles Times*, January 9.

Government Accountability Office. 2009. *Immigration Enforcement: Better Controls Needed over Program Authorizing State and Local Enforcement of Federal Immigration Laws*. Washington, DC: Government Accountability Office.

Gratton, Brian, and Myron Gutman. 2000. "Hispanics in the United States, 1850–1990: Estimates of Population Size and National Origin." *Historical Methods* 33 (3): 137–53.

Greely, Henry, et al. 2006. "Family Ties: The Use of DNA Offender Databases to Catch Offenders' Kin." *Journal of Law, Medicine, and Ethics* 34 (2): 248–62.

Greenberg Quinlan Rosner and American Viewpoint. 2010. "New University of Southern California/*Los Angeles Times* Poll." May 29. http://gqrr.com/index.php?ID=2447.

Greenhouse, Steven. 2010. "Offended Muslims Speak Up." *New York Times*, September 24, pp. B1, B4.

Griffin, John, and Brian Newman. 2008. *Minority Report: Evaluating Political Equality in America*. Chicago, IL: University of Chicago Press.

Griffin, Larry. 2004. "'Generations and Collective Memory' Revisited: Race, Region, and Memory of Civil Rights." *American Sociological Review* 69 (4): 544–57.

Griffin, Larry, and Peggy Hargis. 2008. "Surveying Memory: The Past in Black and White." *Southern Literary Journal* 40 (2): 42–69.

Grimm, Daniel. 2007. "The Demographics of Genetic Surveillance: Familial DNA Testing and the Hispanic Community." *Columbia Law Review* 107 (1): 1164–94.

Groeneman, Sidney. 2001. "Hispanic Ethnicity." Posting on listserv aapornet@usc.edu, October 17.

Gross, Ariela. 2007. "'The Caucasian Cloak': Mexican Americans and the Politics of Whiteness in the Twentieth-Century Southwest." *Georgetown Law Journal* 95 (2): 337–92.

———. 2008. *What Blood Won't Tell: A History of Race on Trial in America*. Cambridge, MA: Harvard University Press.

Gross, Samuel. 2008. "Convicting the Innocent." *Annual Review of Law and Social Science* 4: 173–92.

Gross, Samuel, et al. 2005. "Exonerations in the United States 1989 through 2003." *Journal of Criminal Law and Criminology* 95 (2): 523–60.

Guinier, Lani, and Gerald Torres. 2002. *The Miner's Canary: Enlisting Race, Re-*

sisting Power, Transforming Democracy. Cambridge, MA: Harvard University Press.

Guo, Guang, Michael Roettger, and Tianji Cai. 2008. "The Integration of Genetic Propensities into Social-Control Models of Delinquency and Violence among Male Youths." *American Sociological Review* 73 (4): 543–68.

Ha, Shang. 2010. "The Consequences of Multiracial Contexts on Public Attitudes toward Immigration." *Political Research Quarterly* 63 (1): 29–42.

Hacker, Andrew. 1992. *Two Nations: Black and White, Separate, Hostile, Unequal*. New York: Scribner's.

Hacker, Jacob, and Paul Pierson. 2010. *Winner-Take-All Politics: How Washington Made the Rich Richer—and Turned Its Back on the Middle Class*. New York: Simon and Schuster.

Hagan, John, Carla Shedd, and Monique Payne. 2005. "Race, Ethnicity, and Youth Perceptions of Criminal Injustice." *American Sociological Review* 70 (3): 381–407.

Hajnal, Zoltan. 2007. *Changing White Attitudes toward Black Political Leadership*. New York: Cambridge University Press.

"Hallowed Ground." 2010. *The Economist*, June 10, p. 38.

Handlin, Oscar. 2002. *The Uprooted: The Epic Story of the Great Migrations That Made the American People*. 2nd ed. Philadelphia, PA: University of Pennsylvania Press.

Haney López, Ian. 1996. *White by Law: The Legal Construction of Race*. New York: New York University Press.

———. 1997. "Race, Ethnicity, Erasure: The Salience of Race to LatCrit Theory." *California Law Review* 85 (5): 1143–1211.

———. 2006. "Colorblind to the Reality of Race in America." *Chronicle of Higher Education*, November 3, pp. B6–B9.

Hanna, Sherman, and Cong Wang. 2007. "Racial/Ethnic Disparities in Risky Asset Ownership: A Decomposition Analysis." *Proceedings of the Academy of Financial Services* 53: 113–30.

Hao, Lingxin. 2007. *Color Lines, Country Lines: Race, Immigration, and Wealth Stratification in America*. New York: Russell Sage Foundation.

Harmon, Amy. 2006. "Love You, K2a2a, Whoever You Are." *New York Times*, January 22, sec. 4, pp. 1, 18.

Harris, David, and Jeremiah Sim. 2002. "Who Is Multiracial? Assessing the Complexity of Lived Race." *American Sociological Review* 67 (4): 614–27.

Harris, Frederick. 2006. "It Takes a Tragedy to Arouse Them: Collective Memory and Collective Action during the Civil Rights Movement." *Social Movement Studies* 5 (1): 19–43.

———. 2009a. "Toward a Pragmatic Black Politics." In *Barack Obama and African American Empowerment: The Rise of Black America's New Leadership*, ed. Manning Marable and Kristin Clarke. New York: Palgrave Macmillan. 65–71.

———. 2009b. "Toward a Pragmatic Black Politics? Barack Obama and the New Black Politics." *Souls* 11 (1): 41–49.

Harris, Fredrick, and Gary Langer. 2008. *Survey on Race, Politics, and Society.*

New York: Center on African-American Politics and Society, Columbia University, and the ABC Polling Unit.

Harris-Perry, Melissa. 2010. "Black by Choice." *The Nation*, May 3, p. 10.

Haskins, Ron. 2007. *Immigration: Wages, Education, and Mobility*. Washington, DC: Pew Charitable Trusts.

Hattam, Victoria. 2004. "Ethnicity: An American Genealogy." In *Not Just Black and White: Historical and Contemporary Perspectives on Immigration, Race, and Ethnicity in the United States*, ed. Nancy Foner and George Fredrickson. New York: Russell Sage Foundation. 42–60.

———. 2007. *Ethnic Shadows: Jews, Latinos, and Race Politics in the United States*. Chicago, IL: University of Chicago Press.

Haughwout, Andrew, Christopher Mayer, and Joseph Tracy. 2009. "Subprime Mortgage Pricing: The Impact of Race, Ethnicity, and Gender on the Cost of Borrowing." *Brookings-Wharton Papers on Urban Affairs*, ed. Gary Burtless and Janet Pack. Washington, DC: Brookings Institution Press. 33–57.

Hedges, Chris. 2011. "The Obama Deception: Why Cornel West Went Ballistic." *Truthdig*, May 16. http://www.truthdig.com/report/print/the_obama_deception_why_cornel_west_went_ballistic_20110516.

Heiphetz, Larisa, et al. 2009. "Multiracials May Be Extra Egalitarian: Evidence from the Implicit Association Test." Paper presented at the annual meeting of the Association for Pyschological Science, San Francisco, May.

Henderson, Mark. 2009. "Genetic Mapping of Babies by 2019 Will Transform Preventive Medicine." *Sunday Times*, February 9.

Henning, Anna. 2009. *Compulsory DNA Collection: A Fourth Amendment Analysis*. Washington, DC: Congressional Research Service.

Heredia, Luisa. 2009. *"Welcoming the Stranger": The Catholic Church and the Struggle for Immigrant Rights in Los Angeles*. Washington, DC: Woodrow Wilson International Center for Scholars.

Herman, Melissa. 2010. "Do You See What I Am? How Observers' Backgrounds Affect Their Perceptions of Multiracial Faces." *Social Psychology Quarterly* 73 (1): 58–78.

Hernandez, José, Leo Estrada, and David Alivirez. 1973. "Census Data and the Problem of Conceptually Defining the Mexican American Population." *Social Science Quarterly* 53 (4): 671–87.

Hernandez, Lyla, and Dan Blazer, eds. 2006. *Genes, Behavior, and the Social Environment: Moving beyond the Nature/Nurture Debate*. Washington, DC: National Academy Press.

Hirschman, Charles, Philip Kasinitz, and Josh DeWind, eds. 1999. *The Handbook of International Migration: The American Experience*. New York: Russell Sage Foundation.

Hirschman, Elizabeth, and Donald Panther-Yates. 2008. "Peering Inward for Ethnic Identity: Consumer Interpretations of DNA Test Results." *Identity* 8 (1): 47–66.

Hitlin, Steven, J. Scott Brown, and Glen Elder Jr. 2006. "Racial Self-Categorization in Adolescence: Multiracial Development and Social Pathways." *Child Development* 77 (5): 1298–1308.

Hitt, Jack. 2005. "Mighty White of You: Racial Preferences Color America's Oldest Skulls and Bones." *Harper's* (July): 39–55.

Hjörleifsson, Stefán, Vilhjálmur árnason, and Edvin Schei. 2008. "Decoding the Genetics Debate: Hype and Hope in Icelandic News Media in 2000 and 2004." *New Genetics and Society* 27 (4): 377–94.

Ho, Arnold, et al. 2011. "Evidence for Hypodescent and Racial Hierarchy in the Categorization and Perception of Biracial Individuals." *Journal of Personality and Social Psychology* 100 (3): 492–506.

Hochschild, Jennifer. 1981. *What's Fair? American Beliefs about Distributive Justice.* Cambridge, MA: Harvard University Press.

———. 1995. *Facing Up to the American Dream: Race, Class, and the Soul of the Nation.* Princeton, NJ: Princeton University Press.

Hochschild, Jennifer, and Traci Burch. 2007. "Contingent Public Policies and Racial Hierarchy: Lessons from Immigration and Census Policies." In *Political Contingency: Studying the Unexpected, the Accidental, and the Unforeseen,* ed. Ian Shapiro and Sonu Bedi. New York: New York University Press. 138–70.

Hochschild, Jennifer, and Brenna Marea Powell. 2008. "Racial Reorganization and the United States Census, 1850–1930: Mulattoes, Half-Breeds, Mixed Parentage, Hindoos, and the Mexican Race." *Studies in American Political Development* 22 (1): 59–96.

Hochschild, Jennifer, and Nathan Scovronick. 2003. *The American Dream and the Public Schools.* New York: Oxford University Press.

Hochschild, Jennifer, and Maya Sen. 2011. "Reification or Blurring: The Impact of Genomic Ancestry Testing on Americans' Racial Identity." Unpublished paper, Harvard University, Department of Government.

Hochschild, Jennifer, Vesla Weaver, and Brenna Powell. 2008. "Political Discourse on Racial Mixture: American Newspapers, 1865 to 1970." Paper presented at the Policy History Conference, St. Louis, May 29–31.

Hoefer, Michael, Nancy Rytina, and Bryan Baker. 2011. *Estimates of the Unauthorized Immigrant Population Residing in the United States: January 2010.* Washington, DC: Department of Homeland Security, Office of Immigration Statistics.

Hogan, Dennis, and David Featherman. 1978. "Racial Stratification and Socioeconomic Change in the American North and South." *American Journal of Sociology* 83 (1): 100–126.

Hohmann-Marriott, Bryndl, and Paul Amato. 2008. "Relationship Quality in Interethnic Marriages and Cohabitations." *Social Forces* 87 (2): 825–55.

Hollinger, David. 1993. "How Wide the Circle of the 'We'? American Intellectuals and the Problem of the Ethnos since World War II." *American Historical Review* 98 (2): 317–37.

———. 2003. "Amalgamation and Hypodescent: The Question of Ethnoracial Mixture in the History of the United States." *American Historical Review* 108 (5): 1363–90.

———. 2006. *Postethnic America: Beyond Multiculturalism.* New York: Basic Books.

———. 2008. "Obama, the Instability of Color Lines, and the Promise of a Post-ethnic Future." *Callaloo* 31 (4): 1033–37.

Holmes, Steven. 2000. "New Policy on Census Says Those Listed as White and Minority Will Be Counted as Minority." *New York Times*, March 11, p. A9.

Hopkins, Daniel. 2009. "No More Wilder Effect, Never a Whitman Effect: Why and When Polls Mislead about Black and Female Candidates." *Journal of Politics* 71 (3): 769–81.

———. 2010. "Politicized Places: Explaining Where and When Immigrants Provoke Local Opposition." *American Political Science Review* 104 (1): 40–60.

Horton, Hayward. 2006. "Racism, Whitespace, and the Rise of the Neo-Mulattoes." In *Mixed Messages: Multiracial Identities in the "Color-Blind" Era*, ed. David Brunsma. Boulder, CO: Lynne Rienner Publishers. 117–21.

Horton, John. 1995. *The Politics of Diversity: Immigration, Resistance, and Change in Monterey Park, California*. Philadelphia, PA: Temple University Press.

Hotline OnCall. 2010. "The GOP's Bloody Border War." NationalJournal.com. http://hotlineoncall.nationaljournal.com/archives/2010/05/the_gops_bloody .php#more.

Hout, Michael. 1984. "Occupational Mobility of Black Men: 1962 to 1973." *American Sociological Review* 49 (3): 308–22.

Howe, Neil, and William Strauss. 2000. *Millennials Rising: The Next Great Generation*. New York: Vintage Books.

Howell, Susan, and Huey Perry. 2004. "Black Mayors/White Mayors: Explaining Their Approval." *Public Opinion Quarterly* 68 (1): 32–56.

Hoy, Seth. 2010. "Immigration Reform and a Younger Generation of Voters." Immigration Impact. http://immigrationimpact.com/2010/04/13/immigration -reform-and-a-younger-generation-of-voters/.

———. 2011. "More States Toss Costly Immigration Legislation in Final Days of Session." Immigration Impact. http://immigrationimpact.com/2011/05/20/ more-states-toss-costly-immigration-legislation-in-final-days-of-session-2/.

Hsu, Steve. 2006. "Brains, Genes, Backlash." Information Processing, June 16. http://infoproc.blogspot.com/2006/06/brains-genes-backlash.html.

Hughes, Robert. 1988. *The Fatal Shore: The Epic of Australia's Founding*. New York: Vintage Books.

Hunt, Matthew. 2007. "African American, Hispanic, and White Beliefs about Black/White Inequality, 1977–2004." *American Sociological Review* 72 (3): 390–415.

Hurwitz, Jon, and Mark Peffley. 2005. "Explaining the Great Racial Divide: Perceptions of Fairness in the U.S. Criminal Justice System." *Journal of Politics* 67 (3): 762–83.

Ibrahim, Habiba. 2009. "Toward Black and Multiracial 'Kinship' after 1997, or How a Race Man Became 'Cablinasian.'" *Black Scholar* 39 (3–4): 23–31.

Iceland, John. 2009. *Where We Live Now: Immigration and Race in the United States*. Berkeley, CA: University of California Press.

Ifill, Gwen. 2008. "Nothing Unique about It." *Time Magazine*, September 1, p. 54.

Ignatiev, Noel. 1996. *How the Irish Became White*. New York: Routledge.

Immergluck, Daniel. 2010. "Neighborhoods in the Wake of the Debacle: Intra-

metropolitan Patterns of Foreclosed Properties." *Urban Affairs Review* 46 (1): 3–36.

"Immigration." 2010. *Polling Report.* http://www.pollingreport.com/immigra tion.htm.

Immigration and Customs Enforcement. 2008. *Delegation of Immigration Authority Section 287(g) Immigration and Nationality Act.* Washington, DC: Department of Homeland Security.

———. 2010. *Special Registration.* Washington, DC: Department of Homeland Security.

Ingersoll, Thomas. 2005. *To Intermix with Our White Brothers: Indian Mixed Bloods in the United States from Earliest Times to the Indian Removal.* Albuquerque, NM: University of New Mexico Press.

International Centre for Prison Studies. 2010. *World Prison Brief: Prison Brief for United Kingdom: England & Wales.* London: Kings College London, School of Law.

International Human Genome Sequencing Consortium (IHGSC). 2001. "Initial Sequencing and Analysis of the Human Genome." *Nature* 409: 860–921.

———. 2004. "Finishing the Euchromatic Sequence of the Human Genome." *Nature* 431: 931–45.

Isaacs, Julia. 2007. *Economic Mobility of Black and White Families.* Washington, DC: Pew Charitable Trusts.

Ismaili, Karim. 2010. "Surveying the Many Fronts of the War on Immigrants in Post-9/11 U.S. Society." *Contemporary Justice Review* 13 (1): 71–93.

Itzigsohn, José. 2004. "The Formation of Latino and Latina Panethnic Identities." In *Not Just Black and White: Historical and Contemporary Perspectives on Immigration, Race, and Ethnicity in the United States*, ed. Nancy Foner and George Fredrickson. New York: Russell Sage Foundation. 197–216.

Jackman, Simon, and Lynn Vavreck. 2010. "Obama's Advantage? Race, Partisanship, & Racial Attitudes in Context." Working paper, Stanford University, Department of Political Science.

Jackson, James, et al. 2004. *National Politics Study, 2004.* Ann Arbor, MI: Interuniversity Consortium for Political and Social Research.

Jacobs, Frank. 2008. "306—The Genetic Map of Europe." August 18. http://big think.com/ideas/21358.

Jacobson, Gary. 2009. "The 2008 Presidential and Congressional Elections: Anti-Bush Referendum and Prospects for the Democratic Majority." *Political Science Quarterly* 124 (1): 1–30.

Jacobson, Mark. 2010. "Muhammad Comes to Manhattan." *New York Magazine*, August 30–September 6, pp. 24–32.

Jacobson, Matthew. 1998. *Whiteness of a Different Color: European Immigrants and the Alchemy of Race.* Cambridge, MA: Harvard University Press.

Jiménez, Tomás. 2004. "Negotiating Ethnic Boundaries: Multiethnic Mexican American and Ethnic Identity in the United States." *Ethnicities* 4 (1): 75–97.

Joh, Elizabeth. 2006. "Reclaiming 'Abandoned' DNA: The Fourth Amendment and Genetic Privacy." *Northwestern University Law Review* 100 (2): 857–84.

Johnson, Kevin, ed. 2003. *Mixed Race America and the Law: A Reader.* New York: New York University Press.

Joint Economic Committee. 2010. *Assessing the Impact of the Great Recession on Income, Poverty, and Health Insurance Coverage in the United States.* September 16. http://jec.senate.gov/public/?a=Files.Serve&File_id=d1125f97 -b1c8-441b-b082-6119682ef166.

Jones, Joseph, and Alan Goodman. 2005. "BiDil and the 'Fact' of Genetic Blackness: Where Politics and Science Meet." *Anthropology News* 46 (7): 26.

Jones, Trina. 2000. "Shades of Brown: The Law of Skin Color." *Duke Law Journal* 49 (6): 1487–1557.

Joseph, Peniel. 2009. "Our National Postracial Hangover." *Chronicle of Higher Education*, August 7, p. B6.

Junn, Jane, and Natalie Masuoka. 2008. "Asian American Identity: Shared Political Status and Political Context." *Perspectives on Politics* 6 (4): 729–40.

Kahn, Jonathan. 2005. "From Disparity to Difference: How Race-Specific Medicines May Undermine Policies to Address Inequalities in Health Care." *Southern California Interdisciplinary Law Journal* 15: 105–29.

———. 2007. "Race in a Bottle." *Scientific American* (August): 40–45.

———. 2009. "Beyond BiDil: The Expanding Embrace of Race in Biomedical Research and Product Development." *St. Louis University Journal of Health Law and Policy* 3: 61–92.

Kaiser Family Foundation/Harvard University/*Washington Post*. 2001. *Survey of Biracial Couples.* http://www.washingtonpost.com/wp-srv/nation/sidebars/ polls/couples.htm.

Kaiser Family Foundation/*Washington Post*/Harvard University. 2006. *African American Men Survey.* 2006-WPH021. http://www.kff.org/kaiserpolls/7526 .cfm.

Kalb, Claudia. 2006. "In Our Blood." *Newsweek*, February 6, pp. 47–55.

Kalkan, Kerem, Geoffrey Layman, and Eric Uslaner. 2009. "'Bands of Others'? Attitudes toward Muslims in Contemporary American Society." *Journal of Politics* 71 (3): 847–62.

Kallen, Horace. 1997 [1924]. *Culture and Democracy in the United States.* New Brunswick, NJ: Transaction Publishers.

Kammen, Michael. 1993. *Mystic Chords of Memory: The Transformation of Tradition in American Culture.* New York: Vintage.

Kasinitz, Philip, John Mollenkopf, and Mary Waters, eds. 2004. *Becoming New Yorkers: Ethnographies of the New Second Generation.* New York: Russell Sage Foundation.

Kasinitz, Philip, et al. 2008. *Inheriting the City: The Children of Immigrants Come of Age.* New York and Cambridge, MA: Russell Sage Foundation and Harvard University Press.

Katznelson, Ira. 2005. *When Affirmative Action Was White: An Untold History of Racial Inequality in Twentieth-Century America.* New York: Norton.

Kaye, David. 2009. "Trawling DNA Databases for Partial Matches: What Is the FBI Afraid Of?" *Cornell Journal of Law and Public Policy* 19: 145–71.

Kaye, David, and Michael Smith. 2004. "DNA Databases for Law Enforcement: The Coverage Question and the Case for a Population-Wide Database." In *DNA and the Criminal Justice System: The Technology of Justice*, ed. David Lazer. Cambridge, MA: MIT Press. 247–84.

Kayser, Manfred. 2010. "The Human Genetic History of Oceania: Near and Remote Views of Dispersal." *Current Biology* 20 (4): R194–R201.

Kelderman, Eric. 2010. "Black Colleges See a Need to Improve Their Image." *Chronicle of Higher Education*, July 2, pp. A1, A17.

Kennedy, Randall. 2003. *Interracial Intimacies: Sex, Marriage, Identity, and Adoption*. New York: Pantheon.

Kenski, Kate, Bruce Hardy, and Kathleen Hall Jamieson. 2010. *The Obama Victory: How Media, Money, and Message Shaped the 2008 Election*. New York: Oxford University Press.

Khanna, Nikki, and Cathryn Johnson. 2010. "Passing as Black: Racial Identity Work among Biracial Americans." *Social Psychological Quarterly* 73 (4): 380–97.

Kilgannon, Corey. 2007. "At a Harlem Reunion, a Rancher from Missouri Meets His 'DNA Cousins.'" *New York Times*, March 14.

Kilgore, Ed. 2010. "Why Southern Republicans Are 'Raising Arizona.'" *Democratic Strategist*. http://www.thedemocraticstrategist.org/strategist/2010/05/why_southern_republicans_are_r.php.

Kim, Claire. 1999. "The Racial Triangulation of Asian Americans." *Politics and Society* 27 (1): 103–36.

———. 2000. *Bitter Fruit: The Politics of Black-Korean Conflict in New York City*. New Haven, CT: Yale University Press.

Kim, Claire, and Taeku Lee. 2002. "Interracial Politics: Asian Americans and Other Communities of Color." *PS: Political Science and Politics* 34 (3): 631–37.

King, Desmond, and Rogers Smith. 2005. "Racial Orders in American Political Development." *American Political Science Review* 99 (1): 75–92.

———. 2008. "Strange Bedfellows? Polarized Politics? The Quest for Racial Equity in Contemporary America." *Political Research Quarterly* 61 (4): 686–703.

———. 2011. *Still a House Divided: Race and Politics in Obama's America*. Princeton, NJ: Princeton University Press.

Kleiman, Mark. 2010. "Toward Fewer Prisoners and Less Crime." *Daedalus* 139 (3): 115–23.

Kleiner, Keith. 2008. "Whole Genome Sequencing to Cost Only $1,000 by End of 2009." December 30. http://singularityhub.com/2008/12/30/whole-genome-sequencing-to-cost-only-1000-by-end-of-2009/.

Klinkner, Philip, and Rogers Smith. 2002. *The Unsteady March: The Rise and Decline of Racial Equality in America*. Chicago, IL: University of Chicago Press.

Klor de Alva, José Jorge, Earl Shorris, and Cornel West. 1998. "Our Next Race Question: The Uneasiness between Blacks and Latinos." In *Latino Studies Reader: Culture, Economy, and Society*, ed. Antonia Darder and Rodolfo Torres. Malden, MA: Blackwell. 180–89.

Koerner, Brendan. 2005. "Blood Feud." *Wired*, September. http://www.wired.com/wired/archive/13.09/seminoles.html.

Kohn, Marek. 2006. "The Racist Undercurrent in the Tide of Genetic Research." *Guardian*, January 17, p. 26.

Kolchin, Peter. 2002. "Whiteness Studies: The New History of Race in America." *Journal of American History* 89 (1): 154–73.

Koops, Bert-Jaap, and Maurice Schellekens. 2006. "Forensic DNA Phenotyping: Regulatory Issues." *California Science and Technology Law Review* 9 (1): 158–202.

Kraft, Peter, and David Hunter. 2009. "Genetic Risk Prediction—Are We There Yet?" *New England Journal of Medicine* 360 (17): 1701–3.

Kretsedemas, Phillip. 2008. "Redefining 'Race' in North America." *Current Sociology* 56 (6): 826–44.

Krieger, Nancy. 2005. "Stormy Weather: Race, Gene Expression, and the Science of Health Disparities." *American Journal of Public Health* 95 (12): 2155–60.

Krikorian, Mark. 2009. "NRO's Krikorian on Pronunciation of Sotomayor's Name: 'It Sticks in My Craw.'" *Media Matters for America*. http://mediamat ters.org/blog/200905270012.

Lamason, Rebecca, et al. 2005. "SLC24A5, a Putative Cation Exchanger, Affects Pigmentation in Zebrafish and Humans." *Science* 310 (5755): 1782–86.

Lao, Oscar, et al. 2008. "Correlation between Genetic and Geographic Structure in Europe." *Current Biology* 18 (16): 1241–48.

Lau v. Nichols. 1974. 414 U.S. 563.

Lazer, David, ed. 2004. *DNA and the Criminal Justice System: The Technology of Justice*. Cambridge, MA: MIT Press.

Lee, Jennifer, and Frank Bean. 2010. *The Diversity Paradox: Immigration and the Color Line in Twenty-First Century America*. New York: Russell Sage Foundation.

Lee, Sharon, and Barry Edmonston. 2005. *New Marriages, New Families: U.S. Racial and Hispanic Intermarriage*. Washington, DC: Population Reference Bureau.

———. 2006. "Hispanic Intermarriage, Identification, and U.S. Latino Population Change." *Social Science Quarterly* 87 (5): 1263–79.

Lee, Sugie, Mark Rosentraub, and Timothy Kobie. 2010. "Race, Class and Spatial Dimensions of Mortgage Lending Practices and Residential Foreclosures." *Journal of Urbanism* 3 (1): 39–68.

Lee, Taeku. 2004. "Social Construction, Self-Identification, and the Survey Measurement of 'Race.'" Paper presented at the annual meeting of the American Political Science Association, Chicago, IL.

Lei, Hsien-Hsien. 2007. "DNA-Supported Ancestral Tourism." *Eye on DNA*, June 11. http://www.eyeondna.com/2007/06/11/dna-supported-ancestral-tour ism/.

Levin, Shana. 2007. "Interethnic and Interracial Dating in College: A Longitudinal Study." *Journal of Social and Personal Relationships* 24 (3): 323–41.

Levine, Harry, et al. 2008. *Drug Arrests and DNA: Building Jim Crow's Database*. New York: Council for Responsible Genetics Forum on Racial Justice Impacts of Forensic DNA Databanks.

Levine, Peter, Constance Flanagan, and Les Gallay. 2009. *The Millennial Pendulum: A New Generation of Voters and the Prospects for a Political Realignment*. Washington, DC: New America Foundation.

Lewis, Paul, and S. Karthick Ramakrishnan. 2007. "Police Practices in Immigrant-Destination Cities: Political Control or Bureaucratic Professionalism." *Urban Affairs Review* 42 (6): 874–900.

Lewis-Beck, Michael. 2009. "The Economy, Obama, and the 2008 Election." *PS: Political Science & Politics* (July): 457–83.

Lewis-Beck, Michael, and Charles Tien. 2009. "Race Blunts the Economic Effect? The 2008 Obama Forecast." *PS: Political Science and Politics* 42 (1): 687–90.

Lewontin, Richard. 1972. "The Apportionment of Human Diversity." *Evolutionary Biology*. Vol. 6. Ed. Theodosius Dobzhansky et al. New York: Appleton-Century-Crofts. 381–98.

Li, Jian, et al. 2009. "Whole Genome Distribution and Ethnic Differentiation of Copy Number Variation in Caucasian and Asian Populations." *PLoS One* 4 (11): e7958.

Lim, Dennis. 2009. "Examining Race and a Future Beyond It." *New York Times*, January 25, p. AR14.

Loewen, James. 1971. *The Mississippi Chinese: Between Black and White*. Cambridge, MA: Harvard University Press.

Logan, John. 2003. "America's Newcomers." University at Albany, Lewis Mumford Center for Comparative Urban and Regional Research. http://mumford1.dyndns.org/cen2000/NewcomersReport/Newcomer01.htm.

Logan, John, and Glenn Deane. 2003. "Black Diversity in Metropolitan America." University at Albany, Lewis Mumford Center for Comparative Urban and Regional Research. http://mumford1.dyndns.org/cen2000/BlackWhite/Black DiversityReport/black-diversity01.htm.

Logan, John, Sookhee Oh, and Jennifer Darrah. 2009. "The Political Impact of the New Hispanic Second Generation." *Journal of Ethnic and Migration Studies* 35 (7): 1201–23.

Lomax, John 2005. "Who's Your Daddy? Track Your True Identity along a DNA Trail Left behind by Your Ancestors." *Houston Press*, April 14.

Loving v. Virginia. 1967. 388 U.S. 1.

Lubin, Alex. 2005. *Romance and Rights: The Politics of Interracial Intimacy, 1945–1954*. Jackson, MS: University Press of Mississippi.

Lucas, Samuel. 2000. "Hope, Anguish, and the Problem of Our Time: An Essay on Publication of *The Black-White Test Score Gap*." *Teachers College Record* 102 (2): 461–73.

Luks, Samantha, and Laurel Elms. 2005. "African-American Partisanship and the Legacy of the Civil Rights Movement: Generational, Regional, and Economic Influences on Democratic Identification, 1973–1994." *Political Psychology* 26 (5): 735–54.

Lynch, Michael, Simon Cole, Ruth McNally, and Kathleen Jordan. 2008. *Truth Machine: The Contentious History of DNA Fingerprinting*. Chicago, IL: University of Chicago Press.

MacArthur, Daniel. 2009. "Massive Study of African Genetic Diversity." *Genetic Future*, April 30. http://scienceblogs.com/geneticfuture/2009/04/massive_study _of_african_genet.php.

Magliocca, Gerard. 2009. "The Obama Realignment (and What Comes Next)." Unpublished paper, Indiana University School of Law.

Mahoney, Cardinal Roger. 2006. "Op-Ed: Called by God to Help." *New York Times*, March 22.

Majumder, Partha. 2010. "The Human Genetic History of South Asia." *Current Biology* 20 (4): R184–R87.

MALDEF. 2003. *Diminished Voting Power in the Latino Community: The Impact of Felony Disfranchisement Laws in Ten Targeted States*. Los Angeles: MAL-DEF.   http://www.maldef.org/assets/pdf/FEB18-LatinoVotingRightsReport.pdf.

Marrow, Helen. 2003. "To Be or Not to Be (Hispanic or Latino): Brazilian Racial and Ethnic Identity in the United States." *Ethnicities* 3 (4): 427–64.

———. 2004. "Coming to Grips with Race: Second-Generation Brazilians in the United States." Unpublished paper, Pontifícia Universidade Católica do Rio de Janeiro.

———. 2008a. "Hispanic Immigration, Black Population Size, and Intergroup Relations in the Rural and Small-Town U.S. South." In *New Faces in New Places: The Changing Geography of American Immigration*, ed. Douglas Massey. New York: Russell Sage Foundation. 211–48.

———. 2008b. "Who Are the *Other* Latinos, and Why?" In *The Other Latinos: Central and South Americans in the United States*, ed. José Falconi and José Mazzotti. Cambridge, MA: David Rockefeller Center for Latin American Studies. 39–77.

Martes, Ana. 2008. "Neither Hispanic, nor Black: We're Brazilian." In *The Other Latinos: Central and South Americans in the United States*, ed. José Falconi and José Mazzotti. Cambridge, MA: David Rockefeller Center for Latin American Studies. 231–56.

Marx, Anthony. 1998. *Making Race and Nation: A Comparison of South Africa, the United States, and Brazil*. New York: Cambridge University Press.

Massey, Douglas. 2007. *Categorically Unequal: The American Stratification System*. New York: Russell Sage Foundation.

Massey, Douglas, and Camille Charles. 2006. "National Longitudinal Survey of Freshmen." Princeton University, Office of Population Research, http://nlsf.princeton.edu/index.htm.

Massey, Douglas, and Nancy Denton. 1993. *American Apartheid: Segregation and the Making of the Underclass*. Cambridge, MA: Harvard University Press.

Massey, Douglas, and Magaly Sánchez. 2010. *Brokered Boundaries: Creating Immigrant Identity in Anti-Immigrant Times*. New York: Russell Sage Foundation.

Massey, Douglas, et al. 2003. *The Source of the River: The Social Origins of Freshmen at America's Selective Colleges and Universities*. Princeton, NJ: Princeton University Press.

Massoglia, M. 2008. "Incarceration, Health, and Racial Disparities in Health." *Law & Society Review* 42 (2): 275–306.

Masterson, Thomas, Edward Wolff, and Ajit Zacharias. 2009. *What Are the Long-Term Trends in Intergroup Economic Disparities?* Annandale-on-Hudson, NY: Bard College, Levy Economics Institute.

Masterson, Thomas, Ajit Zacharias, and Edward Wolff. 2009. *Has Progress Been Made in Alleviating Racial Economic Inequality?* Annandale-on-Hudson, NY: Bard College, Levy Economics Institute.

Masuoka, Natalie. 2008. "Political Attitudes and Ideologies of Multiracial Americans." *Political Research Quarterly* 61 (2): 253–67.

———. 2011. "The 'Multiracial' Option: Social Group Identity and Changing Patterns of Racial Categorization." *American Politics Research* 39 (1): 176–204.

Mauer, Marc. 2006. *Race to Incarcerate*. New York: The New Press.

Maugh, Thomas II. 2009. "Gene Therapy Makes Major Stride in 'Lorenzo's Oil' Disease." *Los Angeles Times*, November 6.

MAVIN Foundation. 2006. "About Us." http://mavinfoundation.org/about/mission.html.

McBride, James. 1996. *The Color of Water: A Black Man's Tribute to His White Mother*. New York: Riverhead Books, Putnam's.

———. 2009. "My Mother, Obama, and Me: United and Divided by the Sixties." *The Sixties* 2 (1): 70–72.

McCabe, Kristen, and Doris Meissner. 2010. *Immigration and the United States: Recession Affects Flows, Prospects for Reform*. Washington, DC: Migration Policy Institute.

McCarty, Nolan, Keith Poole, and Howard Rosenthal. 2008. *Polarized America: The Dance of Ideology and Unequal Riches*. Cambridge, MA: MIT Press.

McClain, Carol. 2004. "Black by Choice: Identity Preference of Americans of Black/White Parentage." *Black Scholar* 34 (2): 43–54.

McClain, Paula. 2006. "Presidential Address: Racial Intergroup Relations in a Set of Cities: A Twenty-Year Perspective." *Journal of Politics* 68 (4): 757–70.

McClain, Paula, et al. 2008. "Racial Distancing in a Southern City: Latino Immigrants' Views of Black Americans." *Journal of Politics* 68 (3): 571–84.

McDonnell, Judith, and Cileine de Lourenço. 2009. "You're Brazilian, Right? What Kind of Brazilian Are You? The Racialization of Brazilian Immigrant Women." *Ethnic and Racial Studies* 32 (2): 239–56.

McDougall, Cynthia et al. 2003. "The Costs and Benefits of Sentencing: A Systematic Review." *Annals of the American Academy of Political and Social Science* 587 (1): 160–77.

Mekel-Bobrov, Nitzan, et al. 2005. "Ongoing Adaptive Evolution of ASPM, a Brain Size Determinant in Homo Sapiens." *Science* 309 (5741): 1720–22.

Menjivar, Cecilia, and Leisy Abrego. 2009. "Parents and Children across Borders: Legal Instability and Intergenerational Relations in Guatemalan and Salvadoran Families." In *Across Generations: Immigrant Families in America*, ed. Nancy Foner. New York: New York University Press. 160–89.

Metropolitan Policy Program. 2010. *State of Metropolitan America: On the Front Lines of Metropolitan Transformation*. Washington, DC: Brookings Institution Press.

Miles, Donna, and Gregory Carey. 1997. "Genetic and Environmental Architecture of Human Aggression." *Journal of Personality and Social Psychology* 72 (1): 207–17.

Milkman, Ruth. 2006. *L.A. Story: Immigrant Workers and the Future of the U.S. Labor Movement*. New York: Russell Sage Foundation.

Mittra, James. 2007. "Predictive Genetic Information and Access to Life Assurance: The Poverty of 'Genetic Exceptionalism.'" *BioSocieties* 2 (3): 349–73.

Miville, Marie, et al. 2005. "Chameleon Changes: An Exploration of Racial Identity Themes of Multiracial People." *Journal of Counseling Psychology* 52 (4): 507–16.

Modan, Gabriella. 2007. *Turf Wars: Discourse, Diversity, and the Politics of Place*. Malden, MA: Blackwell.

Mollenkopf, John, and Raphael Sonenshein. 2009. "The New Urban Politics of Integration: A View from the Gateway Cities." In *Bringing Outsiders In: Transatlantic Perspectives on Immigrant Political Incorporation*, ed. Jennifer Hochschild and John Mollenkopf. Ithaca, NY: Cornell University Press. 74–92.

Montejano, David. 1987. *Anglos and Mexicans in the Making of Texas, 1836–1986*. Austin, TX: University of Texas Press.

Moore, Solomon. 2001. "Census' Multiracial Option Overturns Traditional Views." *Los Angeles Times*, March 5.

Moran, Rachel. 2001. *Interracial Intimacy: The Regulation of Race and Romance*. Chicago, IL: University of Chicago Press.

Morgan, Edmund. 1975. *American Slavery, American Freedom: The Ordeal of Colonial Virginia*. New York: Norton.

Morgan State University. 2009. "College Confidential." http://talk.collegeconfi dential.com/african-american-students/651164-why-didnt-you-apply-hbcu. html.

Myers, Dowell. 2007. *Immigrants and Boomers: Forging a New Social Contract for the Future of America*. New York: Russell Sage Foundation.

Myrdal, Gunnar. 1944. *An American Dilemma*. New York: Harper & Brothers.

Nabokov, Peter, ed. 1999. *Native American Testimony*. Rev. ed. New York: Penguin.

Nagel, Joane. 1995. "American Indian Ethnic Renewal: Politics and the Resurgence of Identity." *American Sociological Review* 60 (6): 947–65.

Nash, Catherine. 2004. "Genetic Kinship." *Cultural Studies* 18 (1): 1–33.

National Assessment of Educational Progress. 2010. "Trial Urban District Assessment." http://nationsreportcard.gov/tuda.asp.

National Center for Education Statistics. 1995–96, 2000–2001, 2007–8. *Common Core of Data (CCD), Public Elementary/Secondary School Universe Survey*. Washington, DC: Department of Education.

———. 2004. *Historically Black Colleges and Universities, 1976 to 2001*. Washington, DC: Department of Education.

———. 2010. *Digest of Education Statistics 2009*. Washington, DC: Department of Education.

National Center for Health Statistics. Various years. *National Health Interview Survey*. Atlanta, GA: Centers for Disease Control and Prevention.

National Human Genome Center. 2004. *State of the Science on Human Genome Variation and "Race."* Washington, DC: Howard University.

National Human Genome Research Institute. 2010a. "Cases of Genetic Discrimination." http://www.genome.gov/12513976.

———. 2010b. "Frequently Asked Questions about Genetic and Genomic Science." http://www.genome.gov/19016904.

———. 2010c. *Genetic Nondiscrimination Act of 2008*. Washington, DC: National Institutes of Health.

National Research Council. 2009. *Strengthening Forensic Science in the United States: A Path Forward*. Washington, DC: National Academy Press.

National Science Foundation. 2010. *Science and Engineering Indicators 2010.* Washington, DC: National Science Foundation.

———. Various years. *Science and Engineering Indicators.* Washington, DC: National Science Foundation.

Nellis, Ashley, and Ryan King. 2009. *No Exit: The Expanding Use of Life Sentences in America.* Washington, DC: The Sentencing Project.

Nelson, Alondra. 2004. "'I Bought a Ghanaian Flag That Day': Genetic Genealogy and the Pursuit of African Ancestry." Unpublished paper, Columbia University: Department of Sociology.

———. 2008. "Bio Science: Genetic Genealogy Testing and the Pursuit of African Ancestry." *Social Studies of Science* 38 (5): 809–33.

Nevins, Allan. 1958. "A Historian Predicts: Intermarriage of the Races 'Will Be Inevitable.'" *U.S. News and World Report,* November 14, p. 72.

New American Media. 2007a. "California Dreamers: A Public Opinion Portrait of the Most Diverse Generation the Nation Has Known." http://news .newamericamedia.org/news/view_custom.html?custom_page_id=340.

———. 2007b. "Deep Divisions, Shared Destiny." http://news.newamericamedia. org/news/view_article.html?article_id=28501933d0e5c5344b21f9640dc 13754.

Newman, Ben, Todd Hartman, and Charles Taber. forthcoming. "Foreign Language Exposure, Cultural Threat, and Opposition to Immigration." *Political Psychology.*

Newsome, Melba. 2007. "A New DNA Test Can ID a Suspect's Race, But Police Won't Touch It." *Wired Magazine,* no. 16. http://www.wired.com/print/poli tics/law/magazine/16-01/ps_dna.

Newsweek. 1995. *Newsweek Survey: What Is Black?* Princeton, NJ: Princeton Survey Research Associates.

Nobles, Melissa. 2000. *Shades of Citizenship: Race and the Census in Modern Politics.* Palo Alto, CA: Stanford University Press.

Nordgren, Anders, and E. T. Juengst. 2009. "Can Genomics Tell Me Who I Am? Essentialist Rhetoric in Direct-to-Consumer DNA Testing." *New Genetics and Society* 28 (2): 157–72.

Nosek, Brian, et al. 2007. "Pervasiveness and Correlates of Implicit Attitudes and Stereotypes." *European Review of Social Psychology* 18 (1): 36–88.

Novkov, Julie. 2008. *Racial Union: Law, Intimacy, and the White State in Alabama, 1865–1954.* Ann Arbor, MI: University of Michigan Press.

Obama, Barack. 2007. *Dreams from My Father: A Story of Race and Inheritance.* Reprint. New York: Crown.

O'Connor, Colleen. 2011. "In Denver, St. Patrick's Day Parade Is Multicultural, Latino Celebration." *Denver Post,* March 12.

Office for Civil Rights and Civil Liberties. 2008. *Report to Congress on the Department of Homeland Security Office for Civil Rights and Civil Liberties.* Washington, DC: Department of Homeland Security.

Office of Inspector General. 2003. *The September 11 Detainees: A Review of the Treatment of Aliens Held on Immigration Charges in Connection with the Investigation of the September 11 Attacks.* Washington, DC: Department of Justice.

Office of Management and Budget. 1997. *Revisions to the Standards for the*

Classification of Federal Data on Race and Ethnicity. Washington, DC: Executive Office of the President, OMB Office of Information and Regulatory Affairs.

———. 2000. *Guidance on Aggregation and Allocation of Data on Race for Use in Civil Rights Monitoring and Enforcement*. Washington, DC: Executive Office of the President.

O'Malley, Patricia. 2005. "Ethnic Pharmacology: Science, Research, Race, and Market Share." *Clinical Nurse Specialist* 19 (6): 291–93.

Omi, Michael, and Howard Winant. 1994. *Racial Formation in the United States*. 2nd ed. New York: Routledge.

Oppel, Richard Jr. 2011. "Arizona, Bowing to Business, Softens Stand on Immigration." *New York Times*, March 18.

Oropesa, R. S., Nancy Landale, and Meredith Greif. 2008. "From Puerto Rican to Pan-Ethnic in New York City." *Ethnic and Racial Studies* 31 (7): 1315–39.

O'Rourke, Dennis, and Jennifer Raff. 2010. "The Human Genetic History of the Americas: The Final Frontier." *Current Biology* 20 (4): R202–R207.

Ossario, Pilar, and Troy Duster. 2005. "Race and Genetics: Controversies in Biomedical, Behavioral, and Forensic Sciences." *American Psychologist* 60 (1): 115–28.

Pager, Devah. 2003. "The Mark of a Criminal Record." *American Journal of Sociology* 108 (5): 937–75.

Panter, Abigail, et al. 2009. "It Matters How and When You Ask: Self-Reported Race/Ethnicity of Incoming Law Students." *Cultural Diversity and Ethnic Minority Psychology* 15 (1): 51–66.

Papaioannou, Theo. 2009. "Governance and Justice: The Challenge of Genomics." In *The Limits to Governance*, ed. Catherine Lyall, Theo Papaioannou, and James Smith. Burlington, VT: Ashgate. 21–49.

Pascoe, Peggy. 2009. *What Comes Naturally: Miscegenation Law and the Making of Race in America*. New York: Oxford University Press.

Passel, Jeffrey. 2005. *Unauthorized Migrants: Numbers and Characteristics*. Washington, DC: Pew Hispanic Center.

Passel, Jeffrey, and D'Vera Cohn. 2009. *A Portrait of Unauthorized Immigrants in the United States*. Washington, DC: Pew Hispanic Center.

Passel, Jeffrey, and Paul Taylor. 2009. *Who's Hispanic?* Washington, DC: Pew Hispanic Center.

———. 2010. *Unauthorized Immigrants and Their U.S.-Born Children*. Washington, DC: Pew Hispanic Center.

Patterson, Orlando. 2001. "Race by the Numbers." *New York Times*, May 8, p. A27.

———. 2009. "Race and Diversity in the Age of Obama." *New York Times Book Review*, August 16, p. BR23.

Pattillo-McCoy, Mary. 1999. *Black Picket Fences: Privilege and Peril among the Black Middle Class*. Chicago, IL: University of Chicago Press.

Payne, Perry Jr. 2008. "Currents in Contemporary Ethics: For Asians Only? The Perils of Ancestry-Based Drug Prescribing." *Journal of Law, Medicine, and Ethics* 36 (3): 585–88.

Peery, Destiny, and Galen Bodenhausen. 2008. "Black + White = Black: Hypodescent in Reflexive Categorization of Racially Ambiguous Faces." *Psychological Science* 19 (10): 973–77.

Peffley, Mark, and Jon Hurwitz. 2010. *Justice in America: The Separate Realities of Blacks and Whites*. New York: Cambridge University Press.

Perlmann, Joel. 2002. "The Intermingling of Peoples in the United States: Intermarriage and the Population History of Ethnic and Racial Groups since 1880." Levy Economics Institute of Bard College, Annandale-on-Hudson, NY.

Pew Center on the States. 2010. *Prison Count 2010: State Population Declines for the First Time in 38 Years*. Washington, DC: Pew Center on the States.

Pew Forum on Religion and Public Life. 2010. *Public Remains Conflicted over Islam*. Washington, DC: Pew Forum on Religion and Public Life.

Pew Hispanic Center. 2007. *2007 National Survey of Latinos*. Washington, DC: Pew Hispanic Center.

———. 2008. *2008 National Survey of Latinos*. Washington, DC: Pew Hispanic Center.

———. 2009a. *Hispanics and the Criminal Justice System: Low Confidence, High Exposure*. Washington, DC: Pew Hispanic Center.

———. 2009b. *Through Boom and Bust: Minorities, Immigrants and Homeownership*. Washington, DC: Pew Hispanic Center.

———. 2010. *Illegal Immigration Backlash Worries, Divides Latinos*. Washington, DC: Pew Hispanic Center.

Pew Internet and American Life Project. 2006. *Exploratorium Survey*. Princeton, NJ: Princeton Survey Research Associates International.

Pew Research Center. 1999. *1999 Millenium Survey*. Washington, DC: Pew Research Center for the People and the Press.

———. 2003. *The 2004 Political Landscape*. Washington, DC: Pew Research Center for the People and the Press.

———. 2007a. *Muslim Americans: Middle Class and Mostly Mainstream*. Washington, DC: Pew Research Center for the People and the Press.

———. 2007b. *A Portrait of "Generation Next": How Young People View Their Lives, Futures, and Politics*. Washington, DC: Pew Research Center for the People and the Press.

———. 2007c. "Racial Attitudes in America." http://pewsocialtrends.org/assets/pdf/Race.pdf.

———. 2008a. "Americans Say They Like Diverse Communities: Election, Census Trends Suggest Otherwise." Washington, DC: Pew Research Center for the People and the Press.

———. 2008b. *Young Voters in the 2008 Election*. Washington, DC: Pew Research Center for the People and the Press.

———. 2009a. *Muslims Widely Seen as Facing Discrimination*. Washington, DC: Pew Forum on Religion and Public Life.

———. 2009b. "Trends in Political Values and Core Attitudes: 1987–2009: Independents Take Center Stage in Obama Era." http://people-press.org/reports/pdf/517.pdf.

———. 2009c. *Independents Take Center Stage in Obama Era*. Washington, DC: Pew Research Center for the People and the Press.

———. 2010a. *Many Say Coverage of the Poor and Minorities Is Too Negative.* Washington, DC: Pew Research Center for the People and the Press.

———. 2010b. *Marrying Out: One-in-Seven New U.S. Marriages Is Interracial or Interethnic.* Washington, DC: Pew Research Center Publications.

Pew Research Center and National Public Radio. 2009. *Racial Attitudes in America Survey.* Washington, DC: Pew Research Center.

———. 2010. *A Year after Obama's Election: Blacks Upbeat about Black Progress, Prospects.* Washington, DC: Pew Research Center.

Pinckney, Darryl. 2009. "What He Really Said." *New York Review of Books,* February 26, pp. 10–11.

Plutzer, Eric. 2002. "Becoming a Habitual Voter: Inertia, Resources, and Growth in Young Adulthood." *American Political Science Review* 96 (1): 41–56.

Pluviose, David. 2006. "Study: Most Community Colleges Not Fully Prepared for Demographic Shift." *Diverse,* May 18, pp. 10–11.

Plyler v. Doe. 1982. 457 U.S. 202.

PollingReport.com. 2010. "Immigration." http://www.pollingreport.com/immigration.htm.

Porter, Colleen. 2001. "Hispanics by Race." Posting on listserv aapornet@usc.edu, October 10.

Portes, Alejandro, and Rubén Rumbaut. 1991–2006. *Children of Immigrants Longitudinal Study (CILS).* Ann Arbor, MI: Inter-university Consortium for Political and Social Research.

Powell, Brenna. 2010. "A New Comparative Agenda for Ethno-Racial Politics." Unpublished paper, Harvard University, Government and Social Policy Program.

Powell, Michael. 2006. "Profiles of Men Who 'Fit the Description.'" *Washington Post,* December 14.

Powell, Michael, and Janet Roberts. 2009. "Minorities Affected Most as New York Foreclosures Rise." *New York Times,* May 16, pp. A1, A14.

Prewitt, Kenneth, and Sidney Verba. 2001. "Census 2000 and the Fuzzy Boundary Separating Politics and Science." *Bulletin of the American Academy of Arts and Sciences* 54 (4): 32–40.

———. Forthcoming. *Counting the Races of America: Do We Still Need To? Do We Still Want To?* Berkeley, CA: University of California Press.

Price, Alkes, et al. 2008. "Discerning the Ancestry of European Americans in Genetic Association Studies." *PLoS Genetics* 4 (1): 236.

Public Agenda. 1998. *A Lot to Be Thankful For: What Parents Want Children to Learn about America.* New York: Public Agenda.

———. 2002. *Knowing It by Heart: Americans Consider the Constitution and Its Meaning.* New York: National Constitution Center and Public Agenda.

Public Agenda and Carnegie Corporation of the United States. 2003. *Now That I'm Here: What America's Immigrants Have to Say about Life in the U.S. Today.* New York: Public Agenda.

———. 2009. *A Place to Call Home: What Immigrants Say Now about Life in America.* New York: Public Agenda.

Putnam, Robert. 2007. "E Pluribus Unum: Diversity and Community in the

Twenty-First Century: The 2006 Johan Skytte Prize Lecture." *Scandinavian Political Studies* 30 (2): 137–74.

Putnam, Robert, and David Campbell. 2010. *American Grace: How Religion Divides and Unites Us.* New York: Simon and Schuster.

Qian, Zhenchao, and Daniel Lichter. 2007. "Social Boundaries and Marital Assimilation: Interpreting Trends in Racial and Ethnic Intermarriage." *American Sociological Review* 72 (1): 68–94.

Quillian, Lincoln, and Rozlyn Redd. 2009. "The Friendship Networks of Multiracial Adolescents." *Social Science Research* 38 (2): 279–95.

"Race, Dating and Marriage." 2001. *Washington Post*, July 5.

"Racial Clues in Bowel Cancer Find." 2008. BBC News. http://news.bbc.co.uk/2/hi/health/7319251.stm.

"Ramadan Resolution by US House of Representatives." 2007. *Muslim Observer*, October 4. http://muslimmedianetwork.com/mmn/?p=1382.

Ramakrishnan, S. Karthick, and Irene Bloemraad, eds. 2008. *Civic Hopes and Political Realities: Community Organizations and Political Engagement among Immigrants in the United States and Abroad.* New York: Russell Sage Foundation.

Ramakrishnan, S. Karthick, and Paul Lewis. 2005. *Immigrants and Local Governance: The View from City Hall.* San Francisco, CA: Public Policy Institute of California.

Ramakrishnan, S. Karthick, and Tom Wong. 2010. "Partisanship, Not Spanish: Explaining Municipal Ordinances Affecting Undocumented Immigrants." In *Taking Local Control: Immigration Policy Activism in U.S. Cities and States*, ed. Monica Varsanyi. Palo Alto, CA: Stanford University Press. 73–96.

Ramakrishnan, S. Karthick, et al. 2009. "Race-Based Considerations and the Obama Vote: Evidence from the 2008 National Asian American Survey." *Du Bois Review* 6 (1): 219–38.

Rasmussen Reports. 2010. "58% Favor Welcoming Immigration Policy." April 26. http://www.rasmussenreports.com/public_content/politics/current_events/immigration/58_favor_welcoming_immigration_policy.

Ray, Turna. 2009. "Disruptive But Profitable: PricewaterhouseCoopers Projects 11 Percent Annual Growth for Personalized Rx." *Genome Web*, December 9. http://www.genomeweb.com/print/928871?hq_e=el&hq_m=570143&hq_l=1& hq_v=24ef1e1e03.

Regalado, Antonio. 2006. "Scientist's Study of Brain Genes Sparks a Backlash." *Wall Street Journal*, June 16, pp. A1, A12.

Reich, Gary, and Jay Barth. 2010. "Educating Citizens or Defying Federal Authority? A Comparative Study of In-State Tuition for Undocumented Students." *Policy Studies Journal* 38 (3): 419–47.

Riccardi, Nicholas. 2010. "Arizona Passes Strict Illegal Immigration Act." *Los Angeles Times*, April 13.

Rice University. 2011. "Limitations of Question about Race Can Create Inaccurate Picture of Health-Care Disparities." *ScienceDaily*, April 19. http://www.sciencedaily.com/releases/2011/04/110419151809.htm.

Ridgeway, Greg. 2007. *Analysis of Racial Disparities in the New York Police Department's Stop, Question, and Frisk Practices.* Santa Monica, CA: Rand Corporation.

Robinson, Eugene. 2010. *Disintegration: The Splintering of Black America.* New York: Doubleday.

Rockquemore, Kerry, and David Brunsma. 2002. *Beyond Black: Biracial Identity in America.* Thousand Oaks, CA: Sage Publications.

Rockquemore, Kerry, David Brunsma, and Daniel Delgado. 2009. "Racing to Theory or Retheorizing Race? Understanding the Struggle to Build a Multiracial Identity Theory." *Journal of Social Issues* 65 (1): 13–34.

Rodríguez, Clara. 2000. *Changing Race: Latinos, the Census, and the History of Ethnicity in the United States.* New York: New York University Press.

Rodríguez, Cristina, et al. 2010. *A Program in Flux: New Priorities and Implementation Challenges for 287(g).* Washington, DC: Migration Policy Institute.

Roediger, David. 2005. *Working toward Whiteness.* New York: Basic Books.

———. 2008. "Race Will Survive the Obama Phenomenon." *Chronicle of Higher Education*, October 10, pp. B6–B10.

Rogers, Reuel. 2004. "Race-Based Coalitions among Minority Groups: Afro-Caribbean Immigrants and African-Americans in New York City." *Urban Affairs Review* 39 (3): 283–317.

———. 2006. *Afro-Caribbean Immigrants and the Politics of Incorporation: Ethnicity, Exception, or Exit.* New York: Cambridge University Press.

Romano, Renée. 2003. *Race Mixing: Black-White Marriage in Postwar America.* Cambridge, MA: Harvard University Press.

Root, Maria. 1993. "Bill of Rights for People of Mixed Heritage." http://www.drmariaroot.com/doc/BillOfRights.pdf.

Roper Center for Public Opinion Research. 2010. "iPOLL." http://www.roper center.uconn.edu/.

Rosales, F. Arturo. 1985. "Shifting Self Perceptions and Ethnic Consciousness among Mexicans in Houston 1908–1946." *Aztlan* 16 (1–2): 71–94.

Rosenbaum, Dennis, et al. 2005. "Attitudes toward the Police: The Effects of Direct and Vicarious Experience." *Police Quarterly* 8 (3): 343–65.

Rosenberg, N., et al. 2002. "Genetic Structure of Human Populations." *Science* 298 (5602): 2381–85.

Roth, Wendy. 2005. "The End of the One-Drop Rule? Labeling of Multiracial Children in Black Intermarriages." *Sociological Forum* 20 (1): 35–67.

Rothstein, Mark. 2011. "GINA's Beauty Is Only Skin Deep." *Genewatch.* http://www.councilforresponsiblegenetics.org/GeneWatch/GeneWatchPage.aspx?pageId=184&archive=yes.

"Rough Justice." 2010. *The Economist*, July 22, p. 13.

Royal, Charmaine, et al. 2010. "Inferring Genetic Ancestry: Opportunities, Challenges, and Implications." *American Journal of Human Genetics* 86 (5): 661–73.

Rugh, Jacob, and Douglas Massey. 2010. "Racial Segregation and the American Foreclosure Crisis." *American Sociological Review* 75 (5): 629–51.

Rumbaut, Rubén. 2005. "Sites of Belonging: Acculturation, Discrimination, and

Ethnic Identity among Children of Immigrants." In *Discovering Successful Pathways in Children's Development: Mixed Methods in the Study of Childhood and Family Life*, ed. Tom Weisner. Chicago, IL: University of Chicago Press. 111–64.

———. 2009. "Pigments of Our Imagination: On the Racialization and Racial Identities of 'Hispanics' and 'Latinos.'" In *How the United States Racializes Latinos: White Hegemony and Its Consequences*, ed. José Cobas, Jorge Duany, and Joe Feagin. Boulder, CO: Paradigm Publishers. 15–36.

Sampson, Robert, and Charles Loeffler. 2010. "Punishment's Place: The Local Concentration of Mass Incarceration." *Daedalus* 139 (3): 20–31.

San Martin, Nancy. 2007. "Many Shades of Reaction." *Miami Herald*, June 19.

Sanchez, Diana, and Courtney Bonam. 2009. "To Disclose or Not to Disclose Biracial Identity: The Effect of Biracial Disclosure on Perceiver Evaluations and Target Responses." *Journal of Social Issues* 65 (1): 129–49.

Sandel, Michael. 1994. "Book Review: Political Liberalism." *Harvard Law Review* 107: 1765–94.

Sankar, Pamela. 2008. "Moving beyond the Two-Race Mantra." In *Revisiting Race in a Genomic Age*, ed. Barbara Koenig, Sandra Lee, and Sarah Richardson. New Brunswick, NJ: Rutgers University Press. 271–84.

Sapiro, Virginia, et al. 2007. *American National Election Studies Cumulative Data File, 1948–2004*. Ann Arbor, MI: Inter-university Consortium for Political and Social Research.

Saulny, Susan. 2011a. "Census Data Presents Rise in Multiracial Population of Youths." *New York Times*, March 24.

———. 2011b. "Black and White and Married in the Deep South: A Shifting Image." *New York Times*, March 19.

Savage, Charlie. 2009. "On Nixon Tapes, Ambivalence over Abortion, Not Watergate." *New York Times*, June 24.

Schafer, Chelsea, and Greg Shaw. 2009. "The Polls—Trends: Tolerance in the United States." *Public Opinion Quarterly* 73 (2): 404–31.

Schildkraut, Deborah. 2009. "The Dynamics of Public Opinion on Ethnic Profiling after 9/11: Results from a Survey Experiment." *American Behavioral Scientist* 53 (1): 61–79.

Schnittker, Jason, Jeremy Freese, and Brian Powell. 2000. "Nature, Nurture, Neither, Nor: Black-White Differences in Beliefs about the Causes and Appropriate Treatment of Mental Illness." *Social Forces* 78 (3): 1101–30.

Scholz, John, and Kara Levine. 2004. "U.S. Black-White Wealth Inequality." In *Social Inequality*, ed. Kathryn Neckerman. New York: Russell Sage Foundation. 895–929.

Schor, Paul. 2005. "Mobilising for Pure Prestige? Challenging Federal Census Ethnic Categories in the USA (1850–1940)." *International Social Science Journal* 57 (183): 89–101.

Schorn, Daniel. 2007. "A Not So Perfect Match." *60 Minutes*, July 15. http://www.cbsnews.com/stories/2007/03/23/60minutes/main2600721.shtml.

Schorr, Daniel. 2008. "A New, 'Post-Racial' Political Era in America." National Public Radio, January 28. http://www.npr.org/templates/story/story.php?storyId=18489466.

Schuck, Peter. 2009. "Taking Immigration Federalism Seriously." *The Forum* 7 (3): article 4. http:www.bepress.com/forum/vol7/iss3/art4/.

Schuman, Howard, and Willard Rodgers. 2004. "Cohorts, Chronology, and Collective Memories." *Public Opinion Quarterly* 68 (2): 217–54.

———. 2006. *Cohorts, Chronology, and Collective Memories.* Ann Arbor, MI: Inter-university Consortium for Political and Social Research, Study No. 1318.

Schuster, Stephen, et al. 2010. "Complete Khoisan and Bantu Genomes from Southern Africa." *Nature* 463: 943–47.

Scientific Working Group on DNA Analysis Methods Ad Hoc Committee on Partial Matches. 2009. "SWGDAM Recommendations to the FBI Director on the 'Interim Plan for the Release of Information in the Event of a "Partial Match" at NDIS.'" *Forensic Science Communications* 11 (4). http://www.fbi.gov/about-us/lab/forensic-science-communications/fsc/oct2009/standard_guid lines/swgdam.html.

Seelye, Katharine. 2010. "Candidate Shrugs Off History's Lure." *New York Times,* June 26, pp. A8, A14.

Segovia, Francine, and Renatta DeFever. 2010. "The Polls—Trends: American Public Opinion on Immigrants and Immigration Policy." *Public Opinion Quarterly* 74 (2): 375–94.

Sen, Maya. 2010. "The Role of Race and Gender in Awarding of Subprime Mortgage Loans." Unpublished paper, Harvard University, Department of Government.

The Sentencing Project. 2010a. *Expanding the Vote: State Felony Disenfranchisement Reform, 1997–2010.* Washington, DC: The Sentencing Project.

———. 2010b. *Felony Disenfranchisement Laws in the United States.* Washington, DC: The Sentencing Project.

Seringhaus, Michael. 2010. "To Stop Crime, Share Your Genes." *New York Times,* March 15, p. 23.

Serrano, José. 2004. "Senseless Census: A Congressman Offers an Insider's Take on the Form's Curious Racial Groupings." *New York Post,* December 8, p. 51.

Shelby, Tommie. 2005. *We Who Are Dark: The Philosophical Foundations of Black Solidarity.* Cambridge, MA: Harvard University Press.

Sheridan, Mary Beth. 2004. "Interviews of Muslims to Broaden." *Washington Post,* July 17, p. A1.

Shiao, Jiannbin, and Mia Tuan. 2008. "Korean Adoptees and the Social Context of Ethnic Exploration." *American Journal of Sociology* 113 (4): 1023–66.

Shostak, Sara, et al. 2009. "The Politics of the Gene: Social Status and Beliefs about Genetics for Individual Outcomes." *Social Psychological Quarterly* 72 (1): 77–93.

Shriver, Mark, and Rick Kittles. 2008. "Genetic Ancestry and the Search for Personalized Genetic Histories." In *Revisiting Race in a Genomic Age,* ed. Barbara Koenig, Sandra Lee, and Sarah Richardson. New Brunswick, NJ: Rutgers University Press. 201–14.

Shufeldt, R. W. 1907. "Race Fusion: Dr. Shufeldt Replies to Prof. Giddings on the Negro." *New York Times,* December 23, p. 8.

Shyrock, Andrew. 2008. "On Discipline and Inclusion." In *Being and Belonging:*

Muslims in the United States since 9/11, ed. Katherine Pratt Ewing. New York: Russell Sage Foundation. 200–206.

Silva-Zolezzi, Irma, et al. 2009. "Analysis of Genomic Diversity in Mexican Mestizo Populations to Develop Genomic Medicine in Mexico." *Proceedings of the National Academy of Sciences* 106 (21): 8611–16.

Simmons, Ann, and Abby Sewell. 2010. "Suit Seeks to Open Compton to Latino Voters." *Los Angeles Times*, December 20.

Singer, Eleanor, Toni Antonucci, and John van Hoewyk. 2004. "Racial and Ethnic Variations in Knowledge and Attitudes about Genetic Testing." *Genetic Testing* 8 (1): 31–43.

Skinner, David. 2006. "Racialized Futures: Biologism and the Changing Politics of Identity." *Social Studies of Science* 36 (3): 459–88.

Skinner v. Switzer. 2011. 562 U.S. ___.

Skogan, Wesley. 2005. "Citizen Satisfaction with Police Encounters." *Police Quarterly* 8 (3): 298–321.

———. 2006. "Asymmetry in the Impact of Encounters with Police." *Policing and Society* 16 (2): 99–126.

Slaten, Darci. 2009. "New Forensic Method Aims to Predict What a Person Looks Like from DNA Sample." *UA (University of Arizona) News*.

Smith, Gaddis. 2009. "Life at Yale during the Great Depression." *Yale Alumni Magazine* (November/December): 36–45.

Smith, James, and Barry Edmonston, eds. 1997. *The New Americans: Economic, Demographic, and Fiscal Effects of Immigration*. Washington, DC: National Academy Press.

Smith, Lindsay. 2010. "Identifying Democracy: Citizenship, DNA, and Identity in Post-Dictatorship Argentina." Paper presented at the American Bar Foundation, Chicago.

Smith, Stephen. 2009. "MGH to Use Genetics to Personalize Cancer Care." *Boston Globe*, pp. A1, A7.

Snipp, C. Matthew. 1986. "Who Are American Indians? Some Observations about the Perils and Pitfalls of Data for Race and Ethnicity." *Population Research and Policy Review* 5 (3): 237–52.

Soares, Christina. 2010. "Portrait in DNA: Can Forensic Analysis Yield Police-Style Sketches of Suspects?" *Scientific American*, May 11, pp. 14–17.

Soares, Pedro, et al. 2010. "The Archaeogenetics of Europe." *Current Biology* 20 (4): R174–R183.

Social Science Research Council. c. 2005. "Is Race Real?" http://raceandgenomics.ssrc.org/.

Sollors, Werner, ed. 1989. *The Invention of Ethnicity*. New York: Oxford University Press.

———. 2000. *Interracialism: Black-White Intermarriage in American History, Literature, and Law*. New York: Oxford University Press.

Sonenshein, Raphael. 1993. *Politics in Black and White: Race and Power in Los Angeles*. Princeton, NJ: Princeton University Press.

Squires, Catherine. 2007. *Dispatches from the Color Line: The Press and Multiracial America*. Albany, NY: State University of New York Press.

Squires, Gregory. 2009. "Segregation as a Driver of Subprime Lending and the Ensuing Economic Fallout." Comments before the Joint Economic Committee, June 25. Washington, DC: George Washington University.

Stanfield, Rochelle. 1999. "The Blending of the United States." http://www.4uth.gov.ua/usa/english/facts/ijse0699/stanfld.htm.

Steinberg, Gail. n.d. "Dan O'Brien—The World's Best Athlete: A Transracially Adopted Hero." http://www.pactadopt.org/profiles/obrien.html.

Steinhardt, Barry. 2004. "Privacy and Forensic DNA Data Banks." In *DNA and the Criminal Justice System: The Technology of Justice*, ed. David Lazer. Cambridge, MA: MIT Press. 173–96.

Steinhauer, Jennifer. 2010. "'Grim Sleeper's Arrest Fans Debate on a DNA Use." *New York Times*, July 9, pp. A1, A12.

Stepick, Alex, et al. 2003. *This Land Is Our Land: Immigrants and Power in Miami*. Berkeley, CA: University of California Press.

Stevens, Gillian, Mary McKillip, and Hiromi Ishizawa. 2006. *Intermarriage in the Second Generation: Choosing between Newcomers and Natives*. Washington, DC: Migration Policy Institute.

Stevenson, Seth. 2004. "Customers Like Me." Slate.com, April 26. http://www.slate.com/id/2099476/.

Stiefel, Leanna, Amy Schwartz, and Dylan Conger. 2003. "Language Proficiency and Home Languages of Students in New York City Elementary and Secondary Schools." Unpublished paper, New York University, Taub Urban Research Center.

Stoker, Laura, and M. Kent Jennings. 2008. "Of Time and the Development of Partisan Polarization." *American Journal of Political Science* 52 (3): 619–35.

Stone, Alfred Holt. 1908. *Studies in the American Race Problem, with an Introduction and Three Papers by Walter F. Willcox*. New York: Doubleday, Page and Company.

Straight, Ronald. 2002. "Asset-Accumulation Differences by Race: SCF Data, 1995 and 1998." *American Economic Review, Papers and Proceedings* 92 (2): 330–34.

Su, Rick. 2011. "Immigration as Urban Policy." *Fordham Urban Law Journal* 38 (1): 363–91.

Sugrue, Thomas. 2010. *Not Even Past: Barack Obama and the Burden of Race*. Princeton, NJ: Princeton University Press.

Sulem, Patrick, et al. 2007. "Genetic Determinants of Hair, Eye, and Skin Pigmentation in Europeans." *Nature Genetics* 39 (12): 1443–52.

Sullivan, Meg. 2010. "Facebook Study Finds Race Trumped by Ethnic, Social, Geographic Origins in Forging Friendships." *UCLA News*, October 28. http://newsroom.ucla.edu/portal/ucla/race-less-important-forging-friendships-171171.aspx.

Survey of Consumer Finances. 2009. "2007 SCF Chartbook." http://www.federalreserve.gov/pubs/oss/oss2/92/scf92home.html.

"Symposium on Race, Pharmaceuticals, and Medical Technology." 2008. *Journal of Law, Medicine and Ethics* 36 (2): 443–601.

Tafoya, Sonya, Hans Johnson, and Laura Hill. 2004. *Who Chooses to Choose*

Two? Multiracial Identification and Census 2000. New York: Russell Sage Foundation and Population Reference Bureau.

Tallbear, Kimberly. 2008. "Native-American-DNA.Com: In Search of Native American Race and Tribe." In *Revisiting Race in a Genomic Age*, ed. Barbara Koenig, Sandra Lee, and Sarah Richardson. New Brunswick, NJ: Rutgers University Press. 235–52.

Tang, Hua, et al. 2005. "Genetic Structure, Self-Identified Race/Ethnicity, and Confounding in Case-Control Association Studies." *American Journal of Human Genetics* 76 (2): 268–75.

Tariq, Lila. 2010. "Cultural Chords." *Azizah Magazine* 6 (1): 72–74.

Tate, Katherine. 2010. *What's Going On?: Political Incorporation and the Transformation of Black Public Opinion.* Washington, DC: Georgetown University Press.

Tavernise, Sabrina, and Robert Grebeloff. 2010. "Immigrants Make Paths to Suburbia, Not Cities." *New York Times*, December 15, pp. A13–A15.

Temple, Robert, and Norman Stockbridge. 2007. "BiDil for Heart Failure in Black Patients: The U.S. Food and Drug Administration Perspective." *Annals of Internal Medicine* 147 (1): 57–62.

Terkel, Studs. 1974. *Working: People Talk about What They Do All Day and How They Feel about What They Do.* New York: Pantheon Books.

Terrell, Henry. 1971. "Wealth Accumulation of Black and White Families: The Empirical Evidence." *Journal of Finance* 26 (2): 363–77.

Tesler, Michael, and David Sears. 2010. *Obama's Race: The 2008 Election and the Dream of a Post-Racial America.* Chicago, IL: University of Chicago Press.

Texiera, Erin. 2005. "Multiracial Scenes Now Common in TV Ads." MSNBC, February 15. http://www.msnbc.msn.com/.

Thatchenkery, Tojo, and K. Sugiyama. 2011. *Missing in Mobility: An Analysis of Leadership Invisibility of Asian Americans in Organizations.* Fairfax, VA: George Mason University School of Public Policy.

Thornton, Michael. 2009. "Policing the Borderlands: White- and Black-American Newspaper Perceptions of Multiracial Heritage and the Idea of Race, 1996–2006." *Journal of Social Issues* 65 (1): 105–27.

Tichenor, Daniel. 2002. *Dividing Lines: The Politics of Immigration Control in America.* Princeton, NJ: Princeton University Press.

Tienda, Marta, and Faith Mitchell. 2006. *Multiple Origins, Uncertain Destinies: Hispanics and the American Future.* Washington, DC: National Academies Press.

Tishkoff, Sarah, et al. 2009. "The Genetic Structure and History of Africans and African Americans." *Science* 324 (5930): 1035–44.

Tocqueville, Alexis de. 1966 [1848]. *Democracy in America.* ed. J.P. Mayer and Max Lerner. New York: Harper and Row.

Tonry, Michael and Matthew Melewski. 2008. "The Malign Effects of Drug and Crime Control Policies on Black Americans." *Crime and Justice* 37 (1): 1–44.

Tutton, Richard. 2004. "'They Want to Know Where They Come From': Population Genetics, Identity, and Family Genealogy." *New Genetics and Society* 23 (1): 105–20.

Tutton, Richard, et al. 2008. "Genotyping the Future: Scientists' Expectations about Race/Ethnicity after BiDil." *Journal of Law, Medicine, and Ethics* 36 (3): 464–70.

Uggen, Christopher, Jeff Manza, and Melissa Thompson. 2006. "Citizenship, Democracy, and the Civic Reintegration of Criminal Offenders." *Annals of the American Academy of Political and Social Science* 605 (1): 281–310.

"Undergraduate Diversity: More Minorities More Women." 2010. *Chronicle of Higher Education*, September 24, p. B45.

United Nations. 2009. "International Migration, 2009 Wallchart." http://www .un.org/esa/population/publications/2009Migration_Chart/IttMig_maps.pdf.

United Nations Department. of Economic and Social Affairs. 2003. Poster on International Migration 2002. New York: United Nations Population Division.

United States Conference of Catholic Bishops. 2003. *Strangers No Longer: Together on the Journey of Hope*. Washington, DC: Committee on Migration of the United States Conference of Catholic Bishops.

United States v. Brignoni-Ponce. 1975. 422 U.S. 873.

Urban Institute. c. 2006. "Select Prisoner Reentry Publications as of November 2006." http://www.urban.org/projects/reentry-portfolio/publications.cfm.

U.S. House of Representatives. 1997. *Hearings on Federal Measures of Race and Ethnicity and the Implications for the 2000 Census*. 105th Cong., 1st Sess.

Vallejo, Jody. 2009. "The Mexican Origin Middle Class in Los Angeles." Unpublished paper, University of Southern California, Department of Sociology.

Varsanyi, Monica, ed. 2010. *Taking Local Control: Immigration Policy Activism in U.S. Cities and States*. Palo Alto, CA: Stanford University Press.

———, et al. 2010. "A Multilayered Jurisdictional Patchwork: Immigration Federalism in the United States." http://papers.ssrn.com/sol3/papers.cfm?abstract _id=1656530.

Vasconcelos, José. 1979 [1925]. *The Cosmic Race: A Bilingual Edition*. Baltimore, MD: Johns Hopkins University Press.

Venter, J. Craig, et al. 2001. "The Sequence of the Human Genome." *Science* 291 (5507): 1304–51.

Vigdor, Jacob. 2009. *From Immigrants to Americans: The Rise and Fall of Fitting In*. New York: Rowman and Littlefield.

Vitello, Paul. 2010. "Heated Opposition to a Proposed Mosque." *New York Times*, June 11, pp. A23, A24.

Volden, Craig, and Alan Wiseman. 2009. "Legislative Effectiveness in Congress." Unpublished paper, Ohio State University, Department of Political Science.

Wacquant, Loic. 2002. "From Slavery to Mass Incarceration: Rethinking the 'Race Question' in the U.S." *New Left Review* 13: 41–60.

Wade, Nicholas. 2005. "Researchers Say Intelligence and Diseases May Be Linked in Ashkenazic Genes." *New York Times*, June 3, p. A21.

———. 2009. "Genes Show Limited Value in Predicting Diseases." *New York Times*, April 16.

Wailoo, Keith, and Stephen Pemberton. 2006. *The Troubled Dream of Genetic Medicine*. Baltimore, MD: Johns Hopkins University Press.

Wallace, Rebecca. 2008. "New Breed of Multiracial Poster Children. Literally." *Newsweek*, April 20.

Wallman, Katherine. 1998. "Data on Race and Ethnicity: Revising the Federal Standard." *American Statistician* 52 (1): 31–33.

Walsh, Katherine. 2007. *Talking about Race: Community Dialogues and the Politics of Difference*. Chicago, IL: University of Chicago Press.

Walzer, Michael. 1992. *What It Means to Be an American*. New York: Marsilio Publishers.

Wamba, Philippe. 1999. "While the Lion's at Your Door: American Blacks, Africans, and the Killing of Amadou Diallo." *CommonQuest* 4 (2): 42–49.

Wan, William. 2010. "U.S. Catholic Universities Seeing Influx of Muslim Students." *Washington Post*, December 20, p. A01.

Wang, Sijia, et al. 2008. "Geographic Patterns of Genome Admixture in Latin American Mestizos." *PLoS Genetics* 4 (3): e1000037.

Washington Post/Kaiser Family Foundation/Harvard University. 2001. *Race and Ethnicity in 2001: Attitudes, Perceptions, and Experiences*. Menlo Park, CA: Kaiser Family Foundation.

Waslin, Michele. 2010. "Immigration Enforcement by State and Local Police: The Impact on the Enforcers and Their Communities." In *Taking Local Control: Immigration Policy Activism in U.S. Cities and States*, ed. Monica Varsanyi. Palo Alto, CA: Stanford University Press. 97–114.

Watanabe, Teresa, et al. 2010. "Arizona's Crackdown on Illegal Migrants Feels Familiar." *Los Angeles Times*, April 16.

Waters, Mary. 1990. *Ethnic Options: Choosing Identities in America*. Berkeley, CA: University of California Press.

———. 1995. "Ethnic and Racial Identities of Second Generation Black Immigrants in New York City." *International Migration Review* 28 (4): 795–820.

———. 1999. *Black Identities: West Indian Immigrant Dreams and American Realities*. Cambridge, MA: Harvard University Press.

Waterston, Adriana. 2004. *The Dawning of Multicultural America*. Larchmont, NY: Horowitz Associates Inc., Market Research & Consulting.

Weaver, Charles. 2008. "Social Distance as a Measure of Prejudice among Ethnic Groups in the United States." *Journal of Applied Social Psychology* 38 (3): 779–95.

Weisberg, Robert, and Joan Petersillia. 2010. "The Dangers of Pyrrhic Victories against Mass Incarceration." *Daedalus* 139 (3): 124–33.

Weitzer, Ronald, and Steven Tuch. 2006. *Race and Policing in America: Conflict and Reform*. New York: Cambridge University Press.

Western, Bruce. 2006. *Punishment and Inequality in America*. New York: Russell Sage Foundation.

Western, Bruce, and Becky Pettit. 2010. "Incarceration and Social Inequality." *Daedalus* 139 (3): 8–19.

Western, Bruce, et al. 2004. "Incarceration and the Bonds between Parents in Fragile Families." In *Imprisoning America: The Social Effects of Mass Incarceration*, ed. Mary Patillo, David Weiman, and Bruce Western. New York: Russell Sage Foundation. 21–45.

Whitaker, Monica. 2002. "Tribe Hopes DNA Proves Cherokee Heritage." http://happytrails_2.tripod.com/sitebuildercontent/sitebuilderfiles/dna.htm.

White, Michael, and Jennifer Glick. 2009. *Achieving Anew: How New Immigrants Do in American Schools, Jobs, and Neighborhoods*. New York: Russell Sage Foundation.

Wike, Richard, and Brian Grim. 2010. "Western Views toward Muslims: Evidence from a 2006 Cross-National Survey." *International Journal of Public Opinion Research* 22 (1): 4–25.

Wildeman, Christopher. 2008. "Paternal Incarceration and Children's Physically Aggressive Behaviors: Evidence from the Fragile Families and Child Wellbeing Study." *Social Forces* 89 (1): 285–309.

———. 2009. "Parental Imprisonment, the Prison Boom, and the Concentration of Childhood Disadvantage." *Demography* 46 (2): 265–80.

Williams, Kim. 2006. *Mark One or More: Civil Rights in Multiracial America*. Ann Arbor, MI: University of Michigan Press.

Williamson, Abigail. 2008. *Social Capital, Diversity, and Inequality Community Field Studies: Final Report*. Cambridge, MA: Harvard University, Harvard Kennedy School.

———. 2011. *Beyond the Passage of Time: Local Government Response in New Immigrant Destinations*. Cambridge, MA: Harvard University, Harvard Kennedy School.

Willing, Richard. 2006. "DNA Rewrites History for African-Americans." *USA Today*, February 1.

Wilson, Melanie. 2008. "DNA—Intimate Information or Trash for Public Consumption." *Baylor Law Review, TexSupp*. http://www.TexSupp.com/2008/07/24/dna-intimate-information-or-trashfor-public-consumption/.

Wilson, William J. 1980. *The Declining Significance of Race*. Chicago, IL: University of Chicago Press.

———. 2009. *More than Just Race: Being Black and Poor in the Inner City*. New York: Norton.

Wimmer, Andreas, and Kevin Lewis. 2010. "Beyond and Below Racial Homophily: ERG Models of a Friendship Network Documented on Facebook." *American Journal of Sociology* 116 (2): 583–642.

Winerip, Michael. 2005. "For Immigrants, Math Is a Way to Success." *New York Times*, May 18, p. A19.

Witters, Dan. 2010. *Americans' Life Evaluation Reaches New High*. Gallup Inc., May 27. http://www.gallup.com/poll/126578/americans-life-evaluation-reaches-new-high.aspx.

Wolff, Edward, and Maury Gittleman. 2011. "Inheritances and the Distribution of Wealth, or Whatever Happened to the Great Inheritance Boom? Results from the SCF and PSID." Cambridge, MA: National Bureau of Economic Research.

Womack, Ytasha. 2010. *Post Black: How a New Generation Is Redefining African American Identity*. Chicago, IL: Lawrence Hill Books.

Wong, Janelle. 2006. *Democracy's Promise: Immigrants and American Civic Institutions*. Ann Arbor, MI: University of Michigan Press.

Woodward, C. Vann. 1971. *The Strange Career of Jim Crow*. 2nd rev. ed. New York: Oxford University Press.

WordNet® 3.0. n.d. "Genomics." Dictionary.com. http://dictionary.reference.com/browse/genomics.

Wright, Lawrence. 1994. "One Drop of Blood." *New Yorker*, July 24, pp. 46ff.

Wright, Natasha, and Wendy Roth. 2011. "Aboriginal Claims: DNA Ancestry Testing and Changing Concepts of Indigeneity." In *Biomapping and Indigenous Identities*, ed. Susanne Berthier, Sandrine Tolazzi, and Sheila Collingwood-Whittick. Amsterdam: Rodopi.

Yancy, Clyde. 2007. "The Association of Black Cardiologists Responds to 'Race in a Bottle': A Misguided Passion." *Scientific American*, July 30.

Yen, Hope. 2010. "Interracial Marriage Still Rising, But Not as Fast." Associated Press, May 26.

Yoplac, Maria. 2010. "To Give My Parents, and Myself, a Better Life." *Real Simple*, July.

Yoshikawa, Hirokazu. 2011. *Immigrants Raising Children: Undocumented Parents and Their Children*. New York: Russell Sage Foundation.

Yoshikawa, Hirokazu, et al. 2008. "Access to Institutional Resources as a Measure of Social Exclusion: Relations with Family Process and Cognitive Development in the Context of Immigration." *New Directions for Child and Adolescent Development* (121): 63–86.

"Younger Voters Were Racially Diverse, Voted Democratic, and Approved of President Obama." 2011. *The Circle* 8 (1): 1–3.

Zakharia, Fouad, et al. 2009. "Characterizing the Admixed African Ancestry of African Americans." *Genome Biology* 10 (12): R141.3–R141.11.

Zero Anthropology. 2005. "Freedmen Descendants Use DNA to Show Indian Blood." *The CAC Review*, June 5. http://cacreview.blogspot.com/2005/06/freedmen-descendants-use-dna-to-show.html.

Zhang, Yuanting, and Jennifer Van Hook. 2009. "Marital Dissolution among Interracial Couples." *Journal of Marriage and Family* 71 (1): 95–107.

Zolberg, Aristide. 2006. *A Nation by Design: Immigration Policy in the Fashioning of America*. New York and Cambridge, MA: Russell Sage Foundation and Harvard University Press.

Zwart, Nijmegen Hub. 2007. "Genomics and Self-Knowledge: Implications for Societal Research and Debate." *New Genetics and Society* 26 (2): 181–202.

Index

Note: Numbers in italic type indicate figures; those followed by a lowercase t indicate tables.